Training for the Future:

The Rise and Fall of the Manpower Services Commission

Patrick Ainley and *Mark Corney*

CASSELL

To our parents

Cassell Educational Limited
Villiers House
41/47 Strand
London WC2N 5JE

First published 1990

British Library Cataloguing in Publication Data
Ainley, Patrick
  Training for the future: the rise and fall of the Manpower Services Commission.
  1. Great Britain. Manpower Services Commission
  I. Title   II. Corney, Mark
  354.410083'3

  ISBN 0–304–31861–2

Phototypeset by Input Typesetting Ltd, London SW19

Printed and bound in Great Britain by The Alden Press Ltd, Oxford.

Contents

Foreword

The story of the MSC is important because it amounts to *the* major attempt at large-scale social engineering in Britain since the post-war wave of measures. It is a fascinating tale, well told, and this book is sure to become a 'must' for students of educational and labour market trends. In addition it ought to command a great deal of interest among those on public administration courses.

The details of the plot are modern, though the fate of its heroes has many precedents. The story turns into a mixture of farce and tragedy when 'the mission' represented by the MSC is embraced and then overwhelmed by the wider social system and culture.

The authors are authorities in this field and, provided there are no major twists in the tale still to unfold, this book will be the best on the MSC for some time to come.

Ken Roberts
Head of Sociology
University of Liverpool

Acknowledgements

This book was based on a research project conducted at the Public Policy Unit of Queen Mary College, London University. The authors would like to thank the Unit's Director, Dr Wayne Parsons, and Professor Trevor Smith for their encouragement and support. We are also indebted to those individuals who gave their time and permission to be interviewed in the course of the study. Also to Dr John Stone, Head of the Department of Social Science and Administration at Goldsmiths' College, London University, for the invaluable resources he secured which were vital to its realization in book form.

We would also especially like to express our thanks to Naomi Roth for her help in bringing the manuscript to print. Also to Claire Wallace, Bernard Davies and George Low for their helpful comments and criticisms.

Our final thanks are to Beulah and Janine for their patience and love.

Introduction: A Quango with a Mission

> Today's debate will attract no great headlines in tomorrow's newspapers.[Yet] The setting up of the Manpower Services Commission is a momentous event in Britain's social, industrial and educational history. . . . It is an objective some of us have been working for for many years. . . . Progress has been slow not to say laborious . . . I should like to have seen its birth marked with a little more panache (Sir Paul Bryan MP, then junior Minister at the Department of Employment, *Parliamentary Debates*, vol. 852, c. 1160–1, 13 March 1973).

The Manpower Services Commission was created by the Employment and Training Act 1973 and lasted until its transformation into the Training Commission in 1988. Its short history was rich in controversy and full of intrigue. No other quango (quasi-autonomous non-governmental organization) attracted such critical comment from left and right. Even its name-plate was deemed sexist. Nevertheless its growth was spectacular and its breadth of responsibility ever wider ranging. This contrasted sharply with the MSC's birth as a small public agency which was little known outside the training community. Yet the MSC came to represent a new vision of society and the economy. Its leading personnel emphasized the importance of vocational education and training in economic regeneration. Moreover, by its very nature, as the largest of many quangos, the MSC had a controversial career in terms of public accountability and its overall relationship to the state.

In the turbulent political and economic conditions of the 1970s and 1980s the Manpower Services Commission was to be a quango with a mission; a mission rarely perceived and all too often misunderstood. Caroline Benn and John Fairley (1986), for instance, perceived it as an 'increasingly sinister corporate creature that was changing the nature of British society — in particular jobs, training and education' (p. 12). Another critic was similarly convinced that the strategic purpose of the MSC was nothing less than the 'radical restructuring of the British working class' (Finn, 1986, p. 54). Educationalists also conceived of the MSC as determined upon narrowing the school curriculum and thus ensuring that the middle class received a standard education whilst the working class was entertained by something called training (e.g. Morris and Griggs, 1988). In a short polemic Frank Coffield asked 'Is there work after the MSC?', and relabelled the MSC 'the Ministry of Social Control' (*New Society* 26 January 1984). However, at the ideological level the MSC countered by postulating a simple economic truth — that if Britain wished to regain its status as an industrial power of the first rank, society at large had to rethink its attitude to wealth and its creation. In short, Britain had to have a 'social ethic' which corresponded to its political aspirations for economic modernization.

The implications of this simple message gave the MSC an influence and significance that was more subtle and pervasive than has been generally recognized. Its critics have generally emphasized the short-run economic and political objectives of the MSC, especially because the quango gained a reputation for its expertise in crisis management. But, put into the context of seeking to modernize Britain's attitudes to the world of work and wealth creation, short-term evaluations of the significance of the MSC are somewhat lacking in historical perspective. Hostility to the MSC was aggravated by the fact that many of its ideas were also shared by the 'New Right'. Their emphasis on creating a law-abiding community built upon the foundations of individualism, free markets and financial discipline implied, although this was rarely explicitly stated, a remoulding of the underlying cultural values holding the nation together. Through its insistence upon changing attitudes to work and wealth creation, the MSC was at the forefront of the social engineering involved. But the MSC's ideas about the future of British society were also valid for each of the other main options then available in the political market place: those of the state enterprise system and the social market. Political parties and their advisers preparing Britain for these alternatives failed to incorporate the MSC's message at the risk of appearing outdated and outmoded.

The quango set itself three important tasks. In the widest context of transforming deeply entrenched social values, it aimed to abolish completely the dichotomy between education and training that had emerged during the nineteenth century. Within the policy-making context, the MSC's goal was to elevate the importance of vocational education and training and redefine its contribution to productivity and national development. At the institutional level the MSC attempted the complete overhaul of Britain's education and training system. Predominant attitudes to wealth creation and industry naturally influenced the specific problem of the failure of state and industry to invest in vocational education and training but it was through its control of this vital area of domestic policy that the MSC tried to modernize basic aspects of the economy and to reshape the national psyche.

The MSC argued more convincingly and forcibly as time went by that Britain had consistently underestimated the contribution of the human factor to the economy. The return of mass unemployment in the 1970s and 1980s more than anything else blurred the debate about the role of training in economic performance. As Robinson (1989) indicated, the MSC failed to state clearly the fundamental objectives of many of its reforms of vocational education and training (VET). Any reform of VET had important repercussions, not only for improving the inflation/unemployment trade-off (what economists call the Phillips curve) and redistributing the employment opportunities within the labour market, but also for raising the productive capacity of the economy. Unfortunately, through the part it played in managing the worst effects of mass unemployment, the MSC's concept of vocational education and training came to be associated with sharing existing opportunities in a depressed labour market rather than with productivity and growth. The MSC was left struggling to create a modern and effective training culture while Britain's main competitors — the USA, Japan and West Germany — got on with the job of training and retraining for industrial and technological change.

By concentrating upon the MSC's fire-fighting initiatives in unemployment and incursions into what was seen as the separate area of education, many critics missed the overall intent of the MSC's longer-term ambition of creating what Alan Pike nicely termed 'a pro-training culture' (*Financial Times* 6 May 1986). Consequently the deep-seated nature of Britain's education and training malaise was too readily glossed over and attacks, often emotional, upon the quango ignored what the MSC faced in reality — a multi-faceted and deeply rooted training problem.

At the institutional level the MSC's great rival became the Department of Education and Science. The quango challenged the long-cherished notion of 'education for life' and attempted to replace it with 'education and training for work'. The practical embodiment of these ambitions was the much-plagued Youth Training Scheme for school leavers and the Technical and Vocational Education Initiative within schools. At the specific policy level the MSC's role was to find solutions for the skill shortage problem. Again, however, the MSC had to create a positive attitude whereby policy makers treated resources in human capital as an investment similar to that in plant and machinery. Yet the MSC repeatedly ran up against industry's inertia towards training.

As the MSC's ideas, in particular those of John Cassels, the first Director, and his successor Geoffrey Holland, evolved on the subject of training, other proposals concerned with maintaining full or near-full employment were also developed. After 1974 the MSC successfully managed the unemployment crisis for both Labour and Conservative administrations alike. Many of the new initiatives were the foundations from which it aimed to improve Britain's training policies in the years ahead. This book explains how the MSC has been a catalyst for policy development and adept at establishing and administering new programmes. It also indicates why the outcome of its efforts was not what their instigators had anticipated. For although it has been largely through the efforts of the MSC that the importance of training for industry is now accepted on all sides, it is also a fact that Britain's 'skills crisis' continues unabated. Similarly, despite the MSC's efforts to create a unified education and training system, the role of schools in allocating labour to unequal positions in the workforce has been enhanced.

As Britain's pioneering quango, the MSC, throughout its fifteen year existence, faced the persistent and ambiguous question of public accountability and control. Quangos have in the past been of two distinct types – those that are purely advisory bodies and those having executive powers to manage the day-to-day work of a policy area. The MSC was of the latter type and, like all quangos of this type, exhibited problems in terms of its relationship with other state bodies and parliament in particular. The MSC's relationship was especially controversial because of the very large public resources at its disposal and the increasing range of activities included in its brief. On the other hand the MSC was a tripartite body which was representative of the most powerful groups in British society. It gave a voice to the interests of both organized labour through the TUC and the employers through the CBI. This was critical to its success during a period of growing politicization and the consequent expansion of manpower policy. Membership of the MSC presented a channel, especially for the TUC, for influencing economic policy when other paths were blocked.

While quangos came and went, the MSC marched from strength to strength and this under successive Thatcher administrations which have been resolutely anti-quango and anti-interventionist in outlook. As a powerful strategic organization deep in the heart of the labour market the MSC appeared as anathema to Conservative ideology. Nevertheless two elections seemed to prove that the MSC was 'safe with the Tories'. Its security of tenure was assured because it succeeded in maintaining a degree of consensus of political opinion on seemingly daunting contemporary problems. In many ways the MSC had all the hallmarks of what has been called 'the Thatcher experiment', yet at first glance it appears contrary to Tory thinking. This book describes how the MSC sustained its precarious situation and remained in the vanguard of refashioning attitudes across British society. For as a public institution the MSC mirrored a modern, forward-looking corporation and placed the implementation of new ideas and the achievement of getting the job done above the niceties of public accountability and control. An editorial in the prestigious journal *Political Quarterly* rightly concluded that 'The MSC has demonstrated how a quango can be so arranged that it can play an innovative and energising role in some of the fields where Britain has been backward' (autumn 1986). It was indeed the embodiment of the Thatcher style of government – authoritarian and direct. The MSC also represented, as George Low said, 'a failure of democracy'. Economic success can have its democratic price.

Yet quangos are as easily disposed of as they are created. For an organization that was uncertain of its future from the moment of its creation, to survive as long as it did was a feat in itself. Although the abolition of the MSC caught many by surprise, a government marching on a stomach full of doctrine and dogma can dismiss any public body almost at will. With the return of economic growth in the mid-1980s the quango had outlived its usefulness. It was no longer needed to maintain even the semblance of social cohesion that it had provided for government. Nor was it required any longer to impose changes upon a reluctant Department of Education and Science now that a new definition of relevance to industry's needs had been adopted in the national curriculum for Britain's schools. At the same time enterprise replaced training as competition was unleashed upon schools and colleges turned loose into the educational market place. With the final departure of the trades unions from its decision-making processes, what was now seen as just another relic of Britain's corporate past was dismembered and then made redundant.

The history of the MSC divides into two distinct eras. Between 1974 and 1979 the Commission began, somewhat prematurely, the process of constructing a comprehensive manpower policy. In this guise manpower policy was an amalgam of employment policy (anti-unemployment programmes, employment placing services, labour mobility schemes), training policy (industrial training policy, vocational education and training initiatives) and manpower planning (labour market intelligence and occupational planning). The thinking behind comprehensive manpower policy was that historically uncoordinated labour market policies should be integrated and directed together to improve the efficiency of the labour market. Naturally the concept had crucial implications for combating unemployment and retaining full employment. This 'Grand Design' was the ultimate ambition of the MSC and, under Labour, was conceived as an attendant policy to an overall interventionist strategy whereby monetary and fiscal policy targeted inflation, industrial policy raised economic growth and manpower policy sustained full employment. For it to succeed, however, at least two conditions had to be fulfilled. Firstly, both industry and the state had to invest heavily in vocational education and training in order to enhance the performance of the economy. Secondly, new training and job creation programmes had to be seen in a positive light to enable Britain to have a highly trained and forward-looking workforce. One step built on the other and to a great extent the MSC was too optimistic as to the level of awareness among policy makers about the importance of human capital within industry and inside education. The return of mass unemployment and, ironically, the MSC's relative success in managing the crisis, left the Grand Design in tatters. For all intents and purposes it was abandoned and from 1976 the MSC grappled with its apparent failure.

The arrival of the first Thatcher government ushered in a new beginning for the MSC and for training in Britain. The MSC concentrated on changing attitudes to training and specializing in the field of vocational education and training. It attempted to divorce training from its connection with mass unemployment and to present it as an essential prerequisite for industrial and commercial efficiency. More generally the role of the MSC was to guarantee that Britain's education and training system reflected the needs of modern industry. In terms of economic policy its goal was to place manpower into the context of supply-side economics. Free-trade policies would ensure that industry could import new-technology plant and machinery from across the world; the domain that would give the critical competitive edge to the British economy, argued the MSC, was human capital (MSC, 1981a). Emphasis in Thatcherite ideology on competitiveness and productivity provided ripe conditions for the MSC to spread its gospel that the age of human capital had arrived. But the MSC was learning how difficult it was to administer a comprehensive manpower policy. At the very least it required a commitment by government to integrate manpower with a policy for incomes on the Swedish model and neither Conservative nor Labour governments were prepared to take this on.

Within these contrasting eras of MSC history there have been some discernible cycles in policy making and in outlook. The first period (1974–1976) witnessed the rise and fall of Comprehensive Manpower Policy. A second phase (1976–1982) was notable for the MSC's fire-fighting activities in the labour market. The MSC obtained the reputation for managing the worst effects of unemployment, expanding where it could and being awash with funds. Nevertheless, in the aftermath of the failure of the Grand Design, the Commission made a deliberate policy choice to concentrate on youth unemployment rather than spread resources thinly to cover the less sensitive adult problem. During these years, however, the MSC became less an independent forum on manpower issues and moved ever closer to realms of state, although parliamentary and public control was slight. As Kaufman (1986) argued, 'whatever the formal situation it is still on a tripartite basis, but more or less as an arm of central government' (p. 137). In this vital respect both Labour and Conservative administrations acted with the same political intentions. The 1973 Employment and Training Act conferred on the MSC the role of 'holding company' with powers to review the work of its two operating agencies, the ESA (Employment Services Agency) and the TSA (Training Services Agency). Under Labour this was to change. The Commission was to become the powerhouse, and the old operating arms legal divisions, of the ten-member board. The Tories brought this practical position within the law in their Employment and Training Act of 1981.

The new Thatcher government after some hesitation was also to learn of the fire-fighting capabilities of the MSC. It was soon evident that neither the government nor its policy advisers understood training beyond its connection with managing unemployment. The third phase of the MSC's development (1982–1986) saw the establishment of the first national vocational preparation scheme and was in effect a period of consolidation when some of the quango's other long-term policy goals were achieved. By 1986 the quango had reached its zenith. A consensus emerged over its existence prior to the 1987 General Election and the three main parties each elevated training into their mainstream economic strategies.

However, a fourth and final phase of the MSC's evolution began during the run-up to the 1987 General Election. Its whole existence, its structure and policies were to change beyond recognition. The Tory manifesto dismissed the earlier conception of a powerful strategic force improving the efficiency of the labour market. Instead the MSC was to concentrate on a single policy area – training. It was perhaps fitting for the Training Commission, as the new MSC was called, to specialize in an issue which was once the Cinderella of British economic policy. Moreover, the new role recognized the fact that the old MSC had been the catalyst and think tank for innovative policy ideas in the field of education, training and unemployment. However, this fourth phase in the MSC's development contradicted its founding philosophy of improving the efficiency of the whole labour market, not simply training. But the new Training Commission still faced the task of providing high-quality training schemes and of addressing the skill training problem, which had been aggravated by the (temporary) upturn in the economy. This task was finally returned to employers when the Training Commission was abolished in September 1988 after only ten days of existence.

The purpose of this first comprehensive volume on the Manpower Services Commission is twofold: firstly, the book provides a detailed history of the quango's administrative development and the evolution of its policies; secondly, it assesses the impact of the MSC and explains the underlying reasons for Britain's lamentable post-war training record.

Chapter 1 describes the steps that ultimately resulted in the creation of the MSC. It shows how the concept of a 'Council of Manpower Services' had its origins in the 1950s and 1960s. Central to the philosophy of its creation was a recognition of the need to coordinate the various initiatives directed at improving the efficiency of the labour market. The chapter concludes by discussing the possible future direction for the quango as judged by the views of the time and assesses the main areas of the debate for the 1970s. Chapter 2 follows the development of the MSC under the Wilson/Callaghan governments. Under Labour the MSC was to forgo comprehensive manpower planning in return for the stewardship of the fight against youth unemployment. The chapter closes by estimating the achievements and failures of the MSC under Labour and analyses the state of the manpower debate before the Thatcher era.

Chapter 3 discusses the relationship between Mrs Thatcher's economic policies and training. At first the very existence of the MSC was in some doubt. However, the deteriorating unemployment situation brought about a reprieve and also a remarkable and significant U-turn by Mrs Thatcher's first administration. Cuts were turned into a massive increase in public funding for anti-unemployment programmes. The chapter ends by examining the training debate and the relevance of training to supply-side economics. In 1983 the Tories returned to office with a clearer conception of the role of training in economic development and Chapter 4 relates how the MSC became an increasingly close ally of the second Thatcher government. The MSC found new responsibilities that had an intimate relationship with the dream of a free-enterprise culture. Chapter 5 outlines the history of the MSC until its transformation and eventual abolition. The establishment of the Training Commission severed the main organizational and economic principles of the MSC's existence. The short-lived TC was to administer the single area of vocational education and training, bringing to an end the notion of coordinating labour market strategy as a whole. This has its antecedents in the Conservative Party's original concept of the MSC back in 1973. The Tories' original idea was for a standard-setting body developing training programmes geared to the needs of the labour market. In many respects the MSC had come full circle. Moreover, the abolition of the Training Commission and the establishment of a new Training Agency meant that the control of training was back in the hands of Whitehall, something that policy makers twenty years before had wanted to move away from.

Finally, Chapter 6 evaluates the successes and failures of the MSC. In part this involves a somewhat technical discussion of the economics of training to trace the way in which, in their publications and pronouncements, the key MSC figures (interviews with whom formed the data for the original research upon which this book is based) preserved their original ideal of training policy and attempted to apply it in the very different circumstances which subsequently arose. In part it also criticizes the final outcome of this corporate ideal in practice and places the achievements of the MSC in the context of the social costs of the pursuit of the economic modernization that has been attempted by successive Thatcher governments.

Chapter 1

The Origins of the Quango

TRAINING AND THE STATE – THE VISION OF THE MSC

Like the first attempt at a prices and incomes policy, the first effort to create a unified system of education and training goes back to Elizabethan times. The 1563 Statute of Artificers (repealed 1814) was the only legislation to deal exclusively with training for work until the Industrial Training Act became law in 1964. Between those dates Britain had pioneered an industrial revolution without recourse to any formal training measures at all. This fact is alleged as yet another instance of that supposedly unique national capacity for muddling through without formal planning and central state direction. Pragmatic, down-to-earth, British empiricism could here be contrasted with Continental rationalizations and sweeping, philosophical schemes. What Rosenbrock (1977, p. 391) called 'the marriage of intellectual inquiry and practical skill, which resulted in the industrial revolution' was gloriously consummated without any formal brokerage by the legislature. This union just seemed to happen in the cataclysmic confusions of the time. Yet, however apparently miraculous the wealth generated by the country's lead as the first industrial superpower, the marriage between intellect and handicraft soon ended in a divorce. Indeed, throughout the nineteenth century and ever since commentators have bemoaned the subsequent separation between theoretical education and practical training. The accepted version of this sad story is that the children of those practical men of affairs, the factory owners, abandoned trade to ape the foppish ways of a parasitic and landed gentry. Unlike the founding ironmasters, who could turn their hands to any of the crafts performed by any of their operatives, their sons turned their backs upon manufacture and declined ever to soil their hands with practical affairs. With their fathers' fortunes they bought themselves into the aristocracy and thus saved that social anachronism from extinction. Instead, its continuing dominance over the nation's affairs was secured. Hence the consequent debilitating weakness for valuing the practice of effete arts above the creation of the wealth necessary to sustain them. The result was that schools and colleges put a premium on intellectual and abstract knowledge as opposed to practical skills. According to Corelli Barnett (1979), this situation would have to be reversed to 'keep Britain an advanced technological society and save her from being a Portugal, perhaps even an Egypt of tomorrow' (p. 127).

This widely prevalent diagnosis of 'the British disease' ignores the systems of training which were pioneered by the Ministry of Munitions during the First World War and the Ministry of Labour in the Second. Then the extraordinary demands of war production stimulated the training of men, and more especially women, as rapidly as possible. Between 1939 and 1945 Ernest Bevin, as Minister of Labour and National Service, drafted more than half a million people into government training courses to streamline industry for all-out war production. Yet, despite the recommendations of the 1945 Ince Report for a national apprenticeship scheme and the treatment of all beginning workers as trainees, this war-time experience did not permanently alter training in British industry. Formal training was still seen as a second-class method of instruction and apprenticeships, which had grown from their medieval origins under the control of the workers themselves, remained the route to the coveted status of skilled craftsman for manual employees. Meanwhile, the expansion of education after the Second World War catered almost exclusively for the selection of mainly middle-class youth to preferred non-manual employment in the growing service sector.

Technical schools were included as part of the tripartite system of education established by the 1944 Education Act, but during the 1960s and 1970s they were absorbed into the new comprehensive schools. This loss was regarded by even such a prominent advocate of the comprehensive reform as A. H. Halsey (1980) as 'one of the tragedies of British education after the second war' (p. 214). Or, as Lord David Young expressed it from an opposed perspective, 'In the drive towards comprehensives the technical and vocational end of education somehow got lost' (quoted in McCulloch, 1986, p. 45). As late as 1958 secondary technical schools still contained only 4 per cent of the secondary school population and did not exist in more than 40 per cent of local education authorities (Shilling, 1989, p. 49). Similarly the polytechnics, set up in the expansion of higher education that followed the 1963 Robbins Report, quickly came to be imitations of the universities and followed Oxford and Cambridge in encouraging arts rather than sciences and pure research rather than applied technology. Despite their elders' agonizing over the dangers of a divide between the 'two cultures' of art and science, the middle-class students, who were the main beneficiaries of the increase in educational opportunities, persisted in their preference for the arts over the sciences and their applications. So what remained of technical education in formal institutions took place largely in night schools and further education colleges. Here it became established, as Cotgrove (1958) said, as 'a predominantly part time education for students working in factory and office, concentrated mainly on training the technician, craftsman and office worker' (p. 67). Thus the informal and very varied procedures of time-served apprenticeship remained the main route to acquiring craft skills for skilled manual work and the technical tasks that were based upon it.

Numbers of apprentices peaked in 1966, though the proportion of young workers apprenticed did not decline until its highest (25 per cent) in 1969 – one-third of all boys but less than one-tenth of girls, and those mainly in hairdressing (Further Education Unit, 1980, pp. 34–5). Traditional apprenticeships, like the monarchy and aristocracy and so much else of British life, survived as curious relics of a more glorious past. Yet, particularly for young, working class men, they still differentiated the skilled, regularly employed breadwinner from the irregular and unskilled labourer. Just as in Victorian times, apprenticeships under the control of the craft unions secured the reproduction of an aristocracy of labour, distinguished by its sober and respectable habits from the rough mass of the unskilled. Similarly, distinct labour markets were, as Finn (1987) remarked, 'structured through divisions of sex, age and race' (p. 45), more recent immigrants after the war taking the place of the Irish in the century before.

Of course all this was very different from training arrangements in competitor countries, not only Germany and France, but also Japan, the USA and USSR. Here, with the exception only of the USA, industrialization had been a 'top down' affair. Thus, unlike Britain, 'industrialization was, from the start, a political imperative', as David Landes (1969) indicated in his comparison of technical change and industrial development in Western Europe from 1750 (p. 129). The consequence was that for these rivals 'It was the state that encouraged the immigration of foreign – mainly British – workers and technicians, that mobilized capital for investment, that underwrote loans, that set up industrial enterprises, that established (well before Britain) schools and institutes of scientific and technical training' (Kumar, 1978, p. 128). As Britain's protected markets in its former colonial empire were steadily lost to increasingly independent governments and penetration by rival capitalisms, the problem of modernizing an antiquated domestic industry became more and more urgent. Britain steadily sank down the league table of industrial production, dropping below even Italy among the other Common Market countries and now only just ahead of Spain, followed by Greece and Portugal. The country that had led the world in industrial production was now the sick man of Europe. The sickness seemed terminal as economic malaise repeatedly manifested itself in chronic social and political problems.

Sclerotic class divisions ossified any attempt at modernization and reform. Despite reforming efforts the education system only seemed to reproduce these divisions. In the nineteenth century British education had been dominated by the classics to an extent that the historian Hugh Trevor-Roper (1973) found 'extraordinary':

> For surely it must strike any historian as odd that an industrial revolution, having triumphed at home, was carried over the whole world by the élite of a society bred up on the literature of a city state and an empire whose slave-owning ruling class regarded industry and commerce as essentially vulgar . . .

In the twentieth century 'education policy', as Ken Jones (1983) related, 'failed to create a school system adequate to the tasks of technical and political modernization' (p. 19). Paradoxically, Jones attributed this failure to 'the persistent cultural, even ethical concern to mitigate social differences between classes, and to draw an intractable working class into a unified national experience'. This 'affected policy for most of the post-war period and . . . was in conflict with an approach that wished to prioritise a strengthening of the links between schooling and employment' (pp. 20–1).

Meanwhile the training system of apprenticeships remained under the control of the trades unions, which were identified by government and employers as the foremost obstacle to any rationalization and modernization. The industrial craft unions had been formed, as Edward Lucie-Smith relates in *The Story of Craft*, to help resist the pressure of the unskilled mass below as much as that of the employers above.

In the printing trade, for example, 'a proportional role was enforced, which allowed only two apprentices to every four journeymen. . . . Thus the unions concerned themselves, both here and elsewhere, not only with questions of pay and hours, but also with demarcations between different types of jobs and degrees of efficiency. The differentials they insisted upon were a source of friction between one class of worker and another, and sometimes a cause of disruption within industry itself' (1981, 264–5). Because the unions were organically connected with the Labour Party, every legislative effort at reform of the training system was undertaken by Conservative governments. This was a paradox mainly because Tory rhetoric opposed any interference by the state, particularly with employers' own training arrangements. But it is also surprising that one source of the Conservatives' ideas for reform lay in the British labour movement and the trades unions that are its organizational backbone and chief means of financial support. The unions saw themselves as the parents and guardians of such a tradition as did exist in the historical apprenticeship system. They blamed the employers for not extending its benefits to embrace all sections of the working population. They saw management as preoccupied with the physical side of investment in plant and machinery over the investment, which they saw as equally necessary, in upgrading the responsibilities and skills of the workforce.

The labour movement argument for a comprehensive education and training system was undermined by the actual way in which new technology, when it was at last introduced into industry, was applied by Britain's employers. The loss of Britain's protected markets abroad and the penetration of its market at home revealed the precarious position to which the national economy had sunk. Drastic measures would be necessary to restore profitability and so labour had to be coerced or cajoled into contributing to the reconstitution and accumulation of capital that was necessary. New technology was not therefore brought in with the general agreement and cooperation of workers and their unions but in face of their defensive determination to stick to long-established working practices. Where this resistance could be overcome, new methods of production resulted in the overall shedding and deskilling of labour. The consequences of such an application of new technology were nowhere to be seen more plainly than in the old industrial heartlands of Britain. Here there was mass redundancy of the old craft skills and their replacement, if they were replaced, by semiskilled working in new service industries. The result was the destruction of whole communities and the patterns of life reproduced over decades in relation to traditional ways of working. The majority of the workforce was thus degraded towards an undifferentiated mass of interchangeable and semiskilled labour.

These processes of change were continually at work over a long period. During the 1960s they were apprehended as an opportunity for modernization that offered both the means of personal advance to new and better opportunities for many and the possibility of national progress for all. When this did not materialize the accumulated transformations appeared manifest in the form of a widely felt crisis in society and its institutions. The changes were unacknowledged until they were already having profound effects upon society at many levels. They were also generally misconceived, for it was supposed that since new machinery is more sophisticated and complex than the old it must necessarily require more people with more skills to manufacture and operate it. This was certainly the popular public perception that was encouraged by politicians and media alike but it is not necessarily the case. New technology is

certainly more complicated and scientifically advanced than the old which it super-
sedes, just as a steam engine is, when compared to a water mill. It therefore demands
the mastery of new techniques from those who manufacture and maintain it. However, such is the phenomenal productivity of modern manufacture that the proportion
of technicians and craftspeople involved in designing, producing and repairing new
machinery actually decreases compared with the proportion of workers who are
required to operate it, even though their number is also decreased absolutely. And
such is the sophistication of the new technology that the skills required for its
operation are also reduced. Even maintenance and repair are simplified, so that only
design and diagnosis comprehend greater uncertainties, while routine operations
increase certainty and thereby allow rapid and replicable results. The consequence
of this continuous process of rationalization is a widening division between mental
and manual labour, those who know and those who do. Increasingly, overall understanding of processes as wholes is concentrated in a diminishing élite.

This division of the working population is not inevitable but is a consequence of
the particular way in which new technology has been applied in the overdeveloped,
metropolitan countries. Rather than dividing and directing intensified labour into
isolated and repetitive tasks, new technology has the potential to lighten and diversify
work. This is in fact its most effective use, especially in the case of computer control
systems able to handle vast quantities of data with certitude and mechanical precision.
These require a sharing of resources among those who operate them and an extension
of their creative abilities in new relationships. The development of technology thus
has the potential not only to simplify tasks but also for them to be shared and
integrated, increasing productivity with less laborious and repetitive effort. It thus
presents a real opportunity for the transformation of the ancient division of labour
between workers by hand and by brain.

To take full advantage of this historical opportunity requires a new arrangement
of education and training. Unlike the latest reforms being attempted in the schools
system, this would not attempt to return to the type of selective organization that
existed in the recent or perhaps more distant past. Rather, for the first time, formal,
academic study would have to be intimately related with practical, applied learning
in a unified system of vocational education. This new education/training system would
demolish the traditional divisions between an élite education for the professions and
practical training for the crafts. Such a new, unified system of modernized schooling
and apprenticeship would undermine and eventually abolish the class barriers that
are sustained by an outdated division of labour at work. At the same time new and
more equal social relations could only promote the modernization and revitalization
of the economy, leading to a new industrial revolution.

This vision was shared by many who contributed to the growing debate on education and training in Britain, not least by the economists and planners who became
the driving force behind the Manpower Services Commission. They recognized that
the latest developments of new technology were undermining the immemorial divisions between mental and manual labour and between education and training.
Further, they acknowledged that if new technology was to be used to its fullest
advantage and achieve its potential of effecting a new industrial revolution, this could
only be achieved by extending technical training as universally as possible. This
entailed a corresponding social revolution. Traditional divisions between unskilled,

semiskilled and skilled workers would have to be overcome to create a new, flexible and multiskilled craft worker. Such a new type of worker would combine the mental skills of diagnosis and programming with the manual abilities to effect repairs and maintain production. This implied that it would eventually be necessary to obliterate the distinction between blue and white collar workers, between the office and the plant, managers and managed, those who think and those who do. In turn this required a complete transformation of existing attitudes towards education and training. No longer could they be regarded as separate and once and for all affairs. Instead, they were to be seen as indistinguishable and permanent processes which would be continued throughout everybody's working life. The preconception of a steady career or job would be replaced by the notion of transfer from one occupation to another, employments which the applications of new technology were rendering increasingly similar and more advanced. This visionary notion was in fact a highly ambitious programme to modernize both economy and society. It was a deliberate effort to transform the national psyche in the same way that it had been unintentionally constructed by the first industrial revolution.

1964 AND ALL THAT

Training is evidently a deeply political and therefore highly contentious issue. Like education, from which it cannot logically be separated, it concerns society itself and the skills and values it should develop to shape its future. Yet, unlike education, which was an important issue in both the 1945 and 1964 elections, training for a long time remained apolitical. As Anderson and Fairley (1982) confirmed: 'Generally speaking training has not been a major issue of political controversy in Britain for the post-1945 period, even during those periods when proposals for reform were under discussion in Parliament' (p. 192). The apolitical nature of the policy debate reflected the fact that industry was generally accepted as being responsible for training.

Yet there were two sides of industry and both maintained vested interests which prevented any alteration in the traditional situation. As the trades unions pointed out, employers operated within short time horizons that made them reluctant to spend more on training even in periods of boom, while during periods of slump training was the first item of expenditure to be cut back. When trade recovered, employers found it cheaper to compete with one another for the skilled workers they required. The prevalence of such poaching made them even more reluctant to invest time and effort in training staff who might be lured away by higher rewards elsewhere. As far as employers were concerned, the apprenticeship regulations that craft unions had traditionally used to limit the supply and maintain the price of skilled labour were just another of the restrictive practices and labour market rigidities which trades union intransigence put in the way of efforts at modernization and reform. The result was, as Perry (1976) described, that little changed despite frequent commissions and committees of inquiry at regular intervals over the past hundred years and more. These were indeed set up more in response to public concern about the increasing scientific and technological progress of competitor countries than to any concern from either side of industry. The only exception to this perennial stagnation was during the emergency conditions of war. Even then, the situation speedily reverted to normal peacetime practice. This inaction contrasts strikingly with the series of major reforms in education of 1870, 1902, 1918, 1944 and even 1988.

Technical education had been squeezed out of the schools system and survived in the further education colleges. These developed largely in response to industry's requirements for such training facilities as could not be developed on the job. However, as Perry remarks, the majority of firms did not use the further education colleges and did not offer day release for their employees to benefit from them. Nor did they provide much in the way of in-service training. In practice, smaller firms did not train at all but poached trained personnel from the larger companies. To hang on to their trained staffs, larger firms were often forced to promote them away from the shop floor for which they had been trained in the first place. There was a further contradiction in that while enhanced training benefited the individual, it was the company that generally paid for it. So it was the company that lost its investment if newly qualified employees sold their skills on the open market. Plainly there was here a major failing of the free labour market and some sort of state intervention would be necessary.

A sub-committee of the National Joint Advisory Council at the Ministry of Labour (the grandparent of the MSC) was set up, headed by Robert, later Lord, Carr, a private secretary at the department. Yet when it reported in 1958, while it detailed the familiar failings of the training system, including the narrow and specialized content of most apprenticeships, it recommended no fundamental changes. In fact it concluded that responsibility for training should remain with industry. The Tories clearly considered that industry was doing a splendid job and, moreover, the captains of industry wished to keep their training arrangements free from state interference and on a course of voluntary action.

As Britain's relative economic condition continued to decline with the loss of its empire and protected markets in the 1950s and 1960s, a gathering consensus came to share the opinion that the *laisser-faire* approach to training could no longer be tolerated. As Kenny and Reid (1985) said, 'it had consistently failed to supply adequate numbers of skilled workers, and concern was especially prevalent about the impact of these difficulties on the engineering industries in view of their great importance for the national economy' (p. 273). A number of factors combined to reinforce this dawning realization as the post-war boom slid gradually into periods of alternating stop and go. Then insufficient training during recession resulted in skill shortages during the following recovery. Further, the pay differentials that traditional apprenticeship training had enforced were consistently eroded so that, whereas 'in Victorian times the skilled man's wage rate was normally twice that of the labourer, by 1914 the difference was only 50 per cent, and in 1952 it was 16 per cent' (Harrison, 1983, p. 42). Numbers in apprenticeship were falling, as has been noted. Also there were reports that many of those who were apprenticed were not sticking the course as they supposedly had done in the past but were dropping out to unskilled jobs. These 'dead end' employments paid more immediately, if less later, and the Americanized teen-culture that was such a source of contemporary concern emphasized immediate youthful gratification rather than traditional saving for the future.

Typically the immediate prompting for the Carr Committee had been social concern for the teenager bulge then working its way onto the labour market. Concern for the superfluity of the unskilled outweighed anxieties about the shortage of skilled manual workers. The Committee's brief was to 'consider arrangements for the training of young workers in industry with particular reference to the adequacy of intake into apprenticeship and other forms of training in the light of the expected increase in the number of persons entering employment'. The prime mover then was the threat of youth unemployment, and only when it became apparent that the economic boom would be sufficiently sustained to absorb the excess into the labour market did the Committee go on to consider the second part of its brief, namely 'to ensure an adequate supply of trained workers for future needs' (HMSO, 1958). However, an indication of changing perceptions was the report of a working party set up by the Ministry of Labour in 1961 which concluded: 'While the primary responsibility must remain with industry, the Government may need in future to play a larger role in industrial training' (quoted in Sheldrake and Vickerstaff, 1987, p. 33).

Following consultation on a White Paper two years previously, the 1964 Industrial Training Act established a Central Training Council with six employers and six trades union representatives. It had an advisory and consultative function but no actual control over similarly tripartite Industrial Training Boards. Although set up by a Conservative government, the ITBs were intended to play their part in Labour's national planning processes by liaising with the little National and Economic Development Councils that were to look after the manpower requirements of their industrial sectors. By May 1966 there were 13 ITBs covering seven-and-a-half million workers. Numbers training in manufacturing industry increased by 15 per cent between 1964 and 1969 and faster in those industries covered by the ITBs (Lees and Chiplin, 1970). There was also increased day-release use of expanded further education facilities. Although all this was intended to benefit employers, they complained ceaselessly about the exactions of the grant/levy system which financed the training that the ITBs organized and about the interference of the ITBs in what they regarded as their own affairs. Smaller firms particularly lost out because, although they paid the levy, they did not benefit from the grants which went to the larger companies. This conflict between larger and smaller capitals was in fact the main reason why the 1964 Act broke down. Trades unions meanwhile were characteristically divided between urging greater state planning of training for the benefit of all workers, including the unskilled and unemployed, while at the same time hanging on to the advantageous conditions that they had secured for their craft members.

The workings of the Act were therefore reviewed in 1969, and in 1972 the Department of Employment issued a discussion document 'Training and the Future' (HMSO, 1972). This in turn led to the Employment and Training Act of 1973. Such were the leisurely and consultative ways in which government policy was made in those days which seem so far removed from the system of administrative fiat by which policy, especially training policy, came to be made after 1979. In fact they were not so distant; the new balance of industrial training, which was now intended to lean towards the employers and away from the unions, was one symptom of the Heath government's initial enthusiasm for free-market solutions to economic problems. During this brief reign of Selsdon man, unemployment rocketed towards half a million. Yet Sir Keith Joseph was soon to be arguing in opposition against Heath's capitulation to the unions and the fear of the unemployed lounging along the street corners in their thirties cloth caps. In the changed circumstances of the

1980s the free-market solutions that Joseph urged would indeed be applicable to a Britain ever deeper in economic and social crisis. Then the abandonment of the State's commitment to full employment (enshrined in the 1944 White Paper 'Employment Policy') would mark the adoption of a deliberate intention to roll back the rest of the welfare state. 'Full employment' of course really referred to traditional male employment and, strangely, as male unemployment rose during the recession the number of jobs actually increased, especially if account is taken of part-time and home working, these jobs being undertaken mainly by women.

The ITB system fell foul of the beginnings of this recession, in which training was as usual the first item of expenditure upon which employers endeavoured to make savings. As a consequence numbers in apprenticeship fell rapidly. This alone demonstrated the failure of the 1964 Act to bring about a change in industry's attitude to training. The trades unions too withdrew to more entrenched, defensive positions. Yet technological developments were continuously undermining their traditional protection of apprenticeships for skilled crafts. With the collapse of traditional male industries, especially in the North, and their replacement by 'light' industries staffed by women in the South, the majority of young people entering the labour market performed the increasingly semiskilled tasks that the applications of new technology demanded. The old divisions between skilled and unskilled labour were collapsing. Workers were increasingly required who were able to switch between one and another area of work rendered more similar and simplified by the latest advances in automation and control. At the same time recession was beginning to recast the structure and situation of the workforce as a whole. Different concepts of training and retraining would have to be developed if this new situation was to be contained – let alone seized upon as a new opportunity for industrial renewal, social progress and individual advantage.

THE MAKINGS OF THE MSC (1964–1973)

The 1964 settlement of training was coming under increasing fire from left and right. Enoch Powell, for instance, topically punned that Britain was the victim of a 'Great Training Robbery' (also the title of a much later criticism of YTS by trades unionists in Birmingham and of Ivan Berg's celebrated 1971 critique of the US education system). With characteristic hyperbole, Powell asserted that 'the Act had ignited a prairie fire of bureaucracy and profligate spending' (speech to Nottingham Branch of the Institute of Marketing, 11 January 1971). He went on to prophesy that 'freed from its anchorage in profit and loss, it was predictable that training would rise like a balloon and float up into the stratosphere'. Meanwhile the left argued, as many still do – Maurice Kaufman, for instance – that 'The finance of training must be the central issue in the design of any new national training system . . . taking into account the general lack of training tradition in Britain and the unwillingness of most companies to spend money on it of their own accord' (in Benn and Fairley, 1986, p. 143). The left believed that industry should therefore be taxed to provide the costs of state training, just as employers contributed to National Insurance. The levy/grant system of raising money for the ITBs was denounced as an unsatisfactory fudge, which it was. As Perry (1976) recorded, the 1964 Act 'represented an ingenious compromise in leaving control in the hands of those directly concerned with the results of training and providing a self-financing mechanism, while avoiding direct intervention from the centre' (p. 311). In addition, as has been seen, employers were increasingly dissatisfied with the arrangement.

The Conservative government's 1972 discussion document 'Training and the Future' (HMSO, 1972) considered that the levy/grant system had administered a 'shock treatment' to industry. As a consequence a 'permanent shift in attitude in British industry' had been effected. A modification of the system could therefore now be permitted so that employers should no longer have to contribute to training outside their own needs. Government ministers argued that the ITBs had important achievements to their credit. 'They have focussed the attention of industry on training. New thinking about training has been stimulated and new initiatives taken in many fields. Senior management now recognize the value of training more widely' (para 24). Chichester Clarke, the Minister of State for Employment, echoed the report's optimism when he told the House of Commons in March 1973 that there had been 'a change in behaviour of industry'. On the basis of this sanguine assessment a national training agency along Swedish or West German lines was proposed. (Sixteen years later identical arguments were used to justify the dismantling of the MSC and the handing of control of training back to employers.)

The Conservatives' uncharacteristic interest in a national training body to coordinate the work of the ITB was as much administrative as economic. Prime Minister Heath was especially keen to put into effect the recommendations of the 1968 Fulton Committee on the Civil Service. This had advised the 'hiving off' of individual functional units within departments and the establishment of management units with executive power outside departments. The Businessman Team, led by a manager on secondment from Rio Tinto Zinc, advised Heath on putting these recommendations into effect. In particular the Team worked on the problem of improving the Department of Employment's job placing activities. Yet the government was still wary of creating a Frankenstein's monster that would be beyond their control. 'Initially', as Jackson (1986) records, 'the government's plan had been to create simply a national training agency which would co-ordinate the work of the industrial training boards and take over the government's own existing vocational training scheme, which was to be expanded into a mass Training Opportunities Scheme (TOPS)' (p. 28).

A National Training Agency was to be created by hiving it off from the Department of Employment. There had been some discussion about whether it should not be located in the Department of Education and Science but this was a battle that the then Education Secretary lost. As George Low (1988) laconically remarked, 'That was one of the few battles Mrs Thatcher lost as Secretary of State or since' (p. 215). The MSC was to be headed by a chief executive responsible to the Secretary of State for the day-to-day management and allocation of the grant-in-aid from the Department of Employment. The Secretary of State was empowered by the Act with the authority to employ temporarily out-of-work citizens. This merely legalized the work of the Department of Trade and Industry's Community Industry Programme, which provided direct grants to disabled young workers. This was the acorn from which the mighty oak of the MSC's training empire was to grow.

The Training Services Agency was organized into three operating arms: Industry, Directorate and TOPs, with three support divisions; planning, corporate services, and marketing and public relations. Maurice Macmillan, Robert Carr's successor, declared in a parliamentary debate in March 1973 that the TSA would 'be able to take a national view of training needs, which no Industrial Training Board can do, and be able to give Boards help in taking account of their needs, as well as acting themselves, and will be able to provide a basis for research and manpower planning activities'. However, the forty TSA staff were not content to fulfil such a limited brief and immediately set about producing an ambitious and radical 'Five Year Plan'. A main policy recommendation was the call for a state-funded national vocational preparation scheme (Training Services Agency, 1973, p. 14). This was regarded by one of its authors, John Cassels, as 'a valiant effort to persuade industry, when unemployment was relatively low, of the value of such a programme' (interview, 4 May 1985). Cassels still adheres to the radical commitment of such a unified vocational education scheme: fifteen years later and by then the Director-General of the National Economic Development Council, he argued that

> Britain has never really believed in education for the whole of the nation. . . . How else can we explain our long toleration of an examination system which, being (in the jargon) norm-referenced, is programmed to fail up to half of those who sit exams – however well they do? (*The Economist* 27 January 1986).

He still sees vocational training as equal in importance to academic study and a unified education/training system as the way forward to a modernized technology and a more equal society. At the very least he considers that a vocational A level is needed, similar in status to its academic counterpart.

An independent training services agency to coordinate manpower planning and supply with integrated national training programmes had long been the demand also of many in the TUC. Frank Cousins of the Transport and General Workers' Union, for instance, advocated access to training for all workers, not just for apprenticed craft workers. The previous Labour government also had mooted a 'Council of Manpower Services', suggested by Barbara Castle to oversee manpower policy. (Castle also began thinking about splitting the old unemployment offices from the payment of benefits and relocating job centres into prime high street sites. Later, when the split was complete, an Employment Services Agency was authorized to administer them.) Both the TUC and the Labour Party leaned toward the example of Sweden's enlightened social democracy. In particular, they admired the work of the Swedish Labour Market Board, which was used by the socialist government there to maintain full employment in conjunction with demand management policies. Thus it is no exaggeration to say that this became the blueprint for the future MSC.

However, short of a British LMB, the TUC and Labour Party were against any of the changes that the government and CBI proposed in the existing ITBs. In an effort to break the deadlock, Mr Bury, an official at the CBI, sent a letter to his opposite number at the TUC. This correspondence was duly jointly endorsed and sent to the Secretary of State for Employment, Robert Carr. A National Training Agency was thus sanctioned, but the importance of the letter was that it indicated that both the TUC and CBI were agreed on the creation of the MSC.

> 'The TUC concludes that a National Manpower Board – concerned with training and employment services, and with a say in job creation – is needed to provide a coherent structure and effective results. The CBI did not specify the possibility . . . but is not

opposed to it in principle' (joint letter to the Secretary of State for Employment, CBI Press Release, July 1972, p. 14).

The idea of a National Manpower Board was thus inextricably connected with the creation of both the Employment Services Agency and the Training Services Agency. It is therefore incorrect of Perry (1976) to assert that 'the Manpower Services Commission was introduced as a last minute amendment reminiscent of the way in which the Central Training Council had seen the light of day' (p. 313). Similarly Jackson's account of the formation of the ESA and the TSA jointly into the MSC is somewhat wide of the mark. What these writers, and others – for instance, Stringer and Richardson (1982) – do not appreciate is the political circumstances of the MSC's gestation. For the summer of 1972 had seen a dramatic shift in approach by the Heath government. Chastened by the failure of his Selsdon phase, Heath was now determined to co-opt British management and the trades unions into the economic decision-making process. The MSC, as an organization of a new type, therefore showed, as Maurice Macmillan told the House in March 1973, 'the importance that the Government and others attach to the involvement of those concerned, management and unions. . . . The Government attach great importance to what has become known as the tripartite approach. . . .' In short, the Tories agreed to the MSC's establishment because Heath and his fellow Ministers thought it would be a sweetener for their new attempt at Incomes Policy. Paradoxically, in the opinion of Len Murray, who was to become the Secretary General of the TUC, 'it is less difficult for unions to win from their members acceptance on temporary wage restraint, than it is for them to win changes in manpower practices' (quoted in Taylor, 1982, p. 142).

The task which the MSC was set of comprehensive manpower planning, linking job creation with training for employment, was, as Kenny and Reid wrote (1985, p. 294), unprecedented in peacetime. It gave the Secretary of State for Employment, for example, powers of direct intervention in the education system that the Education Secretary was not to enjoy until Mr Baker's assumption of direct control in the 1988 Education Reform Act. Yet, partly because (as we have seen) it enjoyed all-party support and was therefore not contentious, being approved also by both the TUC and CBI, it received very little attention at the time.

ACCOUNTABILITY AND CONTROL

The first government inquiry into training, the Carr Committee, had brought together an informal training community which comprised the TUC, the employers' federation and specialist interest groups like the Institute of Personnel Management, the Institute of Training Officers and BACIE (the British Association for Commercial and Industrial Education). The passage of the 1964 Act formalized this policy-making network. The 1973 Employment and Training Act brought other government departments into the network, most notably the DES and the Exchequer, plus the Department of Trade and Industry, which had sponsored some small job creation schemes before the MSC took them over. The composition of the MSC itself included representatives from education and the local authorities which led to participation by the local education authorities and to the associations voicing their interests – the Association of Metropolitan Authorities, the Association of County Councils and the Association of District Councils. There were also all the unions involved in teaching and lecturing in the schools and colleges. Added to these national groups the MSC's programmes called for a response from the local community and the establishment of regional and local delivery systems. The depth of the policy-making community, argued Moon and Richardson (1985, p. 125), showed that the quango was in fact a 'multipartite' organization and not simply a tripartite body as indicated by the composition of the Commission.

As to the composition of the Commission itself, since the chairman was supposed to act independently of government, Tom King, then a back-bench MP and a future Employment Secretary, argued that it could not be termed tripartite and that this raised grave questions of public accountability. In fact, a great deal of time was spent on the constitution of the Commission and Mrs Thatcher as Secretary of State for Education made a number of representations to Robert Carr and later Maurice Macmillan to obtain assurances that education would not be left in the cold. The Labour Party and the TUC were appalled that the ITBs had no seat on the 10 person Commission board. Altogether, the final composition of the Commission left the consumers of training ahead of the suppliers of services and hence it was an organization dominated by the employers and the unions rather than by the professional trainers.

In effect, the lines of accountability left the Secretary of State for Employment in overall control. As Macmillan told the House of Commons, 'I must retain general responsibility for manpower policy, but I am proposing to set up a Manpower Services Commission representative of employers, trades unions and other interests which would have direct responsibility to me for employment and training services' (House of Commons Debates, 1972, vol. 846, c. 1293). The Chairman acted as the chief accounting officer and sent financial reports to the Secretary of State. Macmillan allayed Tory fears over inadequate control by stating that 'The Commission will have to work closely with my department since nearly all the money to finance it would come from the departmental vote' (*ibid*, 1466). In addition the quango's activities were subject to the normal processes of parliamentary scrutiny through the Public Accounts Committee.

Caroline Benn and John Fairley (1986) argue that the MSC was monolithic and undemocratic in structure. 'There is no mention of representative elections from those working in the MSC and participating in its schemes. Nothing comes from the bottom up as in properly constituted democratic institutions' (p. 7). However, the architects of the MSC dismissed the notion of direct elections because the Commissioners would be representative of the interests they served. (In the case of the TUC more so than the other groups because their representatives were appointed by elected members of their respective unions.) If the Commissioners could not agree among themselves or refused to put into practice decisions recommended by government, the Secretary of State had the final word. This safeguard, said the first Chairman, Sir Denis Barnes, was similar to that applied to 'other public bodies and the nationalized industries. The power is rarely used and the major responsibility for determining the development of the public employment and training services will rest with the Commission' (in *Personnel Management*, April 1974).

Apart from influence through the power of direction, auditing five-year rolling plans and annual financial accounts and nominating the independent Chairman, the state's influence also took the form of the informal links between staff at the Department of Employment and the MSC. As the quango grew, many staff transferred from the DE to the MSC and those in the highest ranks interchanged frequently. Moreover, appointments to the most senior posts, such as Director of the MSC, required authorization by the Prime Minister. The Employment and Training Act had, however, removed Civil Service status from the MSC on the grounds that the quango would be staffed by experts on training and employment. This was not in fact generally the case; as Kaufman (1986) observed, 'MSC staff were on the whole Civil Service bureaucrats with little or no expertise relevant to training. . . . There were few who could discuss training and training problems intelligently' (p. 138). Thus, for Kaufman, the Labour government's decision to reinstate Civil Service status was a retrograde step that harmed the development of training policy.

The Conservatives had a narrow view of manpower planning and therefore denied the new MSC any wider or more strategic role in economic policy. As far as they were concerned, the objective of the MSC was to reform arrangements for promoting a more efficient working of the labour market. Robert Carr, the principal drafter of the 1972 discussion document, saw the quango setting standards of training and undertaking research into what training was required. If it was to be involved in manpower planning at all, it was to be limited to making planning arrangements for skill shortages. Maurice Macmillan expected that the hardest task would be to try to 'anticipate and eliminate shortages of skilled manpower' (House of Commons Debates, 1972, vol. 846, c. 1148).

By contrast, the TUC and some sections of the Labour Party wanted to see the MSC take over the function of manpower planning and create a separate Manpower Intelligence Agency. This would lead to three agencies of similar status, the ESA, TSA and MIA, coordinated by a super-agency, the MSC. This, Perry (1976) argued, would end the way the 1964 Act had 'put the cart before the horse', since many ITBs in accepting aspects of manpower planning were limited only to a micro-approach within their particular industries.

> This has to be supplemented by some agency capable of taking a macro view of the economy as a whole, and this in turn means that the function of training has to be seen not only as setting the pattern for economic health but as providing a vital supporting role in maintaining and improving productive capacity (p. 313).

For this reason the Labour Party maintained that, as Reg Prentice told the House of Commons,

> such a Commission under the hands of a Labour government would make a substantial contribution to solving the manpower problem, and in the hands of a Conservative government we are bound to say that it would provide no substitute at all for the dynamic policies currently lacking in our employment and training policies (House of Commons Debates, 1972, vol. 856, c. 1149).

The TUC saw the MSC as a job creation agency. They particularly welcomed section five of the Employment and Training Act which, by legitimating funds already granted by Parliament to the Department of Trade and Industry for a small Community Industry Scheme helping young disabled people find jobs, enabled the Secretary of State for Employment to:

> make such arrangements as he considers appropriate for the purposes of providing

temporary employment for persons in Great Britain who are without employment; any such arrangements may include arrangements for making payments by the Secretary of State of grant or loan to persons to provide employment. . . .

However, they were disappointed that these powers were vested in the Secretary of State and not in the MSC. Similarly, Neil Kinnock suggested to the Standing Order Committee that:

If as a society we wish to remove the stigma surrounding unemployment it would be better for the power in the clause to be a function of the Commission rather than a reserve power of the Minister. In a sense it is the difference between having an emergency service which is provided by the Minister and having a national unemployment service perpetually available which is in the hands of the Commission which will be moving not only to meet the need after it has arisen but trying to anticipate the need through its general involvement in unemployment and training. This is one reason why we advocated a manpower intelligence agency (Report of Standing Order Committee A, 1973, p. 166).

Within the labour movement's ranks therefore the MSC was seen as either planning the whole labour market through a national manpower plan, as by the TUC, or as a national unemployment service in perpetual motion, as by Kinnock.

In the event the prescience of the late Labour MP Guy Barnett was borne out, for he had suggested to the House that, although Ministers denied that section five implied any new powers, 'I am sure it is a clause which government, whether Conservative or Labour, will need to use' (Report of Standing Order Committee A, 1973, p. 176).

SUMMARY

This chapter has indicated something of the historical background to what increasingly came to be perceived as Britain's training crisis. This crisis was inextricably bound up with persistent social divisions and traditional cultural attitudes. It could only be resolved as part of a process of industrial modernization. The form this modernization should take was the subject of a debate that steadily politicized training issues. The 1964 settlement of training was a compromise between employers and the state in which the trades unions preserved their own vested interests. It was revised in the 1973 Employment and Training Act that created the Manpower Services Commission. The Heath government had its own administrative interest in setting up such a quango independent of the established civil service departments but gave the MSC only the limited brief of coordinating existing training arrangements. The founding of the Commission also signalled the government's return to consensus management of the economy after a brief attempt to apply free-market policies. The composition of the MSC, however, left employers dominant over training provision with the Secretary of State for Employment in final command. The Labour Party when it returned to government in 1974 shared with the trades unions a conception of the MSC as a national training agency modelled upon the Labour Market Board which played such a strategic role in the Swedish economy. Only the Liberals, and later the Social Democrats who joined them, were prepared to extend this strategic role to include coordination with incomes policy. Among the small staff of the initial Training Services Agency, however, there was a more radical comprehension of the changes which the application of the latest technological advances were inflicting upon traditional divisions of labour. They appreciated the opportunities for modernizing Britain's industry and society which the need for nationally organized programmes of training and retraining offered.

Chapter 2

The MSC under Labour (1974–1979) – Managing the Unemployment Crisis

A FALSE DAWN

Labour's advent to power in the 1974 General Election transformed the political landscape in which the MSC found itself. The support of the new government and its TUC backers for central planning and an industrial strategy suggested a much-enhanced role for the fledgling quango. Labour's election manifesto had promised to turn the MSC into 'a powerful body responsible for the development and execution of a comprehensive manpower policy'. Stuart Holland (1975), who was the main architect of the Party's industrial strategy, described at length in his book *The Socialist Challenge* (1975) how the state was to take over monopoly capital in Britain by planning agreements, sector working parties to improve efficiency and a National Enterprise Board to raise investment. These ideas were also embodied in two White Papers, 'The Regeneration of British Industry' (1974) and 'A New Approach to Industrial Strategy' (1975). 'An enlightened manpower policy', as Perry (1976) could see, 'has an important part to play in this scheme of things' (p. 317). Yet, however bright the MSC's prospects looked at the beginning of Labour's term of office, by the end of it there was a realization that the promise of a rational manpower policy had been lost in pursuit of what Holmes (1985, p. 35) called Labour's shibboleth – Industrial Policy.

Moreover, as Sam Brittan noted (1976, p. 77), there was no immediate change in 'economic philosophy'; Denis Healey followed the same 'corporatist' and 'incomes policy' approach as Heath's government. In the industrial strategy manpower planning was relegated to ensuring a supply of key skills necessary for technological growth. The MSC's function therefore was to promote a 'more effective manpower policy, including measures to provide a better supply of skilled manpower to the growth industries and to cope with the problems of transferring people from contracting to expanding industries. . .' For this purpose 'training and retraining will be crucial both in coping with the problems of the recent recession and in enabling people with the needs of the reorientated British industry' (1975 White Paper). The MSC did not find this essentially servicing role either adequate or self-evident. Its

1976/77 Annual Report stated that it was still awaiting a reply from the government about its exact role in the industrial strategy: 'As yet the sectoral approach adopted has not given a clear indication for manpower policy' (p. 7).

Clearly at least, this subsidiary function in the overall industrial strategy did not amount to the centrally important, comprehensive manpower policy to which the MSC aspired. For one thing there was no longer the public money available to pay for it. Raging inflation, mounting unemployment and a deepening balance of payments deficit left little available for expensive programmes of public spending. The government's task was nothing short of 'balancing incompatibles' (Coates, 1980, p. 39). Labour's programme, which aimed to raise industrial efficiency, by definition presumed a high degree of labour shake-out in the short run. As Denis Healey told the House of Commons in December 1975, 'We can return to full employment and maintain full employment over the years if we can bring down our inflation rate to international levels, and improve our industrial performance. . .' (House of Commons, 17 December 1975). It is important that there was still this commitment to restoring full employment eventually and it fitted quite well into the beliefs of the MSC. While some within the TSA accepted that the era of full employment was finally over, others, most notably within the expanding Office of the Manpower Services Commission, thought it could be maintained with the right macro-economic policies. This difference in opinion found joint expression in the practical policies devised to combat unemployment. On the one hand, fire-fighting measures aimed at managing unemployment through micro-initiatives in a period of macro constraint. On the other, these sorties into the labour market were the foundations upon which to change the face of Britain's education and training system in the 1980s. In the long run enhanced efficiency would restore employment levels but in the meantime the MSC was to manage the worst effects of temporary unemployment for increasing numbers of people. This allowed the Labour government to get off the hook, for the Chancellor had sworn that a strategy which consciously created unemployment was politically and morally evil. This hopefully temporary but actually more and more permanent task fell to the MSC. In carrying it out the organization proved its administrative ability to implement large-scale public programmes that steadily grew in scope and in size. Perhaps more importantly, during these years a shift occurred in the intellectual climate of economic policy that would be critical for the MSC's development. The MSC was to thrive after the collapse of the Keynesian era and also to find a place in the sun of Callaghan's Ruskin revolution.

Both operational arms of the MSC had been hived off from the Department of Employment by the end of 1973. The Training Services Agency was transferred to the MSC in April 1974 and the Employment Services Agency in October of the same year, after the practicalities of separating the unemployment benefit operations from the job placing functions were resolved and completed. The Conservative Secretary of State for Employment, Maurice Macmillan, had appointed the Permanent Secretary of the Department of Employment, Sir Denis Barnes, to the Chairmanship of the MSC. He was a civil servant whose name was known in connection with the (then) Youth Employment Service. This appointment, although it appeared logical and natural to many, aroused deep resentment from the TUC. Congress House was of the opinion that Barnes was too close to the Civil Service establishment and that he would not favour a comprehensive manpower policy of the type that the unions wanted. In fact Barnes was himself surprised to be offered the post of Chairman since in 1972 he had had a sharp disagreement with the then Prime Minister, Edward Heath, over the likelihood of obtaining trades union support for wage restraint and he expected to be relegated to the Department of Agriculture and Fisheries. However, by the time he retired from the Chairmanship in 1976 he had earned the more than grudging respect of the unions, who were highly complimentary of his efforts (see Jackson's account of Barnes' appointment and initial union reaction, in Benn and Fairley, 1986, p. 29).

Barnes wanted to increase the MSC's independence by removing the detailed supervision of the Commission's work by the Department of Employment. This would be resented by civil servants at the Department who were envious of the 'free rein' they felt that the MSC already enjoyed. It should not be forgotten that during the first years of the MSC's existence there was continuous discussion over whether or not the Commission's role should be restricted to that of a lobbying institution, concerned merely with raising awareness of the necessity for training and training measures. The official view of the DE, as upheld by the new Permanent Secretary of Employment, Sir Kenneth Barnes (no relation!), was that the MSC should exercise a limited policy-making role. This view was strengthened by the grudging blessing of the Labour government in the shape of Michael Foot as Secretary of State for Employment. He later recalled: 'Reluctantly I agreed to support the MSC because I knew it was an idea that the Labour movement had been working for over the postwar years'. This was despite his disapproval of 'hiving-off government departments . . . which takes away some of the authority sovereign to Parliament' (interview, 10 May 1985). Nevertheless, MSC officials now at last had the go-ahead to develop their idea of a comprehensive manpower policy. They immediately embarked upon producing a radical and far-reaching strategy for manpower. Partly they had gained this freedom to plan so that Foot could deal with the more important and politically sensitive issues, such as industrial relations, which preoccupied him as Secretary of State. So, while freedom from detailed ministerial interference gave the MSC the opportunity it had been looking for, it did so because manpower policy was not considered central to economic management and the industrial strategy. 'And so it came to pass,' as George Low (1988) recorded in his witty and perceptive essay on the MSC in a chronicle of 'The Wasted Years' from 1973 to 1986, 'the MSC waxed mightily in the house of Michael Foot' (p. 216). Meanwhile the CBI continued to give only token support to the MSC.

GETTING ORGANIZED

Between August and September 1973 the remaining nine commissioners were appointed. There were three from industry and three from the trades unions. This did not make the MSC a tripartite body, as it was often mistakenly called, because the government, as third party, was only indirectly represented through the Chairman 'under the direction of' the Minister for Employment. Both the CBI and TUC nominated one professional official each, their other two commissioners being either managers of large companies or union leaders. (The only woman commissioner on this 'Manpower' body represented the CBI for a year until January 1975.) The

Secretary of State consulted the Association of Metropolitan Authorities and the Association of County Councils before appointing two local authority representatives on the MSC, while a third came from Scotland. Similarly, educational bodies were contacted before their interests were represented by one member on the Commission. The MSC was to meet on a monthly basis with its first official meeting in January 1974. However, a preliminary meeting was arranged just before Christmas at which a Deputy Chairman (the CBI official) was elected. This decision reflected the collective view of the commissioners that they had been given inadequate resources to manage the Commission's work. Indeed the MSC at this time had a secretariat of only 40 staff. Sir Denis Barnes thought this far too few to investigate and administer the work of its operating arms. The TUC too were sceptical of the ability of the MSC to control the executive agencies and wished to see it strengthened.

As Chairman of the Commission, Barnes understood the need for the MSC to put itself firmly in the minds of economic decision makers. He therefore embarked in the early months of 1974 on the first of many advertising campaigns. This first great sell was restricted to the trade journals. For instance, in February Barnes was interviewed by *Industrial and Commercial Training*, where he explained how the MSC intended to include manpower planning in its work.

> There is a fair amount of manpower information around, derived in various ways by a variety of bodies. The first thing I would like to do is to see if all this information could be brought together; then we can examine it, find any gaps and decide what our first step should be to get an overall picture of what is happening in this area.

As well as this, he added the possibility that 'unemployment might increase and we ought to be exploring various ideas and trying to develop some policies in the event of unemployment staying at a higher level than we have been accustomed to for some time.' In particular, 'If unemployment does go up we could have a big school leaver problem; we want to develop some ideas on this subject in good time.'

Barnes had already commissioned Santosh Mukherjee, a labour economist, to outline recent developments and to give a broader perspective to the MSC's labour market policies. Mukherjee saw little prospect of unemployment falling in the near future. However, 'future uncertainty need not produce paralysis. Contingency plans need to be formulated to cope with a range of possible outcomes' (MSC, 1974, p. 6). He therefore argued for an Intelligence Division to coordinate all the sources of manpower information. This recommendation was supported by both the TUC and the Labour Party. Mukherjee also proposed a job-creation scheme to help the young and retraining programmes for adults. He concluded that a new definition of work must be developed allied to a major job creation programme. He thus broke with previous approaches to unemployment which had always linked it to aid to the depressed regions by redefining it as a national problem. Skill shortages were evident in all sectors of the economy and so he urged that 'effort will have to be put into creating new jobs, not just on a regional basis as has been practised hitherto, but for those particular age groups in the country as a whole' (MSC, 1974, p. 4). 'Multiple action' (p. 69) was therefore needed.

Mukherjee's proposals implied a massive injection of public funds to finance his programme of job creation in the new skills required by industry. He justified this by the argument that the net costs of keeping a worker in retraining or job creation were less than the gross cost of keeping that worker idle on social benefits. In this he seconded Keynes (1936), whose 'General Theory', written during the slump of the 1930s, had asserted that

> to dig holes in the ground paid for out of earnings will increase not only employment but the real national dividend of useful goods and services. It is not reasonable however that a sensible community should be content to remain dependent on such fortuitous and often wasteful mitigations when once we understand the influence upon which effective demand depends (p. 220).

Keynes had therefore argued that it would be more productive if labour was set tasks that would not only increase income but output also. However, demand management to sustain full employment via job creation was geared for cyclical recessions, not the second great slump, as the economic crisis triggered by the 1973 OPEC oil embargo was beginning to be called.

In such crises an advantage of job creation, and this included the establishment of retraining programmes for the unemployed, was that programmes could be 'switched on' and 'turned off', given the rapidly changing state of the labour market. For a government facing the evil of stagflation, a strategy for job creation presented policy makers with the opportunity to effect an overall deflationary economic package, but pursue a full employment policy. Critics have argued that the MSC responded in an *ad hoc* manner to the crisis of mass unemployment, but they fail to grasp the fact that its strategy for job creation was based on managing the labour market in such a way. It was a basic component of the MSC's ideology to maintain full employment via *ad hoc* job creation schemes. Barnes, in another of his public relations exercises on behalf of the MSC, told a reporter from *Personnel Management* that he wished to see the MSC acting like its Swedish counterpart, the Labour Market Board, which he described as 'the instrument through which the government deals with the employment problems which are created by fluctuations in their economy and I hope that the MSC will gradually have influence in this area' (April 1974). Only the TUC supported an immediate expansion of job creation schemes by the MSC though, while some Labour backbenchers wanted a separate job creation agency to mount such a crash programme.

Mukherjee's study was not discussed in full at the Commission until May but its contents were well known to the Commissioners before that. Armed with its proposals, Barnes went to the Institute of Personnel Management's London Regional Conference in May to explain the work of the MSC to leading figures in the training community. He began his lengthy address by assuring his audience that the MSC was no mere advisory body but could exercise real executive power in the manpower field. He explained: 'In the last resort the Secretary of State can direct the Commission to do something or not do something. . . [but] The major responsibility for determining the development of the public employment and training services will rest with the Commission'. He then went on to describe how the MSC proposed 'to give more sustained attention to the problems of manpower and the labour market than could the Secretary of State or the Department of Employment . . . [who are] subject to immediate political pressure'. The MSC, by contrast, 'should take a longer term view of some of the problems of manpower and the labour market than governments have done in the past'. The Chairman then told his audience that there would be more public discussion of 'manpower problems and policies needed to cope with them'. In his earlier interview with *Industrial and Commercial Training*, Barnes had given an example of the sort of public discussion he proposed: 'Suppose we had some idea . . . if we thought we could get what we wanted without a public debate we wouldn't promote it, but if not we might wish to muster support publicly. . . . This aspect of promoting public dialogue is an important function of the Commission'. In conclusion to his speech, Barnes asserted as his main aim, 'Firstly . . . we must make sure we establish ourselves as a body genuinely independent of government which is likely to continue whatever government is in power'.

Other speeches and interviews followed: six days later Barnes was again elaborating his own views of the MSC's responsibilities to the British Association for Commercial and Industrial Education National Conference.

> The MSC is much more than just a holding company for the two agencies. It will have to raise issues and tackle problems which could be a source of embarrassment to the government – not just to the Department of Employment but also to the Treasury and the Department of Education and Science (*BACIE Journal*, September 1974).

These personal expectations for the future of the MSC had important implications for its corporate structure. Writing just before his retirement, Barnes stressed how important he believed it was 'to develop a corporate identity for the whole range of the Commission's activities'. Externally this would mean 'fixing the MSC group as an effective organization in the public consciousness. Internally it means . . . we may have to unify the activities of the Commission and each of its agencies' (*International Labour Review*, January/February 1976).

These changes were not long in coming about. In July 1975 Michael Foot approved the appointment of a Director of Manpower Intelligence and Planning. The man appointed, Graham Reid, a former economic adviser to the Scottish Office, initially had a staff of three. He was soon joined by Geoffrey Holland, former Director of the Planning Division of the TSA. Their brief included the unification of all the operations of the MSC group. Reid argued that unification would best be achieved by using the MIP division as a coordinating body for the whole of MSC operations. Consequently the division emerged as a kind of 'broker' between the rival agencies and divisions. Its reorganizational efforts culminated in the ratification of the unification of the MSC by the new Secretary of State, Albert Booth, in April 1978.

In December 1975 Michael Foot had accepted Barnes' recommendation for the creation of a Director of the MSC. Barnes wanted a managing director to take over the day-to-day management of the ESA, TSA and Office of the MSC, coordinate their policies and service the Commission with reports and recommendations. This would relieve the Chairman of his workload and in turn create a situation whereby a part-time Chairman would be appropriate. The TUC were unhappy about rumours circulating that Barnes wished to relinquish his full-time post and ease himself into part-time retirement. This was seen as a move to devalue the standing of the MSC. However, from the outset Barnes was considering moving John Cassels from the TSA to the Directorship, a move for which Foot had to receive clearance from the Prime Minister. As Director, Cassels was to have a powerful influence on the subsequent development of the MSC (see Howells, 1980).

In April 1976 Richard O'Brien replaced Barnes as Chairman. The Employment and Training Act required the Secretary of State to consult interested bodies in the appointment of Commissioners but left him with the final say in the matter of the Chairmanship. In fact both the CBI and the TUC had suggested O'Brien's name to the Minister. In part the consensus was due to the fact that it was 'only fair' that the CBI had Buggins' turn at choosing someone for the MSC since the TUC had just had one of their former officials accepted as the head of ACAS. In part it was due to O'Brien's personality and reputation. As a former staff officer in Montgomery's Eighth Army, 'he had only to stand up before a Select Committee and assure the MPs "We have got this problem in our gunsights" and they would entirely believe that the MSC would knock unemployment for six just as Monty had the Germans at El Alamein' (Low, 1988, p. 216). In any case O'Brien had considerable experience of the Whitehall machine as an adviser to the ill-fated Department of Economic Affairs. He had subsequently become the manager of a large company and Chairman of the CBI's Employment and Technology Committee. He was eventually to fall foul of Mrs Thatcher and then to chair the Church of England's 'Faith in the City' report, which subjected her policies to a sustained and principled critique.

Though he was, as Jackson said, 'a natural manager of consensus', O'Brien brought a new operational philosophy to the MSC. He sought to form what Howells called 'corporate management from the centre'. To this end he created a Chairman's Management Committee which brought together all the Chief Executives and heads of divisions. It enabled the Chairman to take a much greater personal role in the Commission's day-to-day activities. Later a Director of Corporate Services was appointed. In April 1977 a Department of Employment internal report welcomed the establishment of the CMC and recommended in addition a new Special Programmes Division to cover the multiplicity of unemployment schemes that were by now being set up. In the regions these would be overseen by Area Manpower Boards that would replace DE officials on regional employment committees. The report also called for a more unified administrative structure by transforming the agencies into legal divisions of the Commission. Albert Booth recognized that this would make the MSC a stronger organization internally and allow the Commission itself to control the financial arrangements of the agencies. O'Brien played an active part in this unification process which began in mid-1977. He rejected as 'pure fantasy' the residual notion that the MSC could conceivably develop into a pressure group outside the Whitehall machine. 'It was', he said, 'naive in the extreme to suppose that an organization that was nearly entirely funded by central government would then be a turn-coat and openly criticize government economic and industrial policy' (interview 23 June 1985). However, cost effectiveness and efficiency were to replace any grand designs that the TUC had for the MSC to establish a comprehensive manpower policy. Rather, the work of the MSC was to become selective more than comprehensive. This corresponded to a general shift which Pliatsky (1982, p. 150) observed from personal experience overtook the Labour government at this time.

COMPREHENSIVE MANPOWER POLICY

The reorganized quango was keen to prove that it could do something about unemployment. In May 1974 the Training Services Agency was ordered by the MSC to send contingency plans to the Secretary of State in anticipation of the expected increase in the jobless total. A new Five Year Plan duly reported that a working party had been established and that it had concluded that substantial grant-in-aid would be needed to realize its plans. As the 1973 Plan had explained: 'If unemployment rises then it will be necessary for the Agency and the Commission to consider a range of possible activities to respond to the situation' (p. 15). In particular, training would have to be safeguarded 'because training tends to suffer disproportionately when economic activity is low'. This was because of the short-term view adopted by some firms and the necessity for others to cut costs in order to survive. 'Unless the short-term effects are countered, the cutback in training will result later in the shortage of skilled labour that endangers economic growth and makes recurrence of another recession more likely.' Counter-cyclical training was thus again identified as the appropriate response to the onset of recession. As Cassels later said in an interview on 5 May 1985, 'Quite clearly our aim was to train people who would enhance the nation's stock of skills so that we could meet the demand when the economy picked up'. This was to remain an abiding rationale of the MSC's activities but it was to be supplemented by increasingly ambitious proposals to meet the consequences of technological change and for changing the habits and attitudes of the workforce.

The TSA set up a second working party headed by Chris Hayes to look specifically at the problem of youth unemployment. Its report was not published before the Commission sent another memorandum to the Secretary of State but it was hoped that it would be added to this and it also incorporated the new ideas that had arisen from Mukherjee's study for the MSC. MSC officials had also been despatched to North America during the winter of 1974 to study the Canadian Youth Opportunities Programme (YOP) and Local Initiative (LIP). These functioned by channelling central government funds straight into the hands of local groups which bid to run community employment schemes without going through the bureaucracy of the federal authorities. The immediacy of this method for mobilizing direct grass-roots responses to unemployment was not lost upon MSC planners.

The MSC also asked the government for more money to increase the pace of modernization of job centres to meet frictional unemployment caused by people moving from job to job, and an additional £70 million to meet the shortfall in training by industry. The MSC's contingency plan also suggested a work creation programme to meet the rise in unemployment. Again this was by intention an *ad hoc* response,

> since it can be introduced and terminated speedily to mitigate the worst effects of a significant rise, and can be directed at the hardest-hit groups in the labour force and the worst-affected regions. This is particularly important in view of the changing nature of unemployment and the groups involved (MSC Annual Report, 1974/75, p. 24).

The Commission wanted a programme that would be as decentralized as possible, locally administered and targeted at disadvantaged groups but at the same time bypassing the local council bureaucracies and thus remaining under its own control. Costed at £30 million, pay for participants would be between market rates and social benefits with help for materials and equipment given to sponsors centrally. The aim was to create 18,000 jobs in a year and a half. Michael Foot (1983) recorded his endorsement of such training schemes in his autobiographical *Another Heart and*

Other Pulses (p. 118). The Labour government itself finally agreed to the establishment of a work creation programme in 1975. To give it credibility, one TUC Commissioner, Daniel McGarvey, the President of the Boilermakers' Union, insisted that the word 'job' be included in the scheme's title.

Well before its second submission to the Secretary of State the MSC had reviewed its first six month's work. It was decided that its role would have to be widened if the duties outlined in the 1973 Employment and Training Act were to be discharged satisfactorily. A comprehensive manpower policy should be implemented as speedily as possible. By the second general election of 1974 the Labour Party agreed to the MSC's new role. The October Manifesto promised to 'transform the existing Manpower Services Commission into a powerful body, responsible for the development and execution of comprehensive manpower policy'. The MSC sent a paper to the Secretary of State outlining what would be involved in this undertaking, but discussions were complicated and prolonged. As the First Annual Report stated, 'Little progress has yet been achieved' (p. 29). The paper was called 'Towards a Comprehensive Manpower Policy', the title of a later publication that was to make a more mature presentation of the general principles involved.

The MSC's paper canvassed the idea that manpower policy had a dual purpose: first, to enable the country's manpower resources to be developed to the full so contributing to national economic wealth, and, second, to guarantee each worker the opportunities for a satisfactory working life. To these ends there should be, as the 1974/75 Annual Report put it,

> a central authority responsible both for managing and coordinating the executive instruments of manpower policy and for influencing through comment and advice the manpower aspects of other policies – economic, fiscal and industrial – to ensure that they are satisfactorily related to the manpower system (p. 30).

Naturally, the MSC indicated how it was itself best suited to carry out this function. In addition, it also wanted government approval for the development of a manpower intelligence capacity and to bring regional functions hitherto conducted by the Department of Employment under the aegis of the MSC. The Chancellor's announcement in his November Budget speech that he recognized the need for more adequate labour market intelligence to inform an active manpower policy was therefore very welcome to the MSC. But it was not until March 1975 that the Secretary of State officially accepted that the MSC should become the main executive body in the UK labour market.

The year had opened with unemployment at 678,000 and it seemed the MSC was to have a major role in alleviating its worst effects. The Chancellor, Denis Healey, framed his April budget 'to reduce unemployment' and allocated £50 million over two years for industrial training programmes run by the TSA, including special measures for training the unemployed and incentives for job mobility. The TSA had hoped for £70 million but could not be dissatisfied, considering that this was an austerity budget. It was followed by a mildly deflationary budget in July and more drastic measures in November. Coates' (1980) study of 'Labour in Power' argued that the November Budget was an attempt to avoid mass unemployment and began the government's retreat from the 'tight discipline over private firms, price controls and subsidies' and 'constituted a U-turn from his previous budgets' (p. 34). After all, 1976 was the year in which Tony Crosland was to warn the local authorities that 'the party was over' and Callaghan announced similar restrictions for education. Nevertheless, the government was still committed to the goal of full employment, which was still the political benchmark by which success was measured and the MSC aided the Chancellor in managing unemployment when cuts in public expenditure were likely to aggravate it. The April Budget, for instance, cut public expenditure by £900 million at a cost of 20,000 jobs. Healey hoped for 30,000 new jobs to replace them as a result of his measures but warnings were being sounded that the retraining programmes were inadequate to cope with the pace of industrial change (for example, two reports from *Political and Economic Planning*: 'Labour Markets in Crisis' (Herron, 1975) and 'Whatever Happened to Workers in Woolwich?' (Danniel, 1975).

In August 1975 unemployment passed the politically significant and psychologically intimidating one million mark. Labour ministers repeatedly described this as intolerable and unacceptable and pinned their hopes on a pay deal with the trades unions. In July Michael Foot, as Secretary of State for Employment, announced a further package of measures. The MSC was allocated an extra £25 million grant-in-aid and the TSA received another £5 million. Healey took a great interest in the MSC's activities. Before each of his many budgets he requested meetings with the Chairman and commissioners. In his April Budget speech he said that he 'had benefited from much valuable advice from the Commission, supported by its agencies. We shall continue to do this, and our meetings will be underpinned by continuing consultation at official level'. In September another set of measures was announced to mitigate unemployment. Among them was a grant for the MSC to develop the Job Creation Programme. The TSA received £20 million more, while there was a national Temporary Employment Subsidy, another new recruitment subsidy specifically for school leavers, increased grants for an Employment Transfer Scheme and an extra £120 million for building new factories. These measures were all part of the bargain that the government had struck with the TUC in exchange for urging wage restraint upon its members through the Social Contract.

Sir Denis Barnes confirmed that job creation was part of the agreement (interview 5 May 1985). He submitted a detailed programme in July and a central Job Creation Unit was set up to oversee the Programme. *BACIE Journal* went so far as to call the JCP a 'mini-New Deal' (November 75). But government ministers considered the scheme as a necessary temporary evil – a national scheme locally administered that could be switched on and off as required. The Chancellor, however, defended this first of the MSC's many and various temporary measures to meet the crisis. He conceded that 'the programme is no substitute for economic recovery. It is designed simply to blunt the effects of the recession on those groups who suffer most in such times'. He also admitted that

> some of the work is unskilled and the training element may be limited. But if the job creation programme is to provide a range of opportunities for all types of ability, an element of unskilled work is inevitable. . . . At first most of the projects coming forward were for unskilled work, but now more imaginative projects, which have been longer in preparation are being devised (Parliamentary Debates, 17 December 1975).

Healey was speaking in a censure motion and used the opportunity to announce an extra £10 million for JCP with £4 million for Community Industry and £19 million to the Temporary Employment Subsidy. Despite this additional help, there was 'still a long way to go before our training programme can be compared with other countries', in particular Sweden'. So in the new year the February White Paper on Public Expenditure until 1979/80 promised another £30 million each year to sustain the programme at full strength, as well as another £55 million per annum for the TSA.

Despite the receipt of this largesse, a central divergence on policy emerged within the MSC. The Commission, like the government, held to the goal of a comprehensive manpower policy, the central objective of which was the return to and maintenance of full employment. Thinking at the TSA began to question this commitment. The TSA's 1973 First Five Year Plan had questioned whether full employment had been 'temporarily or permanently lost' (p. 6). The Review of 1975 was more explicit and concluded that full employment had not been interrupted but ended (p. 8). The Review also pointed to the area where, once the notion of comprehensive manpower policy had been jettisoned, the MSC was to direct its energies. For

the Commission does not yet have a framework within which to examine together all the options for helping young people, including for example job creation and recruitment subsidies, so as to make choices and take action, making the best possible use of all available resources (p. 9).

The Review prefigured much of the later work of the MSC but it failed to convince the Labour government of its new attitude towards employment and unemployment. The government divided employment into permanent and temporary jobs. The TSA sought to overcome this dichotomy by a new attitude towards future manpower planning. In this future workers would not remain in one employment permanently but would change jobs flexibly to keep up with the latest applications of new technology. Unemployment offered the opportunity of retraining for this future, updating old skills via government-sponsored schemes. Typical of the government's response to such ideas was their refusal in February to provide funds for a vocational preparation scheme 'before the youth labour market entirely collapsed', as its advocates put it. Ministers still thought that youth unemployment would fall along with general unemployment in the anticipated economic upturn. Yet the percentage of young people under 20 who were unemployed rose as a proportion of the total unemployed from 5 per cent in 1974 to nearly 30 per cent in 1977.

In response to what was coming to be perceived as a national emergency, Hayes' report 'Vocational Preparation for Young People' began the so-called Great Debate on Education. It asserted that 'it is becoming increasingly important to help young people to develop the awareness of the world of work and of the way in which wealth is produced and used in society' (MSC, 1975, p. 5). Such an awareness was evidently not being cultivated within the schools system:

In recent years the social environment of a number of schools, with more emphasis on personal development and less on formal instruction, has been diverging from that still encountered in most work situations. There the need to achieve results in conformity with defined standards and to do so within fixed time limits calls for different patterns of behaviour. The contrast is more marked where changes in industrial processes have reduced the scope for individual action and initiative (p. 15).

So, while the MSC was preoccupied with increasingly desperate measures to stem the rising flood of unemployment, the TSA prepared the ground for a radical review of the entire education system and a completely different solution to the problem.

The government meanwhile continued in its traditional approach. It concentrated upon counter-cyclical measures and support for the unemployed. It had neither time nor inclination to diagnose the doubling of unemployment as an indication of structural change. In May 1976 the Chancellor donated £15 million more to the MSC and told the House of Commons that

> Since the last TUC Annual Congress I have brought forward four separate sets of selective measures in September and February and again in my budget, to improve the prospects for employment directly, through the introduction and improvement of the temporary employment subsidy, and indirectly for example, through the additional expenditure on industry schemes and to extend facilities for training.

He estimated that as a result of these measures 'more than 100,000 people already have jobs or training places'. Despite cuts in public spending of £1,000 million to meet the conditions of the IMF loan he had negotiated in June, MSC schemes remained untouched. Indeed, he promised that a new set of anti-unemployment measures would be announced later in the month.

There was an atmosphere of panic at the inability to contain the surge in unemployment, let alone force it down below one million. Only Sir Keith Joseph, amongst the reorganizing right of the Conservative Party, was convinced that government had nothing to fear from high unemployment. He argued that circumstances had changed since the 1930s and that the jobless could be contained, even used to the advantage of monetarist policies. This belief was of course officially anathema to the Labour Party, even while its government can be said to have pioneered monetarism in practice. The problem of unemployment was given the highest priority especially at the Department of Employment. Here, as the Deputy Secretary at the time later confirmed, 'new schemes and new ideas of many kinds were discussed' (interview with Donald Derx, 6 June 1985). The pressure was on the MSC to produce results. Labour backbenchers were pressing for a job creation agency, independent of the Department of Employment and beyond Treasury interference. Sir Richard O'Brien was determined to get a scheme off the ground for the young unemployed. But the idea of a vocational preparation scheme for all young people – first suggested by the TSA in 1974 – had been shelved in February, due to wrangling between the Ministries of Education and Employment over who should run it. The most that could be agreed was a pilot Unified Vocational Preparation scheme to be run jointly by the TSA and the DES.

Meanwhile the surprise resignation of Harold Wilson (see Wright, 1987) elevated the supposedly left-wing Albert Booth to the Ministry of Employment. It was summer before he announced a series of measures aimed at reducing unemployment. The School Leavers' Subsidy was replaced by a more comprehensive Youth Employment Subsidy. Yet more sums were made available to the TSA to increase the numbers of trainees on the Training Award Scheme. In addition there was a new Work Experience Programme 'designed to give young people a realistic introduction to the requirements, disciplines, and satisfactions of working life' (*Employment Gazette*, August 1976). This was O'Brien's idea. Targeted at young people, it was administered by a central unit at the office of the MSC, headed by a manager from ICI. Along with the Job Creation Programme, the unit delegated capital grants to sponsors who paid the wages of participants. The Treasury had made £19 million available but because of the savings on Social Security payments and funds from the EEC, the cost was much less.

By the end of 1976 the MSC thus had two schemes providing temporary employment. Yet the Commission still sought to impress upon the government the virtues of comprehensive manpower planning rather than such temporary arrangements. A new report, 'Towards a Comprehensive Manpower Policy' (MSC, 1976), elevated the position of manpower in the economy to a level hitherto unattained: 'Manpower is a key resource, perhaps the country's most valuable asset, and it should be in the forefront of government, industry and company strategy and not as a residual factor as so often happens at present' (p. 12). Manpower planning functioned not only to contribute to national economic health but also to the individual well-being and opportunities of each worker. 'It views people as a factor of production, means towards the end of producing goods or providing services. It views them also as individuals, each with needs centred around his or her working life' (p. 8). The MSC's role in manpower planning 'cannot be limited to carrying out the traditional functions of manpower policy, the public employment services and retraining in the traditional way. Nor should manpower policy be regarded as a 'fire-fighting' activity to deal with the short-term problems. . .' (p. 13). What was needed was a 'strategic approach'. This was not intended as interference in the workings of the labour market. Rather the MSC's role was to comprehend the interactions of its many facets and all areas affected by them. In order to facilitate labour mobility for instance, 'I suppose that the really crucial problem is housing', as Barnes told the Public Accounts Committee (20 April 1975). Most importantly, the MSC had to be involved in the analysis and formulation of pay structures and collective bargaining if full employment was ever to return.

Ironically these grandiose assertions were the last that was to be heard for some time of comprehensive manpower policy. Henceforward the MSC was to act on behalf of the Secretary of State in a much more limited capacity, fire-fighting the consequences of mass unemployment. The MSC was thus 'blown off course' as its work evolved into selective responses to this one overwhelming problem. Yet even within the threat presented by rising unemployment, there was a growing awareness of the particular dimension of youth unemployment which outweighed concern for the long-term adult unemployed. It was here that the MSC, while it sacrificed what it saw as its role of implementing Active Manpower Strategy, gained the opportunity to win a new empire in tackling the problem of mass youth unemployment. The MSC now attempted to apply comprehensive manpower policy in its provision for young people both in and out of work and at all levels of education and training.

LOSING A ROLE AND FINDING AN EMPIRE

After 1976 the MSC became preoccupied with the management of youth unemployment. The attempt to change attitudes to manpower planning in Britain as projected in the TSA's Five Year Review was discarded. Disagreements within the training community were left unresolved and a coherent approach to the training crisis could not be constructed. Instead, the political pressure to do something about youth unemployment led to the establishment of a new Special Programmes Division within the MSC. Consequently the powerhouse of the MSC shifted from the TSA. It was at this point that the MSC can be said to have been 'blown off course'. The long-term goal of comprehensive manpower policy, which the TUC had supported and regarded as their own, now had to be abandoned. All efforts were henceforward channelled into the immediate, practical problems of getting large unemployment schemes off the ground.

The TSA's 'Vocational Training for Young People', published in May 1975, sought collective arrangements for youth. It proposed a vocational preparation scheme for young people jointly financed by industry and central government. The idea of 'pump priming' for such a scheme was introduced for the first time with the suggestion that government funding would decline as industry acknowledged the value of the programme. A new means of funding apprenticeships jointly between employers and the MSC was suggested to run alongside an amended grant/levy system, but this was abandoned owing to lack of agreement with the CBI. The TSA also approached the government for resources to establish a vocational preparation scheme as suggested in their Report but this too was rejected. Undeterred, TSA officials presented pro-posals in January 1976 to Albert Booth and Shirley Williams at Employment and Education respectively for 'Gateway' training for all young people. As seen, the Ministers eventually agreed but only to a pilot scheme of Unified Vocational Pre-paration (see below). The view within the government was still that youth unemploy-ment was a temporary phenomenon that would disappear once the economic cycle turned up.

Attitudes at the CBI were hardly more encouraging: Michael Bury, Chairman of the CBI's Employment and Training Committee, argued that employers were scepti-cal of the benefits of mass youth training because it represented training beyond the actual needs of industry. If any such scheme was ever set up it should be financed by the government and not at all by employers. Rather the CBI preferred that the attitudes and performance of young people which affected their employability should be dealt with by the schools. It was the schools and not industry that was to blame for the 'unemployability' of school leavers which, it was suggested, was the reason for the rise in youth unemployment. For example, Arnold Weinstock declared beneath the headline 'I Blame the Teachers' in the *Times Educational Supplement* (23 January 1976), 'Employers are firmly of the view that shortcomings in the vocational preparation of young people are basically an educational problem which cannot be passed on to the employers under the guise of training and induction.' This contrasted sharply with the view of German employers, for instance, who paid over 90 per cent of the cost of training all young people in employment.

Such statements were partly intended to fend off the TSA's proposals for 'Gateway' training, which employers saw as state interference in their affairs. They also con-firmed the scapegoating of the schools, which were now held to be the major factor in causing youth unemployment and a brake upon Britain's adaptation to new tech-nology. This presentation of the problem of course absolved employers themselves of any responsibility for the situation. Their assertion was taken up and repeated not only by the popular (and increasingly populist) press, but was solemnly repeated by Labour ministers, especially the Prime Minister in the Ruskin speech that launched the so-called Great Debate on Education in the autumn of 1976. However ridiculous it appeared, such an explanation of the country's economic decline merely inverted the exaggerated claims that Labour had made for education ten years previously. Then Harold Wilson had promised that the new comprehensive schools and colleges were the solution to antique class divisions and that they promised a bright new future of scientific technology for all. But Callaghan's Ruskin speech was more than a mere inversion of opportunistic rhetoric. It signalled, as Stuart Hall (1983) recorded, 'the fact that Labour's historical programme in education, which had spanned the post-war period, and can be summed up under the banner of "universal provision" or "comprehensivization", had reached some sort of terminal point' (p. 2). Indeed, following the publication of the White Paper 'A Framework for Expansion', the education system underwent a decade and more of contraction.

Certainly the TSA's 'Vocational Preparation for Young People' sent a shock wave through the DES, where rivalry with the DE was intense. The DES was still reeling from a damning indictment by the prestigious Organisation for Economic Co-operation and Development. This had recorded the lack of 'a balanced analysis of persisting and new trends in society, in technological development and the role of the state, and of the place of education and science in the process of production' (OECD, 1975, p. 74). It had also lambasted the Department for its 'passivity', 'inertia' and 'obsessive secrecy'. This criticism was followed up next year by a House of Commons Select Committee which endorsed the criticisms and recommended substantial changes. In answer to these changes, the DES conceded that it had 'erred in encouraging schools to prepare pupils for the "social" rather than their "economic" role' (DES, 1976, p. 10). This concession was only repeated as an admission of guilt in the Prime Minister's Ruskin speech.

By the time Ken Cooper arrived as Chief Executive at the TSA in December 1975 he described the atmosphere between the two Ministries as one of 'war' (interview 12 October 1985). According to one leading educational correspondent, the MSC was trying to 'put the skids under the DES' (Phillip Venning, *Times Educational Supplement* 2 January 1976). The official view at the Manpower Planning Division of the TSA was that the DES was 'intellectually bankrupt' of ideas on vocational preparation and youth unemployment. Yet the TSA was not yet strong enough to act without cooperation from the education establishment. It still had to go out of its way to appease and reassure the various educational interests that it was not in the business of a takeover. Ken Cooper had recourse to the pages of the *Times Educational Supplement* to describe such suggestions as 'emotional' (9 April 1976). But the TSA had disturbed the further education colleges by demanding that TOPs courses should be run throughout the year and not just during academic term times. Cassels then had to make it clear that his Agency wanted 'close cooperation but not interference' in the colleges (*Times Educational Supplement* 5 November 1976). However, the proposals for vocational preparation for young people at the levels suggested would in practice mean a major challenge to both the further education sector and secondary schools.

The response of the DES was to hold a belated conference in March 1976 entitled 'Getting Ready for Work' (DES library 1976). (This document became known as the 'Bird Report' after J. Bird, its author, an Under-Secretary at the DES.) The conference eventually, after much interdepartmental wrangling, led to Albert Booth and Shirley Williams jointly announcing a pilot Unified Vocational Preparation scheme to be run by the TSA together with the DES. It was intended that this practical interdepartmental cooperation would reconcile the differences between the two Ministries. However continuing lack of coordination between the two contributed to delays in implementing UVP and a lack of provision for it. It would be another six years before the MSC could go ahead with a comprehensive scheme of vocational preparation, this time without the involvement of the DES.

Callaghan's Ruskin speech fundamentally shifted the balance between Employment and Education. It set the terms of a new agenda which the MSC was increasingly able to dictate as it grew in strength and confidence, with only one brief interruption, for over a decade until 1987. Callaghan endorsed the employers' complaint that 'new recruits from the schools sometimes do not have the basic tools to do the job that is required of them'. Even 'many of our best-trained students who have completed the higher levels of education . . . have no desire or intention of joining industry'. The remedy was obvious: 'There seems to be a need for a more technological bias . . . that will lead towards practical applications in industry'. For, 'There is no virtue in producing socially well-adjusted members of society who are unemployed because they do not have the skills' (reported in the *Times Educational Supplement* 22 October 1976). This was the language that created the atmosphere and political conditions in which the MSC was to thrive. The old slogan of equal opportunities was replaced by the new watchword of relevance (to the needs of industry) that the MSC was to make its own. If the history of English education since the war can be periodized from the 1944 Butler Act until 1964, when comprehensive schools began to replace the tripartite system, then a new era of vocationalism was inaugurated by Callaghan's speech at Ruskin in 1976. This period was only terminated in 1987 by the Conservatives' drastic change of education policy towards free market competition between schools and colleges to privatize the successful and close the least fit as a means of reintroducing a selective system (see Ainley, 1988).

The exercise in public participation that followed Callaghan's speech summarized what was to be the new dogma for the next decade.

> In addition to their responsibility for the academic curriculum, schools must prepare their pupils for the transition to adult and working life. Young people need to be equipped with a basic understanding of the functioning of our democratic political system, of the mixed economy and the industrial activities, especially manufacturing, which create our national wealth.

The Green Paper 'Education in Schools' (HMSO, 1977, p. 44) embodied the wisdom of the 'Great Debate', in which Mrs Williams presided over assemblies of headteachers, educational administrators and other worthies who cogitated upon Callaghan's Ruskin message at a variety of regional meetings. It was typical of this tedious peripatetic precursor of the SDP's founding conference that the way it was envisaged that the new orthodoxy could best be enforced was through the schools – although the task was too great for schools alone, and so 'industry, the trades unions and commerce should now be involved in curriculum planning processes' (HMSO, 1977, p. 22). The machinery whereby this could be achieved, beyond some modest projects provided as examples by the Schools Council, was not suggested in the Great Debate. Its proposals were left to be implemented by the education service itself. Even when

Shirley Williams began talking about a possible government-funded scheme offering all those under 18 without work the alternative of education or training, it was imagined that the scheme would be run primarily by her Ministry together perhaps with some voluntary youth agencies.

Yet the MSC had already designated youth as a priority group 'of special national importance' in 'Towards a Comprehensive Manpower Policy'. For,

> The unemployment amongst young people is so serious (and likely to remain so) that it should become an objective of the Commission to ensure that all young people of 16–18 years of age, who have no jobs, or have not engaged in further or higher education, should have the opportunity of training, or participation in a job creation programme, or work experience (p. 22).

A working party to study 'all the current measures of helping young people' was set up headed by Holland. At the press conference promoting the review it was stated that youth unemployment was 'the most overwhelming task of the Commission' (as reported in the *Times Educational Supplement* 5 November 1976). The government welcomed the publication of Holland's report in the new year of 1977 when, in the context this time of a controlled reflationary budget, more resources were again placed at the disposal of the Secretary of State for Employment. 'Young People and Work' followed the TSA's earlier recognition that full employment had 'not been interrupted but ended'. It therefore proposed new and permanent measures to deal with the permanent problem of youth unemployment. Mass youth unemployment was recognized as a structural feature of the economy and no longer conceived of as a temporary, cyclical phenomenon that would vanish once trade picked up and full employment was eventually restored. The government still tended to think of it in this way, however. So did the Conservative opposition, relentlessly harrying Labour (and the Liberals once they joined the government in the Lib–Lab pact to sustain it in office) for allowing unemployment to rise so high. To deal with the permanent problem of youth unemployment, Holland wanted a permanent, medium-sized scheme for low school attainers, rejecting what he regarded as the delinquent element of school leavers. However, Albert Booth and his Under-Secretary at Employment, John Golding, both insisted upon a commitment to all school leavers as a condition of Ministerial acceptance of the scheme. The TUC backed this demand for comprehensive provision for all young people, though argument raged with the DES over the definition of comprehensiveness. Meanwhile Shirley Williams continued throughout the remaining years of the Labour government to press the Cabinet without success for Educational Maintenance Allowances so that pupils who wished to remain at school after 16 would not be lured away by training allowances.

The scheme that eventually emerged was a larger operation than Holland had wanted, but it was still targeted at low school attainers, for 'young people with low qualifications are the most vulnerable to unemployment' (Holland Report, p. 4). A national scheme was proposed to start with 130,000 places rising to an estimated 350,000 to 400,000 places for 16–18-year-olds. Budgets were to be agreed annually and the programme would build on the experience of the Job Creation Programme which it was to supersede along with the Work Experience Programme. It was to be supervised by a new national board headed by the Chairman of the MSC. Local area boards would supervise the administrative aspects of finding sponsors and allocating grants on the Canadian model. The MSC would be responsible for payment of these grants and of allowances to the young people who participated. A new Special Programme Division, headed by Holland, took immediate responsibility for the new Youth Opportunities Programme and also for the simultaneously introduced Special Temporary Employment Programme for adults.

The Holland Report was formally endorsed by Cabinet in June to start the Youth Opportunities Programme in September the following year. It was announced as 'positive action for the plight of young people' by Harold Walker (in the *Times Educational Supplement* 17 June 1977) and as the first of many 'a New Deal for the nation's unemployed' by Albert Booth, reported in the same. (On 'New Deals' generally, see Finn, 1987). Booth claimed in Parliament (26 June 1977) that YOP would meet 'the criticism that existing provisions do not provide adequate training for young people by integrating series of measures for young people in the 16–18 age group, which will provide them with a combination of training and work experience'. Despite TUC backing for the programme there was widespread scepticism and dissatisfaction among the trades unions with the predictable consequences of YOP. It threatened displacement and substitution of adult workers, would be likely to reduce their wage rates and made the unionization of young workers more difficult. (See Gregory and Noble (1982) for a general discussion of union responses to and dissatisfaction with YOP.) However, the persuasiveness of the TUC, and especially Ken Graham, the TUC's long-standing Commissioner, obtained the support of the General Council.

As seen, Booth's 'New Deal' for the unemployed in Britain shifted the focus of attention away from the TSA, the original power house of the MSC. The Special Programmes division of the MSC headed by Holland now took the lead both in terms of ideas and action. 'His earnest protestations about the young unemployed', George Low (1988) maintained, 'made him a favourite in Labour local government circles, where he was a frequent speaker' (pp. 216–17). The accent was heavily on youth: by the time YOP had risen to 350,000 available places, STEP for adults offered only 25,000. The 1978 'Review and Plan' explained the key difference between the work of the division and the other programmes provided by the MSC:

> Its work is characterised by three features not found to the same degree in other MSC operations. Its focus is on the needs of the individual, particularly the unemployed individual; it is organised to be highly flexible and responsive to local needs; its success depends critically on its ability to mobilise others, rather than itself to undertake large operations.

Yet sheer weight of numbers overwhelmed Holland's intentions for the programme. It began by offering work preparation and pre-vocational training to one in eight of all school leavers, 80 per cent of whom graduated to employment or further full-time training. But as the numbers on the scheme rose towards half a million by 1981/82 when half of all school leavers were joining it, its placement rate fell below 25 per cent. There was a corresponding fall in the quality of the training provided. This was a pattern that was to be repeated with other subsequent programmes, especially the Youth Training Scheme. Just as on these future occasions, Holland craved the indulgence of critics with the excuse that was later repeated: new innovations were not like the goddess Athena. They did not spring fully-armed from the

head of Zeus. Rather, 'It must build towards its objectives'. After all, this 'construc-
tive alternative to unemployment' was a 'major new route into employment for many
young people'. It '. . . marked a major opportunity not just for the unemployed
young people, but for our society, and for all the education and training services'.
And yet in this defensive article for the *Times Educational Supplement* (14 April
1978), Holland could not but imply that the MSC was attempting what others had
failed to do, 'to help precisely those young people whom the education and other
services and programmes have failed to enthuse and help, that third of any age group
whom we have neglected for too long'.

Many educationalists resented such implicit criticisms and despised and ostracized
the new programme. It was seen as channelling the least able into low-status, practical
work and undermining the principles of comprehensive education. The first battle
occurred over Educational Maintenance Allowances. As seen, Shirley Williams, the
Minister of Education, had argued that EMAs would complement, rather than conflict with, the Holland proposals. Allowances for sixth formers should be the same
as those for the Youth Opportunities Programme and so the two options for 16-year-
olds would be presented on equal terms. The schools were indeed worried that the
Youth Opportunities allowance (which was equivalent to £40 at prices current with
the later YTS allowance of £27.50) would deter youngsters from staying on into the
sixth form. Particularly the schools hoped for an influx of 'new sixth formers' as
youth unemployment rose. In fact Williams was refused her Educational Maintenance
Allowances for those remaining at school or college because it would have been
prohibitively expensive. As the Chief Secretary to the Treasury, Joel Barnett (1982)
recalled:

> I had to fight another major expenditure battle literally throughout the whole of 1978. . .
> Fred Mulley had first raised the issue when he was Secretary of State for Education, and
> had been defeated, and I thought that the question would not be raised again. Shirley
> Williams not only raised the issue but gave it very high priority in her budget. She also
> tried to say that it should be seen as similar to Albert Booth's Youth Employment
> Measures. I was able to kill the argument on the grounds that Albert's schemes were
> supposed to be temporary . . . where the EMAs were . . . clearly permanent (p. 149).

The MSC would not have welcomed this defence of what it saw as a permanent
institution, but the YOP could only benefit from not having to compete on equal
terms with the schools. Moreover, Shirley Williams accepted defeat with good grace
and issued a Department Circular asking the Local Educational Authorities to cooperate with the new programme. The most that she gained in return was a committee
to study the possibility of setting up a new examination at 17 for the new sixth
formers. Another disagreement arose over the six week rule, whereby a young person
had to search for work for that time before being allowed on a government scheme.
The Manpower Services Commissioners would have preferred to draft school leavers
straight into YOP and asked the government to waive the rule but Ministers insisted
on a tougher line.

Despite this antagonism from educational interests and the criticisms that YOP
increasingly aroused in other quarters, particularly the Labour Party's own youth
wing and among rank and file trade unionists, the programme put the MSC firmly
on the map of the nation's affairs. Whatever its failings, the MSC had succeeded in
delivering the programme. This was an achievement of which none of its critics would

have been capable, and they knew it. It demonstrated the technocratic skill of a quango on a war footing. Only the MSC had been able actually to do something about rising unemployment, a mounting catastrophe before which the government had appeared powerless to act. Even the failings of the programme, which, as noted, Holland assured its critics would be remedied in time, could be presented as virtues. They illustrated the traditional Dunkirk spirit of rising to a national emergency with creative invention. Indeed the Youth Opportunities Programme had all the hallmarks of crisis management, especially with all its initial confusions and uncertainties. Yet a structure had emerged and for the MSC it represented an opportunity to remind politicians and industry yet again of the values of training. The MSC's increased influence would enable it to assert more forcefully its solution to the crisis of employment and to present it as an opportunity for industrial modernization and national renewal.

THE END OF THE GRAND DESIGN

Despite the MSC's success with YOP an opportunity had been lost. Because of the intense political pressure generated by the return of mass unemployment the Labour government had overlooked the central message of the MSC. Albert Booth, the Employment Secretary, thought that 'it will be a long time before the Labour movement came to terms with the experience of the Labour Government 1974–1979. Some successes were industrial democracy under another name – ACAS and the Manpower Services Commission for example' (quoted in Holmes, 1985, p. 170). Despite supposedly representing the British worker, the Party was unable to incorporate manpower policy within its economic and industrial strategy and to raise manpower onto the same platform as physical investment. From Labour's point of view YOP was a temporary managing exercise that was awaiting the upturn in the economy and the return of prosperity and full employment. It was not conceived as the foundation for a permanent scheme. Moreover, unable to persuade industry of the desperate need for high-quality internal manpower planning, the MSC evolved into the 'trainer of first resort', substituting for rather than supplementing industry's training requirements.

The Labour experience showed that a major revision of policy was essential to create a modern pro-training culture. In fact Labour's policies hindered any advance in the field of training. The government's industrial strategy confused the employment debate by spawning a rhetoric of 'permanent' and 'temporary' jobs. Within this dichotomy the role of training in national economic development was lost. In short, whilst the MSC was 'blown off course' in managing the unemployment crisis, it enabled the Labour government not to be destroyed by 'the unemployment bogey' that dogged Heath's Selsdon Man (Holmes, 1985). Holmes argued that in fact it simply meant 'the political buck of unemployment was passed to the new Thatcher government'. However this view neither accounted for the long-run development of MSC schemes – JCP, WEP, WEEP, YOP – into the possibility of a vocational preparation programme, nor the technical ability of the quango in administering the schemes while at the same time gaining kudos from the disaster of the unemployment crisis. Indeed, it is doubtful whether the MSC's later innovative policy proposals would have been conceived without the mass unemployment phenomenon. It needed mass unemployment to press policy makers to take training seriously and to assess its role in economic development. Thus, Lodge and Blackstone (1983) applauded the MSC for improving the provision for the 16–19-year-old group and Tipton (1983) pointed to the fact that YOP and youth unemployment had undeniably changed the nature of the training debate.

In the five years under Labour supervision, the MSC had grown dramatically but many of its basic aims were lost. Firstly, the aim of changing attitudes to training was missed. Secondly, the dream of maintaining full employment through training and retraining was shelved. In connection with this, no policy maker saw the benefits of integrating a policy for incomes with a policy for manpower. Indeed, the MSC itself argued that it did not wish to enter the field of overall economic policy making. However, policy makers failed to comprehend the strategic importance of connecting a strategy for manpower with incomes policy. Hawkins (1976) argued that 'one cannot help concluding that if only half the energy that has been spent on prices and incomes policy and collective bargaining had been directed to the development of a manpower policy, the British economy would be less precarious. . .' (p. 116). Yet Hughes and Pearlman (1978), like most economists, simply concluded that 'like incomes policy manpower policy is complementary to aggregate demand policy and vital to its success' (p. 59). Instead of putting manpower policy at the centre of the Social Contract, the MSC was a mere appendage awaiting fresh funds for new tasks that stretched its competence to the limit. As a consequence, job creation as a strategy to reach full or near full employment was put back a decade. However, the DES had been brought to book by the MSC over youth training, but the Treasury was still awaiting attack. For if full employment, or near full employment, was to be maintained, a body like the MSC, commissioned to prepare a manpower policy that included job creation on a mass scale, would need to be in on discussion for any new incomes strategy. Indeed, the MSC itself, representative of industry, government and unions, could have been the regulatory organization for a new integrated strategy that assailed inflation and sustained employment.

The MSC had begun life with a vision of transforming society and modernizing the economy through a new vocational education and training system. The end of Labour's government witnessed a quango over-worked and over-stretched, unable to achieve its basic goals. The MSC awaited a new beginning that emphasized manpower planning for economic efficiency and growth. A fresh assault on Britain's training culture had to be made. More to the point, the era of the 'Grand Design' was over.

SUMMARY

Under Labour the Manpower Services Commission had embarked upon an ambitious comprehensive manpower strategy intended to ease the return to full employment via programmes of training and retraining. Its organization into a centralized and virtually independent body was designed to facilitate the speedy implementation of this national strategy. At the same time leading officers of the Commission developed a coherent house philosophy that emphasized the importance of the whole workforce, and especially the new entrants to it, acquiring new skills to meet the challenge of modernization for new technology. This ideology had far-reaching implications for restructuring the traditional divisions of labour in industry, for habitual cultural attitudes to work and employment and, above all, for education. Those who shaped this ideology came to accept the structural permanence of mass unemployment, especially youth unemployment, as an opportunity to effect this modernization. The government, however, continued to see the rise in unemployment as a purely cyclical feature that would be overcome with the next upturn of the economy. The recession that followed the 1973 oil crisis scuppered such hopes of an immediate recovery. Instead of putting its own ambitious plans into action, the MSC was sent in pursuit of a series of increasingly permanent temporary job creation schemes. For the rapidly rising numbers of young unemployed, job training schemes replaced job creation as more and more the Labour government substituted a guarantee of training for the socialist goal of the right to work. The Labour government found in the reorganized MSC an efficient instrument for the speedy delivery of a series of work experience and training programmes which it offered to the trades union leaders in exchange for the wage restraint they attempted to impose upon their members in the social contract. While the delivery of these programmes boosted the MSC's funding exponentially during a period of budget cuts, so that its organization and staff grew rapidly, the pursuit of short-term solutions to the crisis of unemployment lost the MSC's grand design of comprehensive manpower strategy.

Chapter 3

The MSC under the Tories (1979–1983): Learning to Love the Quango

THE MSC AND MONETARISM

The years under Labour were a 'false dawn' for the MSC. However, the years under the first Tory government were to be a tale of a quango going from rags to riches. Nonetheless, a feeling of mutual understanding and rapport within which the Prime Minister felt she could do business with the quango took more than one Parliament to materialize. The MSC looked distinctly out of place in the Thatcherite scheme of things, representing the embodiment of consensual politics and not the politics of conviction. The MSC seemed a relic of Britain's corporatist past and the eccentricity of beer and sandwiches at Number 10. In short, the MSC was a classic example of 'big government in an overloaded democracy', which would have to be rolled back in the interests of national survival (Parsons, 1984). Thus, it was not surprising that rumours spread that the new administration would abolish the quango. But, once it was secured inside the Thatcher experiment, the MSC would be a practical example of 'the return of *laissez-faire* assisting in the birth of a new form of state interventionism' (*Political Quarterly*, March 1986). Moreover, the MSC was to be instrumental in supporting Sir Keith Joseph's goal of achieving 'a law-abiding free enterprise reconstruction of Britain's social relations of production' (Coates and Hilliard, 1986, p. 354).

The MSC had to postpone its more grandiose and visionary plans of fostering a new training culture that would contribute to a new industrial renaissance. Instead it had been diverted into fire-fighting youth unemployment, desperately trying to smother the smouldering flames of revolt that it was feared would break out at any moment from the angry and defrauded young. Demoralization of youth was also anticipated as a danger to the work ethic. Once lost, this would sap any future economic revival at source. The schools were the obvious place to attempt a moral re-education of the future generations. The MSC fully appreciated the importance of the schools and colleges and also knew that, since Callaghan's Ruskin speech, educational opinion was swinging in the Commission's direction. From the MSC's perspective, the importance of vocational goals over vague social objectives was at last being appreciated by all but the most idealistic and recalcitrant teachers and lecturers. Moreover, the MSC's new vocationalism, as piloted by its collaborator within the DES, the Further Education Unit, offered a new solution to what was coming to be perceived as the crisis in education.

The MSC's opponents within the educational establishment could only offer more of the same, an extension of the comprehensive reform that had plainly failed to achieve what it had set out to do. The same could be said of the Labour government as a whole, faced with the neo-liberal radicalism presented by the Conservatives in the 1979 General Election. The Tories promised an easy answer to the number one election issue of unemployment. 'Labour isn't working', their posters declared. Yet, of course, the monetarist solution to recession required a rapid increase in unemployment as market forces were given free reign. Allowing unemployment to find its 'natural' level meant an end to temporary employment measures and a labour shake-out to reduce 'overmanning' so that only 'real jobs' would survive. All this portended the termination of what was now seen as the MSC's interference in the free labour market. Under Labour there had been a reluctance to admit to the permanence of such high levels of unemployment, a clinging to the post-war commitment to full employment. This commitment was a part of the Welfare State which had been instituted with all-party support after the war. The new realism of monetarism now established a new consensus. If 'Thatcherism' from its inception was more than a rigid determination to impose a particular economic policy and aimed from the beginning at a deconstruction of the Welfare State into what has been called a residual welfare state, then this abandonment of full employment marks its first point of departure. Correlli Barnett, whose ideas were so influential on the new right, blamed 'Beveridge more than any other (including Keynes)' for 'committing future governments to full employment' – a commitment which he said by handing over power from the employer to the workforce led to Britain's appalling post-war record on productivity and the adoption of new technology (*Daily Telegraph* 1 December 1986). Certainly it was now widely accepted that, as Andrew Sinfield (1981) said, 'The days of "full employment" are not only over; they are as much a part of social history, which we may regard with nostalgia or contempt according to taste, as hoolahoops and spats' (p. 1). So the change of government also marked a turning point: 'On the one hand the very existence of the MSC was confirmed along with its major programmes; on the other, its period of almost uninterrupted growth was clearly at an end' (Howells, 1980, p. 305). In June 1979 the Department of Employment announced substantial cuts in MSC spending.

When the new Chancellor of the Exchequer, Sir Geoffrey Howe, proclaimed a reduction of planned expenditure of £1.5 billion in his first Budget, the Department of Employment was expected to make savings of £172 milions. Cuts were ordered in the Special Temporary Employment Programme, which, in a return to the old policy of regional aid, was now only to be applied in the Development Areas. TOPs and the YOP also suffered reductions and further cuts of £114 million were declared later in the year. For the first time MSC staffing levels were to fall from their peak of 26,450 in 1979 to a planned figure of 22,665 by 1983. The MSC's Corporate Plan had previously anticipated reaching a plateau of 30,000 staff by 1983/84. In the new year it was stated that 1,710 more staff were to go, along with another £30 million annually. The government made no apology for these measures, claiming that they fulfilled its manifesto commitment 'to reduce public expenditure and to concentrate aid', as James Prior told the House of Commons (21 June 1979). In an interview with *Personnel Management* in July he went further: 'Even if I was not looking for savings in public expenditure, which I am, I would see that the time had come to consolidate in these areas and possibly retrench.' He put the government's standard argument that 'unemployment will stop being a problem if industry is allowed to get on with the job. . . Unemployment will only be solved by improving economic performance and growth; that was the purpose of the public expenditure cuts which have been applied to the Commission as to other bodies.'

The MSC Commissioners complained bitterly about these piecemeal reductions, which they said created an atmosphere of apprehension and uncertainty about the government's continued support, making forward planning impossible. The TUC representatives were especially incensed and, not surprisingly, the General Council totally opposed them. A delegation from the Council went to the government to put the case that 'a period of increasing unemployment was a time to be consolidating the activities of the MSC' (TUC Annual Report 1980, p. 46). Yet they retained their seats on the MSC, although the TUC was, according to Ken Graham – then Secretary of the Employment Committee – 'under no illusions about the sphere of influence the MSC gave the TUC in economic decision making' (interview 17 May 1985). Their support was sustained by their favour of a strong centralized labour market planning agency. This they presented as 'our agency' to which 'the whole movement should show loyalty' (see Eversley, 1986). Similarly the Labour Party saw YOP and STEP as 'Labour schemes' and vented their anger at the cutbacks to them with a supply day motion.

During the election there had been rumours that the Tories would abolish the quango and all its programmes. Many MSC officials thought that 'the chances of abolition were strong' (interview with Geoffrey Holland, 10 June 1985). The promise to reduce bureaucracy and waste threatened all of the quasi-autonomous non-governmental organizations, especially the largest of them. As Gamble (1988) records, 'During its first 18 months in office . . . fifty-seven quangos were axed, among them the Price Commission' (p. 102). However, shortly after the Conservative victory, James Prior was at pains to assure the new House of Commons that these were in fact 'scare stories': 'The idea put about during the campaign that we would destroy the Manpower Services Commission came ill from a Party that knew we had set up the Commission' (Parliamentary Debates 21 May 1979). Nevertheless the quango's very existence appeared contrary to the free market philosophy of Mrs Thatcher and her intellectual guru, Sir Keith Joseph. The Conservative election victory of May 1979 had therefore automatically jettisoned any opportunity for an acceptance of comprehensive manpower policy. Although many critics have pointed to the fact that monetary policy under the first Thatcher government was merely an extension of Denis Healey's financial management after 1976, the new government, unlike Labour, did not hide its enthusiasm for monetarism but appeared openly to embrace monetarist dogma and declared itself against government intervention in the economy of any kind. The possibility of stabilizing employment levels when the Medium Term Financial Strategy dictated financial prudence was anathema for the new zealots.

Even the debate (such as it was) between the 'dries' and the 'wets' in the Thatcher cabinet over unemployment and public expenditure did little to the nature and context of the training issue. For example, Sir Ian Gilmour (1982), in the most literate of the many attacks upon the new Conservatism from within the Party's ranks, emphasized that 'Britain can work' because 'an economic policy does not stand by itself. It cannot be separated from its political and moral context' (p. 2). He therefore extolled intervention in the labour market primarily for social and political reasons. He considered it an 'important principle that the unemployed . . . should remain part of society' and 'they may not remain part of society if the rest of us think that our obligation to them is merely met by paying them the lowest possible level of unemployment benefit' (p. 182). For his opponents, like Sir Keith Joseph, even the young unemployed could safely be ignored and would eventually 'price themselves back into work'. The MSC's view of the contribution that state investment in human resources could make to national economic development was not even considered. Indeed, as Stringer and Richardson show (1982, p. 29), the Tories did not enter government with any firm plan for training except that they were committed to a radical review of the Industrial Training Boards. They wanted responsibility for training returned fairly and squarely to the hands of employers. This was as far as their immediate objectives went and was the sum total of their training policy when they entered office. The unemployment issue only figured in terms of its likely consequences in social unrest and disorder and the desire to be seen to be doing something about it. So the government's initial feelings about MSC schemes and their future development were summed up by Sir John Hoskyns, a chief policy adviser to Mrs Thatcher, when he stated,

> We know there is no prospect of getting unemployment down to acceptable levels within the next few years . . . (so) we must show we are willing to salvage something – albeit second best – from the waste involved. There are many who would like to do something, even if it is of only marginal economic value (quoted in Riddell, 1986, p. 50).

Training therefore appeared to have no place save as part of a paternalistic way of taking care of the potentially explosive issue of unemployment.

So the new government was initially sceptical of the value of the MSC and its ambitious plans for manpower policy. However, the Pliatsky Report on Non-Departmental Public Bodies, which many in the MSC had anticipated with foreboding, in the event made no substantial policy recommendations for the MSC. It criticized the repeated shortfalls in allocated resources but said the conventional forms of parliamentary control were adequate (HMSO, 1980, p. 39). Abolition was therefore postponed. In fact the MSC was given an extra £183 million for 1980/81 to rise to £271 million in 1981/82. With this new lease of life the Commission was able to announce in February an expansion of the Youth Opportunities Programme by 40,000 places. The unrelenting rise in unemployment had already forced the government to reallocate resources and the Secretary of State for Employment came to appreciate, just as his predecessors had done, how agile the MSC was in its administration of these temporary work schemes. Indeed, in response to questions from the Employment Committee in the House of Commons about the supposed lack of MSC response to unemployment, Prior conceded that 'in fairness to the MSC they would probably say that the only lack of response from their point of view is the lack of money available' (9 July 1980).

In place of abolition the government decided upon greater ministerial control of the MSC. This was symptomatic of Mrs Thatcher's general approach to public institutions. Again, however, in many respects the process of centralization, at least as far as the MSC was concerned, had originated under the previous Labour administration. Albert Booth authorized the unification of the operating arms (ESA and TSA) as legal divisions of the Commission. The Conservatives merely incorporated a clause to make Booth's decision lawful within the 1982 Employment and Training Act.

Central control of state institutions did not of course extend to the workings of the labour market, although one exception to this prohibition was in the area of trades union reform. Trades union combinations were seen by some reborn Manchester school economists as themselves obstructing the operations of a free market in labour and thus artificially raising its price. Sir Keith Joseph's views were well known and in an October meeting of the NEDC he explained:

> Trade union attitudes make good management difficult. Many at shop floor level seem hostile to the need for industrial efficiency. Many are encouraged to feel that reductions in working hours or increases in real pay are feasible without improvements in productivity . . . restrictive practices – reflected in a reluctance by labour to agree to the elimination of unnecessary work and rules – are too prevalent (quoted in Taylor, 1982, pp. 141–2).

As John Eversley remarked (1986, p. 209), the Thatcher government came into power with 'a deep hostility to any trade union influence', including influence over the ITB system and apprenticeship arrangements. And, as Robinson showed in his dispassionate and detailed account, 'Monetarism and the Labour Market' (1986), this hostility has been the one constant and guiding thread in all the labyrinthine twists and turns of the government's monetarist policies.

Here then was a chance for the MSC officials who were waiting in the wings, still ready to attempt their radical reshaping of industrial training in Britain. They were determined to place the training debate, which they had begun under Labour, together with their much-maligned schemes that Labour had sponsored, into the context of national economic development. For them, monetarism's abiding hatred of trades union influence together with Mrs Thatcher's stress on the need for moral revaluation to stimulate free enterprise and business profitability created the conditions for a new wave of training reform. In May 1980 the government 'Think Tank', the Central Policy Review Staff, published a report 'Education, Training and Industrial Performance'. This castigated existing training arrangements generally, and trades union control of apprenticeships particularly, as a means of maintaining restrictive labour practices. It suggested creating a 'modernized apprenticeship' system by redesignating and reclassifying all tasks in all occupations to facilitate the transfer of flexible labour from one job to another. John Cassels saw this as an opportunity for the MSC to reconsider Britain's vocational education and training. In an interview he revealed that the most important factor in his decision to think again about the country's training institutions was what was happening in the industrial relations arena. In the long term Cassels hoped that the construction of a high-quality Youth Training Scheme would ultimately restructure Britain's skill training system. In the short term the MSC was content for the debate on youth training to feed into the discussion of skill training and apprenticeships. In addition, the challenge to the Industrial Training Boards had the appeal to the government of reducing public expenditure. For, as Cassels also said, 'I think it was clear that antipathy to the ITBs stemmed to a great extent from a feeling that they were bureaucratic – a traditional preoccupation for the Conservatives – though the desire to reduce public expenditure no doubt played a part' (interview 5 May 1985).

Significantly Cassels left the Directorship of the MSC to move to the Cabinet Office as one of the two permanent secretaries there. He was succeeded by Geoffrey Holland, the head of the Special Programmes Division and the author of 'Young People and Work', which had prepared the way for the Youth Opportunities Programme. By far the most important change in personnel, however, was the removal of Sir Richard O'Brien from the Chairmanship of the MSC. O'Brien's general outlook favoured the Labour government's consensual and tripartite approach to public affairs. Even if he had not supported the Social Contract, he was a firm believer in incomes policy. He grew increasingly worried by the successive reductions in public expenditure imposed upon the MSC by the Conservative government and was publicly critical of the threat of further cuts in his foreword to the MSC's 1979/80 Annual Report. As this explicitly stated, 'market forces alone will not produce training of the quality or quantity required' (para. 14). In O'Brien's view MSC programmes should have been expanded with the government intervening more and not less in the labour market. Indeed, he saw incomes policy as essential to returning to full employment. He resented the more direct control that was now imposed upon the MSC itself. As he explained (interview 23 June 1985),

> Under Labour policy making was a relaxed affair with a free flow and exchange of ideas across both departments (MSC and DE), and between senior civil servants and ministers. But under the Tories, especially when Norman Tebbit became Secretary of State, senior civil servants at the MSC were not asked for their views or ideas relating to the conduct of policy. The principles of policy were already set.

Nevertheless, he made very clear to his superiors that he wished to stay on but Tebbit, after congratulating him for his leadership during 'six challenging years', sacked him. The other nine Commissioners expressed their disappointment but could only agree with the general press comment on O'Brien's departure that it cleared the way for the government to appoint its own man to run the MSC.

The government's own man was a former property developer who had returned from the USA to head the Conservative Party's research unit and advise Sir Keith Joseph at the Department of Trade and Industry. David (later Lord) Young's only qualifications to chair the MSC seem to have been that he was for a time the British Chairman of the Organization for Rehabilitation and Training. ORT is an Israeli-based charity now operating in more than thirty countries, which moved to Britain from Geneva in 1979. It began training unemployed young refugees from Tsarist Russia in useful trades such as cobbling and tailoring. Its approach is narrowly utilitarian and its trade schools in France seem Young's immediate inspiration for his ambition to create a vocational preparation programme for the 14–18-year-old group throughout the education system and catering for young people both in and out of employment. As he told the magazine *Education*, 'As a leading figure in ORT, I have a good knowledge of technical high schools in France and elsewhere' (19 November 1982). Sir Keith was also a patron of ORT and it was the Director General of the World ORT Union, Joseph Harmatz, who introduced Young to him. During the summer of 1982 ORT held private briefing sessions attended by Joseph, Tebbit and Baker on Young's ideas for setting up a range of technological high schools in the inner cities. ORT was subsequently involved in the Technical and Vocational Education Initiative and in planning curricula for the City Technical Colleges, which succeeded the TVEI as the government's main technical venture in schools. It was widely reported that Young told the General Secretary of the TUC, Len (later Lord) Murray, that he was only trying to give the education service a badly needed shock. To which Murray replied that 'one shock would not be enough' (Jackson, 1986, p. 36). Lord Young became, in the words of the *Times Educational Supplement* editorial, 'the polished bogeyman of the education world', who 'personified the attempted take-over of the classroom by the training world' (19 November 1982).

Young brought not only a new outlook to the MSC but also a new style of management. O'Brien had regarded his post as representing the government in the UK labour market but he had been prepared to criticize government plans if they appeared illogical or impossible. Instead of trying to secure a consensus over policy issues as O'Brien had always tried to do, Young saw himself as 'having the final say in policy' (Jackson, 1986, p. 37). He strengthened his control on the MSC by working closely with Peter Morrison at the Department of Employment, who took a close interest in the details of MSC policy and was soon proclaiming himself 'the Minister for Training'. In fact Young and Morrison worked as 'Joint Managing Directors' of the MSC, allowing for 'greater control of resources' (interview with Peter Morrison 26 October 1985). 'At a more risible level, Morrison was even allowed to dictate the way in which MSC staff signed their letters' (Jackson, 1986, p. 37).

Young's appointment indicated that the future development of the MSC would be in strict accordance with the overall direction of government economic policy. The MSC might be used to deal with political crises, as and when they arose. Otherwise, its main function was to keep the anti-inflationary strategy on course. Training would be left to the market and would aim to encourage industry to develop and apply the new technologies. The forces of the international market place and free trade policies allowed capital equipment to be cheaply and easily imported. There was as yet no recognition of the MSC's philosophy that how the nation deployed its human capital and how it was developed and nurtured could gain Britain a crucial competitive edge on its rivals. Nor was this vision of a flexible workforce, able to adapt through training and retraining to the rapidly changing conditions of a new industrial revolution, yet connected by the government with its own rhetoric of enterprise and individual initiative.

Education policy under a Tory of the old school, Mark Carlisle, went no further than the habitual effort to preserve the country's remaining grammar schools and some aid to the private sector in the shape of an Assisted Places Scheme of scholarships to the public schools. The first parliamentary Act of the new government was to repeal legislation Labour had introduced to make comprehensive education universal (though in the view of a prominent advocate of extensive comprehensive reform, Caroline Benn, 'the legislation was so ineffective, they needn't have bothered' (interview 19 July 1988)). Wilder spirits in the government, such as former Black Paper writer Rhodes Boyson, attempted to devise complicated voucher systems as a means of restoring selective schools, and the Prime Minister certainly favoured their efforts. Before the election Carlisle too had endorsed Black Paper demands to 'set up national standards in reading, writing and arithmetic. These standards would be set by the Assessment of Performance Unit at the DES and monitored by a bank of tests at set ages' (as reported in *Education* 27 April 1979). However, at this time, as Ken Jones noted (1983, p. 85), the introduction of such sweeping changes would have challenged 'beliefs and practices that are deeply rooted in the education system' and would have entailed 'a confrontation with almost the entire apparatus of state education' for which the government was not yet ready. Insofar as all this emphasized traditional standards and discipline, Conservative education policy tended to work against the new tasks and methods of assessment that the vocational approach to education had begun to introduce into the schools and colleges since Ruskin. Nevertheless, as the ennobled Sir Keith Joseph later recognized, with that speech 'Callaghan can claim to have started to build on the Black Papers' (interview 24 July 1989), and all the elements were to hand for a new solution to the problems of the schools. The new order would connect the education crisis with the crisis of youth unemployment and present them as a new opportunity to attempt a general remoralization of the workforce beginning with the youngest entrants to it. The government was not at first ready to rely upon the MSC to bring these elements together into a coherent strategy, and the quango had first to prove itself essential to the management of mass unemployment.

IN FROM THE COLD

The immediate effect of the new government applying its monetarist medicine to the economy was a rocketing rate of unemployment. The dole queue rapidly trebled to reach and remain at a plateau of three, possibly four, million. The figures have been much disputed, but certainly the total numbers unemployed exceeded the previous record set in the great slump of the 1930s. Within a year of the government taking office the level passed the 10 per cent mark. Despite Sir Keith Joseph's reassurances that times had changed, weaker spirits within the Cabinet began to quail at the social consequences of the economic policies they had espoused. The precedents from the 1930s included not only the Jarrow marches but the even more dire consequences for the future of democracy, which in Germany had collapsed under the combined impact of inflation and mass unemployment. Even the monetarist theorists from whom the new Conservatism drew its inspiration were convinced that democracy could not survive alongside continuing high levels of unemployment. As Hayek (1984) wrote, 'I doubt that any government could persist for two or three years in a policy that meant 10 per cent unemployment for most of that period'. But this was published after the Conservatives had persisted with unemployment at this level for three years and had even been re-elected in spite of it. As the Chancellor of the Exchequer explained in the same year, this success proved the validity of 'the British experiment . . . the demonstration that Trade Union power can be curbed within a free society, and that inflation can be eradicated within a democracy' (Lawson, 1984).

One way to deal with the human cost of such a disastrous rise in unemployment was simply to deny that it existed. As the government's critics repeatedly indicated, the unemployment totals have been recounted downwards nineteen times to the time of writing. There are now two estimates of unemployment: government figures and the unofficial estimates made by various independent organizations. In the depths of the recession during 1986 unemployment was officially estimated at 3.4 million, while independent analysts suggested a figure over 4 million. Even when the economy eventually picked up, if only temporarily, the authoritative Lloyds Bank *Economic Bulletin* for September 1987 stated that 'Unemployment in the widest definition has fallen by only about 135,000 over the past year and is now about 3.9 million or over 14 per cent of the working population.' Robinson (1986) remarked of the largest of the government revisions that 'Prime Minister Thatcher was able to reduce the official count of unemployment by a quarter of a million at the press of a computer switch' (p. 247).

However, denying the reality of the situation could not hide it for ever and in 1981 the long anticipated and much dreaded consequence of such continuing high levels of unemployment erupted in a series of urban riots. These 'uprisings', as some of their participants and supporters called them, continued intermittently over some weeks, threatening even to distract media-focused public attention from the preparations for a Royal wedding. The riots were exactly the response to mass unemployment, especially mass youth unemployment, that the previous series of temporary employment measures had been designed to avoid. They had an impact even at the highest levels of government. As Sir Leo Pliatsky (1983) recorded,

> Sentiment against expenditure cuts crystallised further among non-monetarists as the summer brought with it fresh outbreaks of rioting by young people in one inner city after another. There was a fairly general belief that unemployment among the young, and especially young coloured people, and the urban squalor in which they lived were among the causes of the riots and that there was a need to spend more money, not less, on dealing with them (p. 191).

In July 1981 the Prime Minister announced a major expansion of the Youth Opportunities Programme and other MSC measures at a cost, though limited to the current year, of £500 million extra spending. The irony of this turnaround was not lost upon Sir Leo: 'The budget of the Manpower Services Commission, a quango which earlier in the government's life had been under a cloud overhead and suffered cuts in staff and programmes, was now being re-expanded as an essential instrument in their measures' (Pliatsky, 1983). In fact a real surge of expenditure now occurred. Under Labour spending on the MSC had increased by £382 million in real terms, but under Mrs Thatcher money expenditure rose by £610 million and real expenditure by £683 million. Most of this money was spent on the expansion of the Youth Opportunities Programme. Yet even these increases were to be surpassed by her second government.

Whilst the MSC was pouring money at youth unemployment, Conservative ministers prepared to fulfil their manifesto commitment to return the already diluted Industrial Training Board system to the employers. The only problem was that, as the Secretary of State for Employment, James Prior, admitted, 'it was highly unlikely that employers would agree to shoulder the financial burden' (quoted in Stringer and Richardson, 1982, p. 28). If the government was not careful, Britain would be left without any skill training system at all. It was partly the collapse of apprenticeships that had fuelled youth unemployment and deprived many working-class young men of their only route into skilled employment. Pliatsky's report agreed with the MSC in urging a new training system to administer the Youth Opportunities Programme but this recommendation only encouraged speculation that the Industrial Training

Boards were to be abolished. Both *The Guardian* and the *Daily Telegraph* ran a series of articles criticizing the ITBs, whilst Perry defended them in the Journal of the training establishment (*BACIE Journal*, September 1979).

Labour's attitude towards skill training between 1974 and 1979 had been simultaneously to praise the work of the ITBs and at the same time seek an agreement between employers and the state on new financial arrangements for training. However, when the MSC under O'Brien failed to get the go-ahead for collective funding of skill training, a detailed review of the ITBs was begun in July 1979. The MSC resented the fact that the ITBs drained funds from its grant-in-aid and also that the ITBs would not pursue policies that reflected the social remit of the MSC. Chris Hayes had also argued 'that all but the larger Boards failed to plan strategically' (interview 4 May 1985). However, the review was conducted by representatives of both sides of industry and failed to find agreement. Hence the resulting reassessment of the 1973 Employment and Training Act (MSC, 1980) recommended no radical changes save that costs should be transferred to each industry. As Stringer and Richardson (1982) commented, 'from the MSC's view point the absence of a definite training policy from the Government showed that the MSC itself ultimately controlled the review process and presented an ideal opportunity for the exercise of organizational self interest' (p. 29). However, Prior wanted industry to decide on and pay for the training that it required so he ordered a second inquiry to investigate the transfer of the ITBs to employers. A 'Sector by Sector' review subsequently recommended this course of action but not the abolition of the Boards. Prior's banishment to Northern Ireland was a crucial event. His successor, Norman Tebbit, firmly intended to put Britain's skill training arrangements back to a voluntary system. With characteristic brusqueness he abolished sixteen of the twenty-three ITBs and was only narrowly persuaded to keep the remaining seven within the statutory framework for a time. These included the Engineering Industry Training Board, the largest and most prestigious. Len Murray in *The Times* (12 November 1982) accused Tebbit of 'wantonly throwing away a decade of work by the Boards'.

There was another underlying reason for the government's decision to change the industrial training system yet again. In an interview of 26 October 1985 the former Minister of State for Employment, Peter Morrison, argued that 'the economic recession of the 1970s had proved that the ITB system had not radically altered Britain's attitude towards training since the recession had made resources so scarce that employers as usual reduced in the first instance finances allocated to training'. Morrison believed that the country had to start from a new approach which began 'from the bottom up so to speak'. This view was increasingly being presented to government by MSC officials, especially John Cassels, the author of the consultative paper 'A New Training Initiative' (MSC, 1981), who was now in the Cabinet Office. Even James Prior, before his departure for Ulster, echoed the characteristic language and phrases that many in the education and training worlds associated with the MSC: 'Training and retraining', he told the House of Commons during the third reading of the Employment and Training Bill, 1982,

> are areas where it is absolutely vital to introduce a much greater sense of flexibility in responses. There will be new demands, new processes and new opportunities. Our duty therefore must be to design a system which can adapt and respond to them, and which can thus enable us not only to keep up with the pace of change, but to make the most

of the opportunities which lie ahead . . . this Bill . . . is only one element in the Government's overall policy on training . . . one essential part in a package of measures, designed to establish an effective systematic system.

Prior had already said that the foundation of the government's new training policy would be the Youth Opportunities Programme, which would evolve into a comprehensive vocational preparation scheme. This idea originated in Cassels' 'A New Training Initiative'.

This document, with its appealing logo and the rather flashy format that was fast becoming the house style of MSC publications, rehashed ideas about human capital and the need for a training revolution that had been around in the MSC since its inception. Now the new crisis situation of mass, structural unemployment that particularly affected the young offered the opportunity to put these ideas into practice. At last the Commission would be able to move away from what Kenny and Reid (1985) called its 'former proactive policy, variously described as "training for stock", "speculative" or "countercyclical" training, i.e. training undertaken in anticipation of an increased demand for skills following an upturn in the economy' (p. 297). In its place the MSC's aim for the various temporary employment schemes that it had provided in growing numbers under Labour and that had culminated in YOP was to translate them into a permanent, national and comprehensive training programme for all young people. This was the modernized apprenticeship system that would at last replace the outmoded, skill-specific, craft training of the ITBs. In its stead the New Training Initiative would produce the flexible, multiskilled worker of the future, able to move across old craft boundaries to apply core skills in a variety of circumstances. This approach accepted the criticism that it is in fact impossible to predict long-term skill requirements. As Mukherjee (1974) had said, 'the task of forecasting how much change there will be in demand at any date in the future and to what extent there may be a shortfall or excess of supply is so formidable as to verge on the impossible' (p. 46). Now the MSC made a virtue of this admitted weakness by proclaiming the adaptability and flexibility of the new workforce that was required to meet the unpredictable challenges of the new industrial revolution.

In addition, the New Training Initiative presented a solution to the crisis of education by building a bridge between school and work. More than that, it offered a chance to break down the traditional divisions between mental and manual work, between academic education and practical training. Now every school leaver could be offered a foundation that combined both areas. No longer would irrelevant study in arcane subject specialisms for test by written examinations be separated from practical applications tried and tested in the workplace. The least qualified could also be given an equal chance in the new apprenticeship system which they had been denied by the old. And all this would eventually bring about far-reaching social change, dissolving antique class divisions and outmoded social attitudes to lay the basis for a new culture combining theory and practice, science and technology. Individuals would be freed to exercise their initiative unrestricted by the old barriers between subjects at school and crafts at work. Neither would they be forced to remain in one occupation for all of their working lives. Indeed, the applications of new technology were making such an attitude increasingly unrealistic. Individuals had to be versatile and adaptable if they were to grasp the opportunities unleashed by the latest technological advances that were being applied in so many areas.

A New Training Initiative presented other advantages also. The idea of a vocational preparation scheme for all young people had first been suggested by the TSA in 1974. Again, in 1977, the TSA's 'Review and Plan' had proposed reducing the supply of labour by designating ages 16–19 a 'learning period' for all young people, while Geoffrey Holland, in an interview with *Personnel Management* (December 1981), indicated that 'if we are to move forward, we might have to look at keeping young people in some way out of the labour market until they are eighteen'. The Labour government too had considered introducing such a compulsory scheme. Now the crisis of youth unemployment presented the opportunity to launch it at last. Raising the age of entry to the labour market, if only at first by one year, gave Britain the chance to approach the investment that its competitors, particularly West Germany and Japan, made in their young workers. In addition this had the appeal to government of removing hundreds of thousands of young people from the unemployment register. Even Sir Richard O'Brien had conceded the value of youth employment schemes in preventing the young from becoming 'the enemies of society' (Josiah Mason Lecture, Birmingham University, 29 November 1977). If this attitude concealed the old belief in finding work for idle hands, at least the NTI would combine useful occupation with training funded by the European Social Fund in the latest technology.

So a vocational training scheme for all school leavers was an idea whose hour had come round at last. For the MSC this modernization of the apprenticeship system was an essential part of its pursuit of training policy and an increase in its own influence. To its TUC partners youth training could be represented as a widening of access to training for all young people. For employers, state-subsidized youth training gave them a cheap means of recruiting young people with the right attitudes to work. Young people and their parents might find in the new MSC schemes an alternative to the hopelessness of life on the dole. To the opposition and other critics the New Training Initiative appeared to do something immediate about youth unemployment. It might at the least take unemployed youths off the streets of the riot-torn inner cities. As the *Times* editorial (2 September 1983) welcoming the announcement of the scheme stated, it was in part a short-term 'anti-riot device keeping sixteen-year-olds off the unemployment record and off the streets'. But in the long term a state-run youth training scheme promised a solution to the crisis of permanent and structural youth unemployment. So, as *The Times*'s leader-writer continued,

> the short term expedient must be used as a vehicle for a longer term policy and equipping the workforce of the 1980s and 1990s with a new array of skills required by an economy open to strong competition from Far East, Far West and the Continent. . . . YTS could be a step on the path back to sustained competitiveness.

For the government the NTI filled a vacuum in training policy that had been created by its hostility to the ITBs. It also indicated a new way to undermine trades union power and, as the government's own 'Think Tank' had suggested, to introduce new working practices. It also presented a new answer to the problem and whole purpose of schooling. Potentially here was a means of by-passing the schools and the educational establishment to reach the rising generations and imbue them with the values of enterprise and individual initiative that the new Conservatism held so dear.

This happy coincidence of ideas and motives might still never have found the means to be put into practical effect but for the coincident conjuncture of key personnel so placed as to translate plans and possibilities into reality. It has been seen that the MSC had averted the threat to its existence and had reestablished itself in the favour of the government. The Commission had already demonstrated its administrative abilities in the speed with which it had responded to the previous emergencies of rising unemployment. Now it was headed by a government appointee unambiguously committed to monetarism and the peculiar amalgam of new and old Conservatism that was coming to be known as Thatcherism. David Young was a protégé of Sir Keith Joseph, the original prophet of this new philosophy, who now became the Minister of Education. In addition the government's hatchet man, Norman Tebbit, was strategically placed at the equally crucial Ministry of Trade and Industry. As he gleefully told the *Financial Times*, 'Now that Keith Joseph is at the DES and David Young is at the MSC I think you will soon find the Vandals stabling their horses in the temples' (15 October 1982). Lastly, of course, there was the Prime Minister herself. She endorsed the new approach not only because of her personal enthusiasm for the quick-fire style of David Young – 'the only man,' she said, 'who brings me solutions and not problems' – but because an emergency situation demanded urgent action and her own experience as Minister of Education in the previous Conservative administration had taught her the hopelessness of relying upon the entrenched block of educational interests that still dominated the Department of Education and Science. 'Education', she was heard to declare in the early days of her premiership 'is a disaster area' (see Wolpe and Donald, 1983). So for the next six years, until the departure of Sir Keith and the subsequent feuding between Tebbit and Young, this Gang of Four really made policy in the crucial area of education and training. Under their aegis the MSC rose to the height of its power and influence and played a large part in the permanent transformation of the British economy and society that is the legacy of Mrs Thatcher's government.

THE NEW TRAINING INITIATIVE – A FRESH START

'A New Training Initiative' (MSC, 1981a) gave the MSC the opportunity for which its leading officers had been waiting for so long to assert its vision of the essential part that training could play in Britain's industrial regeneration. The document expressed their philosophy as a new social ethos: in the turbulent situation of rapid technological change, life was a vocational education and work was a training scheme.

> For too long we have treated training and education as a once and for all experience at the start of life as if circumstances and requirements would remain unchanged. . . . There have been few chances for adults to start afresh or add to what they have. Employers have too often taken or been forced to take a short term view and relied heavily on being able to buy in the skills they need from the market place. Training has been seen as a dispensable overhead rather than an investment for the future (pp. 4, 5).

In place of this traditional unplanned, market approach, the NTI argued that systematic training and retraining for the entire workforce was not only important for the survival of individual firms and also for employment prospects but that training and retraining were actually a cure for unemployment. To this end the document promulgated three interrelated national training principles:

1. 'We must develop skill training, including apprenticeships, in such a way as to enable young people entering at different ages and with different educational qualifications to acquire agreed standards of skill appropriate to the jobs available, and to provide them with the basis for progression through further learning;
2. 'we must move towards a position where all young people under the age of 18 have the opportunity, either of continuing in full-time education, or of entering training, or a period of planned work-related training and education;
3. 'we must open up wide opportunities for adults, whether in employment, unemployed or returning to work, to acquire, increase or update their skills and knowledge during the course of their working lives' (p. 6).

The framework of this New Training Initiative implied a significant increase in resources for training. The real question, however, was the relative balance between state funding and finance from industry. The NTI proposals followed the decision to abandon the statutory structure of the ITBs and levy/grant system that had characterized the two previous attempts at reform. As Sheldrake and Vickerstaff (1987) recorded,

> The resulting NTI policy has been a mixture of state involvement and private provision, the corporatist element, remaining symbolically at least in the form of the tripartite MSC. . . . The state contribution to NTI is concentrated in the youth policy area, whilst primary responsibility for adult training remains with industry. . . . NTI represents a contradictory mixture of the recognition that government action is needed (YTS) and a disavowal of it on principle (adult training).

They argued therefore that 'NTI does not provide a framework for a national training strategy' (pp. 58 and 64). This may have been the result but it was certainly not the intention.

While the NTI was aimed at a transformation of the entire workforce, the MSC's priority remained with young people. New entrants to the labour market were the obvious people with whom to begin the new cultural revolution. At the same time the MSC was faced with the immediate task of building a permanent bridge from school to work over the alarming, structural mass unemployment that had resulted with the collapse of the youth labour market and what was left of the old apprenticeship system. The establishment of a modernized apprenticeship system was therefore its first priority. Such a system would emphasize the 'portable' skills, transferable within and between particular 'occupational training families' about which Hayes and others at the Institute of Manpower Studies had written for the MSC (Hayes, 1982 and 1983). However, the object of the MSC's policies for adults remained to encourage training for skill shortages. Here the long-term, detailed, human resource planning approach to tackling national skills shortages was abandoned and the MSC based its policies for the adult training strategy on reacting to demand. The result was that, as Kenny and Reid (1985) commented, 'The MSC . . . now follows two different policies in seeking to meet future demands for skills (p. 52).

From the beginning there was a danger that one of these approaches would be seen as 'real' training and the other not. Particularly as, ever since the merger of the Employment Services Agency and the smaller Training Services Agency, the MSC had combined two policy areas – those designed to combat unemployment and training policies. As Moon and Richardson (1984) noted,

Training policies have not simply been used as a means of preparing members of the workforce for new jobs, but also as a means of removing large numbers of people from the unemployment register. This merger has been most obvious in the case of schemes for youth (p. 73).

The MSC had always been open to the accusation that its youth training programmes were mere make-work schemes and this was indeed all that the Youth Opportunities Programme had ever intended to be. The Youth Training Scheme was to present itself as something fundamentally different, a one year foundation programme for all school leavers whether in or out of work. Yet the addition of a training element appeared to many as purely cosmetic. As Swann and Turnbull (1978) had said, in earlier days 'the able bodied poor were set to work though in more recent years this phrase has been replaced by the euphemism of training' (p. 162). It was ironic that the more imaginative and far-sighted of the MSC's two approaches to training was to be dogged by this accusation, while the traditional approach of training for the limited and specific skills demanded by employers for their immediate needs continued to be regarded as the only 'real training'. Yet youth training could successfully establish itself as the natural route to employment for school leavers if it were of such quality that it would not only guarantee its graduates jobs but would be equally valued by trainees and their parents when compared with the alternative educational route to secure employment through academic study. Whether these two necessary preconditions for the success of the Youth Training Scheme would ever be met remained highly problematic.

The new Secretary of State for Employment, Norman Tebbit, began discussions on the New Training Initiative during the summer of 1981 after his predecessor, James Prior, had given the proposals approval. A period of consultation had also begun at the MSC. On December 7 the Commission published 'A New Training Initiative: An Agenda for Action' (MSC, 1981b), a more uncompromising restatement of the first consultative policy statement. 'Firms and individuals', it said, 'must adapt to change or become its victims' (p. 7). The response to these proposals from the government was immediate. In fact Tebbit published a White Paper on 'The Youth Training Scheme' (Cmnd. 8455) the same day! In it he effectively accepted responsibility by the state for provision of a £1 billion scheme of vocational preparation for young people between the ages of 16 and 18. After this, according to the White Paper, 'the cost of training is basically a matter for the individual employer' (p. 3). Since it was up to each employer to keep his training costs down, adults retraining for higher technical skills through the Open Tech Programme would have to pay for their own self-improvement. This approach only served to emphasize the difference between state and private provision, as did the proviso that state funding was only temporary: 'in the longer term the responsibility for training must lie mainly with employers' (p. 13). The criticism that state funded youth training was not training at all but merely continued the make-work Youth Opportunities Programme was levelled at the new proposals by right and left. For example, hard-line monetarists Miller and Wood (1984) argued that

the New Training Initiative or 'Tebbit' scheme . . . which is due to start in 1983 at an annual cost of £1 billion, will replace YOP on a larger scale, but is little different from it in principle. Unfortunately, it is open to the objection that it provides training rather than proper jobs, which are being demanded and its cost is likely to destroy jobs and job opportunities elsewhere in the economy (p. 103).

In answer to such criticisms the MSC had long argued that training was a vital component of employment stability and corporate growth. In the long term a better-motivated workforce and enhanced manpower utilization would increase productivity and therefore over time exert a marginal influence upon pricing. This in turn would gain more orders for the firm concerned so increasing the demand for labour. Tebbit began putting forward this line of explanation from the beginning of 1982. 'Unless we make better use of our people we are doomed to a steady downward decline', he wrote in an article for *Personnel Management* in February.

> That requires the constant change of skills needed in advanced industrialised economies, and workers who are also better informed, better motivated, more realistic and more adaptable . . . labour is a product which needs to be improved like any other. . . . We must therefore look carefully at the types of training which are and will be needed. We have to get rid of artificial restrictions on age of entry and length of training, and increase flexibility by making refresher and retraining courses available. But that will be possible only if we first make sure that everyone has the essential basic training on which to build as requirements change.

Similarly David Young, in an interview soon after he became Chairman of the MSC, re-emphasized the relationship between training and economic efficiency. Young also outlined what he saw as the specific role of the MSC to 'help prepare for economic recovery through providing efficient training and job placement services'. The MSC would achieve this by 'concentrating on people', particularly those 'at risk such as youngsters, the disabled, the long-term unemployed'. To do this 'we must work in partnership with employers and unions to come to terms with the new technologies'. To these general aims of the MSC he added his own enthusiasms for 'initiative, enterprise and self help' and 'our faith in small businesses' (*The Director* December 1982). Both Young and Tebbit grasped the cultural importance of the changes proposed by the NTI, a vision that they shared with the Prime Minister and Sir Keith Joseph. To this end they both agreed that 'Britain will have to train its way out of the recession' (Peter Morrison interview 26 October 1985).

The first step in this programme was, as Tebbit told the 1981 Conservative Party Conference, to transform the YOP into a high-quality youth training programme. Thus, 'we can turn the tragedy of youth unemployment into an opportunity to create a better trained and skilled workforce for the future', so that 'for the first time . . . unemployment among this age group should have become a thing of the past'. This foundation programme would be for one year in the first instance, though the MSC's Task Group, which reported in the spring of 1982, wanted a two year scheme.

> The scheme we propose will make a central contribution to economic survival, recovery and growth. Our aim is to provide for what the economy needs, and what employers want – a better equipped, better motivated, better qualified and educated workforce. And it is to provide young people with what they themselves need to actively seek greater opportunities to equip themselves to make their way in the increasingly competitive and uncertain world of the 1980s (p. 11).

The supposition that what the economy needed and what employers wanted was a better-qualified and educated workforce was questionable in view of the effect that the application of new technology was actually having on the workforce. Although new technology did create a few new and higher-level skills, the occupations where these were required declined in relation to the greater numbers of skills that were displaced when new technology was introduced into a given industry. Deskilling, if not unemployment, was the order of the day in the traditional industry that survived the rigours of the depression into which the government allowed the economy to slide unhindered. Skilled craft work was increasingly replaced by the reiterated demand for semi-skilled, 'flexible and adaptable' workers, able to cross the old demarcation lines between trades and turn their hands to all the various activities that were progressively simplified by the new technology. The sum of skills of one of these new generalized workers might add up to the particular skills of a former specialized craftsman but in the majority of cases there was a loss of skill. The new tasks, even if spread over what were formerly discrete areas, were more easily acquired by new employees. Employers increasingly preferred therefore to employ part-timers, especially women, rather than youngsters who needed to be educated to sustain their motivation at what were increasingly low-paid, irregular and semi-skilled peripheral jobs. This pattern was especially apparent in the service sector, the only expanding sector of the economy, in which the government was occasionally tempted to place its hopes for the whole future of the British economy.

The rhetoric of quality training for higher skills was somewhat belied by Norman Tebbit's initial approach to the new scheme when he announced that the training allowance which YTS trainees would receive would be £10 less than the wages paid on the YOP and that those who refused to join the scheme would lose their right to supplementary benefit altogether. Of course Tebbit justified this by the assertion that the training quality of YTS would be so much higher than YOP, which it was admitted had had no formal training content, hence the distinction between training allowance and YOP wage. He told the House of Commons Employment Committee (21 June 1982)

> It is important, that we are not cutting the income of an individual youngster. We are not going to some youngster today who is receiving £25 a week and telling him he will get £15 tomorrow. What we are doing is to say to a new youngster who will be coming into the scheme is that we are going to give you training where it is at least twice as good as YOP . . . and in addition we are still going to give you £15 a week.

However, the whole farrago of Tebbit's announcement of the new training allowance to the House of Commons without first consulting either the MSC or its Task Group was merely a ploy identical to his declaration that all the Training Boards would be abolished forthwith. As in that case, when the shouts of protest had died down, Tebbit appeared to make a great concession to his opponents by allowing a limited number of the Boards to remain (see page 55) – only to go on and abolish them later. Similarly in the case of the YTS training allowance, the initial announcement that it would be cut to only £15 drew the sting of his critics, most of whom were prepared to accept a partial victory when the allowance was restored to the £25 that the MSC had in fact originally suggested. As for benefits, although the right to them was not abolished altogether until after the 1987 election, sanctions were introduced against those who refused or prematurely left a place on YTS (a 40 per cent reduction in benefit for 6 weeks, subsequently increased to 13 and then 26 weeks). The MSC also cautioned against removing benefit rights to force youngsters onto YTS, recognizing that this would jeopardize the acceptability of the new scheme (Task Group Report, paras 7. 14 and 15).

Pressure from the TUC and its representatives on the MSC in particular demanded that the allowance be set at the same level as on the old YOPs scheme. Once Tebbit had made this apparent concession, the TUC, as it said in its Annual Report for 1982 (p. 58), conditionally accepted YTS but would continue to monitor the situation closely. Gavin Laird, the Boilermakers' leader, expressed the typical trades union reaction when he declared:

> Let it be said, unequivocally, our union recognises, and the trade union movement recognises, that training schemes are a poor second best for permanent jobs. . . . But having said that, you cannot afford to throw the baby out with the bathwater. The Youth Training Scheme, with all the deficiencies the scheme has that is now being implemented, is far better than that which was produced originally by the Department of Employment and Mr Tebbit. The three TUC representatives have done a magnificent job when you compare how the scheme was originally (Labour Party Report, 1982/83, p. 231).

Others were not so easily satisfied. Mr Tebbit's sudden announcement of the reduced training allowance produced something of a revolt among careers officers, who would be expected to cajole reluctant school leavers into accepting it. Meetings were held in central London and elsewhere protesting at the proposals. The left, in and out of the Labour Party, together with most rank-and-file trades unionists and many parents and working-class youth, at whom YTS was in practice almost exclusively aimed despite its claims to universality, all greeted the new scheme with suspicion if not outright hostility. This submerged opposition to YTS continued to dog the scheme even when concessions appeared to be made. It was the focus of a prolonged debate over the value of state training schemes that rumbled on in what is loosely called the labour movement (see, for example, the Report of the National Labour Movement Inquiry into Youth Unemployment and Training, Birmingham Trades Council Union Resource Centre, 1987).

The hierarchy of the TUC, however, did not see the Youth Training Scheme as a poor substitute for jobs. Ken Graham told the TUC Youth Conference in 1983 that:

> The scheme is fully consistent with TUC policy on training for all, but we have to ensure that something which is consistent when written down is consistent in practice. . . . The more that schemes are established within the unionised sector, the greater the ability to ensure these young people are not treated as cheap labour' (reported in the *Times Educational Supplement* 25 February 1983).

TUC responsibility was therefore clearly to remain on the Commission, especially as Graham saw 'a sound YTS and a strong apprenticeship system . . . developing hand in hand'. Yet clearly, traditional apprenticeships of the type familiar to the trades unions and the modernized apprenticeship system intended by the youth training scheme were mutually incompatible, as the future development of the YTS was to show.

THE YOUTH TRAINING SCHEME – FROM RHETORIC TO REALITY

To facilitate the transition from grand conceptions in a glossy brochure to existence in the real world, the MSC set up fifty-five local Area Manpower Boards to administer the YTS. Each AMB advised the MSC on the planning and implementation of its programmes locally, including manpower intelligence on the types and quantities of training required. They also approved and monitored local MSC projects, although a Large Companies Unit could also perform this function for national schemes in particular firms. The AMBs were not intended merely to be concerned with the YTS but in practice this became their main function. Recognizing this, the Institute of Personnel Management called in 1985 for an expansion of their role. The Institute noted that in the early years of the YTS the demands placed upon the Boards had been so great that they had not been able to 'fulfil their role as local focusing agents for the whole range of training and development activities'. These included 'establishing training and development as an essential, and normal, feature in the lives of each individual in the UK', not just concentrating upon young people. However, it was also recognized that

> an important advantage claimed for the AMB system is that the human resource problems of organisation of all sizes can be more readily identified and tackled. This is particularly important in relation to small businesses which are seen as being the locus for many of the new opportunities for employment (quoted in Sheldrake and Vickerstaff, 1987, p. 298).

The way that the AMBs set about organizing the YTS certainly gave incentives to a new type of small business: that providing the training for the many poorly qualified, working-class school leavers for whom YTS offered the only alternative to a life on the dole. Private training agencies launched themselves into business with the grants of £1950 that the MSC initially gave them for every trainee whom they could place on their schemes. They contracted trainees out to local employers for 'work experience' while they bought in suitable training or else provided it themselves. When the anticipated numbers on YTS did not approach the profitable, many of these small, private managing agencies became bankrupt. However, they established a significant precedent for the future privatizing of education as a whole, while the extensive training empires built up by successful agencies, like Community Task Force, made them indispensable for running the YTS. Large companies also ran their own Youth Training Schemes, though the original intention that the scheme would apply to all youngsters, whether in or out of work, was never realized. From forecast numbers of 33 per cent of all trainees, employed trainees sank to just 5 per cent of all those on the scheme. In many inner-city areas where Labour-controlled local authorities were left by the demise of traditional industries as the largest local employers, council schemes topped up the basic youth training allowance to up to £40 per week. Local-authority-controlled further education colleges also became large-scale providers of youth training, expanding their previous courses for special school leavers to include the influx from YTS. The resulting provision was, as Sheldrake and Vickerstaff remark (1987, p. 58), 'a mixture of state involvement and private provision, the corporatist element remaining symbolically at least in the form of the tripartite MSC'.

Amongst this *mélange* of different types of YTS locally a clear hierarchy of schemes quickly emerged. This followed the pattern that already existed for YOP. Despite the common elements all schemes were supposed to share, YTS quickly became not so much a unified national system as a collection of different schemes with the Information Technology Centres at the top and the old Mode B2s for the disabled and disadvantaged at the bottom. ITeCs and higher-level courses in further education provided training in occupationally specific skills in demand in the labour market. They actually did provide some of the training in new technology that the public image of YTS advertised, rather than mere 'hands on' 'keyboard familiarity'. However, the cost of applying such hi-tech training to all schemes was obviously prohibitive. In any case there were not the job opportunities in such skills for all YTS trainees. Other highly selective schemes in large companies were mainly converted apprenticeships brought within YTS. They offered employment to trainees subject only to their gaining minimum levels of performance. The YTS, contrary to the stated intentions of NTI, therefore tended to divide into schemes providing training for real employment and other schemes that offered no certainty of acquiring marketable skills or of finding work.

Where the NTI had proclaimed YTS was 'first and last a training scheme' and 'not about youth unemployment' (Task Group Report, p. 1), in reality many managing agents used the scheme only for the unemployed and many trainees only signed on as a last alternative to the dole. The small employers with whom the majority of trainees were placed used them mainly to screen potential recruits should vacancies arise. At the very bottom of the pile, former Mode B YOP schemes (paid for a time an additional 'premium' by the MSC) operated in their own 'workshops' entirely detached from the processes of recruitment and selection of labour. Raffe (1986) observed that in Scotland these included 'Mode A schemes on employers' premises set up largely as an expression of social responsibility by the employers . . . where the additional "goats" are from the start distinguished from the "sheep" who comprise the normal intake'. 'Such stratification', as Finn and Markhall had commented on YOP (1981, p. 65), 'was never the intention of the programme but was nevertheless discovered to be its effect in practice'. Its existence undermined another of the aims of the NTI, which was to raise the age of selection for employment above 16 years. In fact, again contrary to the intentions of the NTI, school qualifications, or the lack of them, continue to be the main factor affecting the employment and training prospects for most school leavers.

Rather than there being the uniform national scheme that was intended, the level of take-up of YTS also reflected the state of local labour markets, being lowest in the South-East and highest in areas of high unemployment. Evidence from the MSC's YTS Leavers' Survey for April 1985 to January 1986 showed a reduced chance of finding a job after YTS for young people in the depressed regions and localities, for young people with no qualifications and for young black people. Within local labour markets, despite repeated statements of intent by the MSC, patterns of discrimination continued to be reflected in YTS. There were repeated complaints (starting with one from the Commission for Racial Equality in 1984) that YTS relegated black youth to schemes from which there was less likelihood of leaving for employment. Similarly, young women continued to be over-represented on schemes training for low-paid, traditionally feminine work (see Cockburn, 1987). For instance, in 1984 64 per cent of girls on YTS were in administrative/clerical or sales/personal service work ('Report on YTS Leavers Survey', MSC, October 1984), while the largest remaining apprenticeship – in hairdressing, now being steadily incorporated into the YTS – was also overwhelmingly female.

However, as Peter Morrison, 'the Minister for Training', told the House of Commons in July 1983,

> The scheme is not a social service. Its purpose is to teach youngsters what the real world of work is all about. This means arriving on time, giving of their best during the working day, and perhaps staying on a little longer to complete an unfinished task.

Indeed, Morrison emphasized that the 'beauty' of YTS 'for employers is that they will be able to tailor the training to their own needs'. At the same time, Young explained in *The Director* (April 1983), 'Training should not be confused with education. Training is about work related skills and is intimately concerned with employment. It is for this reason that training in this country must be employer dominated and employer led'. Therefore 'the young should be a source of cheap labour because they can be trained on the job'. With such attitudes from those in command of the scheme it is not surprising that, despite the best efforts of many of those involved in it, the YTS came to mirror the worst conditions existing in the depressed and divided UK youth labour market. In fact the MSC made a virtue of this necessity by disclaiming arguments that it engaged in any sort of social engineering or direction of labour by claiming to be responsive to market forces and to be providing industry with the skills that it required.

Yet although it was provided for employers' benefit, employers obstinately persisted in their reluctance to contribute towards the costs of youth training. It was the original intention of the New Training Initiative that when YTS expanded to a two-year scheme, employers would pay for its second year. However, when the second year was introduced in 1986, this suggestion was forgotten. The first major survey of employers' relations to YTS found that 'the most important advantage to employers participating in the YTS is the opportunity it gives them to look at or screen young people before offering permanent employment. Also very important are the savings that result on labour costs' (Sako and Dore, 1986). Nevertheless, employers were more than ever loath to fund training. Especially in the depths of a recession, when many firms were already pared to the bone, it was cheaper to poach the few skilled employees who were required from rival companies. Also many employers preferred to continue with their traditional methods of recruitment rather than become involved with YTS. This was especially the case for the small businesses that together make up the majority of employers. Nevertheless, most YTS placements continued to be in the same small shops and businesses that had provided the majority of YOP places. These were hardly at the cutting edge of new-technology skills, however much they may have imbued their trainees with the entrepreneurial values of small business enterprise.

Selling the scheme to employers was one of the first tasks for the quango. Advertising for it was first aimed at parents to convince them of its worth but also tried to sell YTS to employers. To make things easier for those running the scheme the government excluded trainees from the Employment Protection Acts as well as most of the race relations legislation and Sex Discrimination Acts. In addition employers retained complete control over the hiring and firing of trainees. Yet employers, as the trades union representatives on the MSC continued to point out, gave very little in return. They were especially reluctant to abandon their traditional procedures and cooperate with developing the national training to agreed standards, which it was one of the aims of the New Training Initiative to encourage. Let alone were they willing for the new vocational qualifications ever to equal in value the traditional academic qualifications which they continued to prefer as indicators of real worth for posts of responsibility. As it was, the YTS had to start without any qualification at the end of it. The YTS leaving certificate, which is still the only standard, national accreditation, 'certainly presents itself as a most superficial document'. Indeed, as Jack Mansell, the head of the FEU was arguing in the *Times Educational Supplement* as late as May 1984, 'the outcomes of YTS are unclear. They have not been generally agreed except in the most superficial terms'. Although something in addition to a leaving certificate was repeatedly promised, it has not yet materialized.

Instead of a recognized qualification, David Young declared, the criterion of success for the scheme would be how many people found jobs at the end of it. It was very unlikely that the criterion could ever be met and critics alleged that the scheme would even increase unemployment. In fact 'additionality', by which the government paid employers to replace two young workers by five trainees, endorsed job substitution. By subsidizing employers who gave young people menial tasks and then returned them to the dole queue, YOP and YTS increased employers' reliance upon state monies to employ temporary trainees whom they did not have to train.

The YTS was therefore seriously flawed from its inception. These faults were disguised in the run-up to the 1983 general election in which heady atmosphere the scheme was prepared and soon after which it was launched. A pilot scheme ran parallel with YOP from April to August 1983 after which all new entrants went to YTS. In May Norman Tebbit told an election press conference that young people were 'enthusiastically enrolling for the government's new training opportunities'. But come September, national estimates suggested only 40 per cent of places were filled. Young was driven to deny that school leavers 'preferred the dole' (*Times Educational Supplement* 30 March 1984). The MSC admitted that the scheme needed improvement, which would come with time and experience. It claimed to have anticipated a 20 per cent shortfall in take-up, which it attributed to 'poor advertising and suspicion of the scheme among the young' (*The Times* 13 October 1984). 'Rome was not built in a day' became its motto. 'Teething problems' would be overcome in time. For, as far as the MSC was concerned, the YTS was merely a first step in transforming the training culture of the entire economy, while for the government the scheme was a great success against which it was not prepared to hear any argument.

YTS had taken the wind out of the opposition's sails. Partly with the TUC's cooperation the MSC had been successful in substituting the demand for a 'right to training' for the traditional labour demand for the right to work (described in the Labour Party's 1983 election 'Programme for Recovery' as 'a fundamental principle of democratic socialism'). Similarly, the MSC had kept ahead of its critics by thinking up Labour's policies before Labour could. Thus the YTS guaranteed, as Labour had also promised, a programme of quality training for all young people not in full-time education. Yet what was really indicative of the MSC's achievement was the way the speeches of government ministers increasingly echoed previous MSC pronouncements. The Tories had come to accept the need to 'create a new attitude to manpower' by implicitly relating training to improved industrial and corporate performance. In reality, however, the ability of the MSC to achieve this view of the value of training was ironically dependent upon the circumstances of mass unemployment and economic recession. Although these circumstances helped the MSC to get schemes off the ground, they constrained its attempts to persuade industry that training constituted an economic investment.

The MSC's dilemma also presented the government with an eventual problem in its fundamental attitude to the quango. After their initial estrangement, the happy couple seemed to have consummated a beautiful relationship in the joint creation of the NTI and its chief issue the YTS. Both MSC and government ministers had together adopted a new approach to training policy based upon long-term objectives rather than short-term success. Yet the government valued the MSC's ability to manage youth unemployment rather than the quango's house philosophy concerning the importance of vocational preparation and manpower planning for the future of the British economy. If the Thatcher government's new brand of Conservatism had created an atmosphere in which the MSC could realistically link investment in vocational training to national economic development, the same political and economic undercurrents negated any major expansion of job creation. Geoffrey Holland, the MSC's Director, had labelled the old Labour job creation programme, STEP, the 'programme of the future'. He had argued that 'with long term unemployment rising to record postwar levels the Special Temporary Employment Programme will become crucial in helping to contain the worst effects' (Department of Employment *Gazette*, July 1980). Yet he was over-optimistic about the future development of STEP. Although the new emphasis on supply-side economics did much to help the MSC launch YTS, it did little to help it persuade ministers of what those at the Commission saw as a potential scheme to reduce long-term unemployment substantially.

Along with other shibboleths of the old consensus, Mrs Thatcher's first government had deliberately abandoned the Welfare State's founding commitment to maintain full employment. The catastrophic consequences of the monetarist experiment had forced one of many U-turns in the originally declared policies. Funding was now directed at areas that were thought to be prerequisites for high and stable employment levels. The MSC's achievement had been to ensure that training occupied a commanding position within these policy prerequisites. However, the way in which YTS in particular was perceived depended upon whether it was agreed that the state could and should restore full employment and create new jobs. The new Conservatism held that this was not the business of government.

THE TRAINING DEBATE – HALF-TERM REPORT

Writing in 1979 John Lockwood, a professional trainer, recognized 'that the MSC is a potential powerhouse and a catalyst for change. We should', he continued, 'sing its praises, recognise its achievements and lament that it has been eliminated from its central objective of creating a new attitude towards manpower' (pp. 467–71). James Prior, giving evidence to the Employment Committee of the House of Commons, similarly conceded

the MSC has had a lot of really bad luck since it was set up, in that it was set up at a time when unemployment was comparatively low, with a view that it would coordinate manpower policies but that it would not engage itself in dealing with special measures.

Prior concluded, 'In a way this has resulted in that it has not been able to fulfil its proper role. . . . I don't think it's any real criticism of the MSC, it is just one that has really been used a great deal' (Eleventh Report of the Employment Committee, 9 June 1980).

However, the training debate had greatly benefited from the rise of supply-side economics and had come a long way under the Tories largely because of the change in the intellectual climate and the opportunism of the MSC. The New Training Initiative placed training at the heart of a profit-making, free enterprise and competitive market-orientated economy. This idea was expressed by 'NTI':

> For prosperity and growth we need to invest, to innovate and exploit new technologies . . . have products and services people want at prices they will pay . . . and exploit growing markets to replace those that are declining. . . (This) must be done as well as it is by our competitors who are now more and stronger than before (p. 1).

This could have been a speech by the Prime Minister or any of the 'blue bunnies' who she said made up her front bench team. Only Luddites disputed the case that training was a precondition for employment and growth. Mrs Thatcher's deliberate abandonment of the commitment to the welfare state's basic foundation, full employment, produced the approach where funding was directed at particular areas thought to be capable of generating greater economic efficiency that would in the long term sustain higher employment levels.

Critically, opinions were changing with regard to youth training. Coates and Topham (1986) argued that the YOP and YTS replaced the full-employment goal by mitigating the worst effects of permanent unemployment, while Miller and Wood (1984) had called for Norman Tebbit to resist spending £1 billion on the YTS and to cut public expenditure and national insurance contributions by an equal proportion. The new Conservatism rejected the goal of restoring full employment but became increasingly aware of the role of human capital in the growth of business and competitiveness. Others suggested that training was an institutionalized response to mass unemployment (e.g. Parsons, 1986), but more optimistic commentators credited the MSC and YTS with the intention of improving the long-run international competitive position of the British economy through a better-trained workforce (e.g. Ashton, 1986). Thompson (1986, p. 206) argued that one of the most positive features of the Conservatives' approach was that their industrial strategy had been 'disengaged' from simply maintaining employment. This was in contrast with Labour's programme, which shored up state industries with public money to sustain employment in declining industries (Redwood, 1984). The second Thatcher administration was to press home this disengaged approach but the relationship with the quango remained potentially fraught, for the leading policy makers at the MSC had further grand designs for mitigating the worst effects of long-term unemployment in Britain and for improving the nation's human capital stock. It was some time before the interests of the quango and the government were openly to diverge, however, and the next four years represented a golden age for the MSC as it continued to grow spectacularly and found a warm and considerate partner in the second Thatcher government.

SUMMARY

The Manpower Services Commission had survived the initial anti-statist hostility of the new Conservative administration, despite the embodiment of old-fashioned corporatism which the Commission represented. Although its finances were cut at first and the growth in the numbers of its personnel was halted, the quango was not abolished. Instead, the government brought it more directly under its control by appointing its own man to chair the Commission. The MSC soon found a ready reception for its ideas of modernizing the skill base and work practices of British industry through a comprehensive programme of training and retraining. This fitted with the new government's hostility to the trades unions and the Prime Minister's distrust of the Education Department, where she had previously been Minister. The emphasis upon youth training afforded a means of cultural revaluation for the new generations beyond the ideologically suspect schools and colleges. Youth training on an unprecedented scale became a political necessity as a response to the nationwide riots in 1981. These marked a real turning point in the quango's fortunes. Under their impetus the MSC's New Training Initiative proposed to convert the temporary Youth Opportunities Programme into a permanent Youth Training Scheme for the mass of working-class school leavers. This would incorporate and replace what was left of the Industrial Training Board system and institute a new and modernized state apprenticeship for all. On the ground, though, the YTS failed to develop into a coherent national training scheme and it never met the goals that were set for it by the MSC. Despite the use that they made of each other, the close relationship between quango and government remained flawed by the MSC's adherence to the ideal of comprehensive manpower strategy as a means of restoring full employment, a commitment which the government had deliberately abandoned.

Chapter 4

The MSC under the Tories (1983–1987): The Marriage Consummated

THE MSC AND ENTERPRISE CULTURE

The Conservatives' triumphant victory in the 1983 General Election signalled a fuller espousal of the free enterprise solution to Britain's economic and social affairs. For example, the Chancellor, Nigel Lawson, speaking in July to Brian Walden on 'Weekend World', declared that 'unemployment is not an economic problem but a social problem'. And Peter Jenkins in the *Guardian* of 11 October 1984 was undoubtedly right when he told his readers that the government was 'hitting on the cultural revolution solution' to economic crisis. No member of the Tory cabinet was more representative of this approach than the soon-to-be-ennobled David Young. Fresh from experience in business in 'the flagship of enterprise', as Mrs Thatcher called the United States of America, Lord Young was appointed Minister for Enterprise and later Secretary of State for Employment. In 1985 the Conservatives were formally to renounce the state's commitment to full employment in the White Paper 'Employment, the Challenge for the Nation'. The MSC had a direct influence on the creation of an enterprise economy with its sponsorship of the growing Enterprise Allowance Scheme. But training was to have a keener refashioning effect on social attitudes as the government began linking policy areas together. This was shown most strikingly in the Technical and Vocational Education Initiative (TVEI) and the ambition of connecting a new two-year YTS with this new incursion into the schools.

A major influence on the development of training policy under the second Conservative government was the continuing reform of Britain's industrial relations. In an interview in *The Times* 5 May 1983, shortly before the election, the Prime Minister had said, 'I cannot accept responsibility for those who strike themselves out of jobs, who refuse to accept new technology, or have not good management. . . . What I do accept responsibility for is inventing the right financial framework and the right legal framework'. Even those within the ranks who had been horrified by the desolation of British industry over which Mrs Thatcher had presided and which had earned for her their nickname of 'Atilla the Hen' conceded that 'the government's approach to trade union legislation has been an outstanding success' (Pym, 1984, p.

161). This success was to be vindicated in the agonizing year-long show-down with the miners, the big battalion of the army of traditionally organized labour. The back of the beast would be broken with this defeat. These changing conditions in Britain's industrial relations certainly helped the MSC to press on with its plans for education and training as part of a comprehensive manpower strategy.

The Conservatives returned to power with a new emphasis to their old employment strategy. Macro-control of the economy was to be supplemented by a micro-approach to employment (Riddell, 1986, p. 248). The main areas for the new initiative were a further round of trades union reform, a further reduction in costs for industry, special assistance to small business, help with the development of the new techno-logies and increased provision for training. These measures, including moves to abolish the Wage Councils and so 'price the unemployment back into work', were embodied in Lawson's 'Budget for Jobs', but as Riddell noted, the measures would take some time to work their way through and were not intended to be expansionary in macro terms. This new approach elevated training on the political agenda and stimulated the high profile assumed by the presentation of the Youth Training Scheme and other MSC programmes for the young and unemployed. Thus the MSC continued to make the political headlines throughout Mrs Thatcher's second term of office.

James Prior, the sacked Tory Cabinet Minister, argued (1986, p. 141) that the new two-year YTS programme was a long overdue reform of Britain's industrial training practices. Prior envisaged YTS reshaping both the country's vocational education and training system and at the same time influencing the debate on skill training. Confidence in YTS was strengthened when the Public Accounts Committee reported in 1983 that it saw the scheme as a means of alleviating the worst effects of the unemployment crisis but argued that it was vital to the economy irrespective of the appertaining employment conditions.

Yet although the Conservatives entered the 1983 election with a much clearer training policy than the rather vacuous and simple intentions that it has been seen they possessed in 1979, it would take some time before the rhetoric of ministers explicitly associated training with business efficiency, productivity, competitiveness and employment stability.

Unsurprisingly, the main input into the training debate was still unemployment. Many continued to see MSC training schemes as window dressing (e.g. Holmes, 1985b). However much the YTS was sold during the election and however many glossy brochures and stylish videos Young's publicity department churned out, the unemployment syndrome was hard to shake off. In the nation's classrooms teachers inverted Shaw's old saw by saying 'Those who can teach and those who can't produce flashy brochures'. Or, as Edward Pearce put it in the *New Statesman* 11 March 1988), 'If you put a duff property speculator in charge of a major department you get an expensive prospectus'. There was, as Lindley (1983) explained:

> . . . a feeling that a major diversification of provision for the education and training of young people is desirable as an end in itself. If only unemployment were not so high, the whole development could have been presented and received as perhaps one of the most *creative* policy initiatives yet in the field of post compulsory education and training. It will take some time, and probably a new government, however, for the Youth Training Scheme to shake off the suggestion of making a virtue of necessity (p. 360).

The schools were the obvious place to start weaning the British people away from their aberrent attachment to 'collectivist values' and their debilitating dependence upon 'socialism' and the Welfare State. However, Mrs Thatcher knew from her own experience as a minister how long was the way and hard through the entrenched interests and labyrinthine bureaucracy of the educational establishment at the Department of Education and Science. These people had long been in a *de facto* alliance with the Labour-dominated local education authorities and the teacher unions. The National Union of Teachers especially had enjoyed what Sarup (1982, p. 59) had called 'a cosy symbiotic relationship' with the DES 'from the 1944 Act until the Great Debate of the 1970s'. DES officials were, in short, hopelessly tainted with the spineless sixties spirit of permissiveness and were therefore ripe for 'cleansing'. Their efforts to extend 'equal opportunities' to all were a bottomless pit for government finances, as even Labour's Tony Crosland had recognized. Now equal opportunities were to be translated by Mrs Thatcher into 'opportunities to be unequal'. At all levels the education system could be seen to be encouraging attitudes of egalitarian lassitude in the majority. Even the élite within higher education were not being adequately prepared to take their place at the commanding heights of a dynamic economy. The colleges and schools were full of subversive lecturers and teachers sapping the morale of the nation's youth. To the difficult dilemma of how to get around this leviathan, with its notorious British duplication of central and local control through the Ministry and the LEAs, Lord Young presented the quango as an obliging and pliant instrument.

The MSC had already engaged with the educational debate that constructed what was popularly apprehended as 'a crisis in education'. To this crisis situation it had offered its own solution in the shape of the New Training Initiative. This proposed an institutional 'bridge' between the two supposedly distinct worlds of school and work. As has been seen, Chris Hayes' report for the Training Services Agency on 'Vocational Preparation for Young People' was instrumental in initiating the Great Debate. It noted the demands from industry for workers with generalized and flexible abilities rather than the former apprenticeships in particular skills. 'A more responsible attitude' was required for this adaptation and it was in their failure to cultivate this attitude that the schools were identified as failing the national economy. The MSC therefore appropriated the accepted notion in educational debate of the 'transition from school to work' being supposedly problematic for the majority of school leavers, together with the need for more 'relevant' and less academic schooling to overcome this problem. A sea-change was then effected in their use so that what had seemed previously the terms of a progressive critique of existing education became justifications for a new economic rationalization. School culture, on the one side, was presented as an influence from which the young had to be institutionally desocialized. On the other side, the world of work was seen as the unproblematic and natural arena in which individuals found their self-fulfilment and achieved 'vocational maturity'.

This exercise in sophistry was not the work of the mandarins of the MSC alone. As Paul Grosch (1987) wrote, 'The MSC has little or no refined educational image; its pronouncements on education smack more of the director's boardroom or the manager's office, than of the professor's study or the teacher's classroom' (p. 141). The breadth of Lord Young's vision, for instance, was shown by his opinion that 'just as Latin was vital to the educated of the fourteenth century, so a knowledge of taxation and marketing is to the educated of the twenty-first century' (quoted in Jones, 1989, p. 102). In fact the MSC relied heavily upon others to develop the ideas which became its *raison d'être* in education. Its analysis of changes in the economy borrowed from the work of the Institute of Manpower Studies at Sussex University, which specialized in applying American training theory to a British context. The MSC contracted the IMS to undertake a number of studies of the developing economy, but its educational inspiration derived largely from the Further Education Unit. This was a unit within the DES set up in 1977 by Labour's Shirley Williams. The FEU became a willing partner of the MSC because it was involved in a sectoral dispute within the DES on behalf of further education against Schools Branch. Grosch calls it 'the acceptable face of vocationalism', steering a middle course between the MSC and the Schools Council. Sir Keith Joseph of course abolished the latter and set up in its place a Secondary Examinations Council and a School Curriculum Development Committee, with which the FEU was to work closely. However, the FEU first spread its influence widely throughout the further education sector with a number of Regional Curriculum Bases that in the Unit's own estimation 'represent the first systematic attempt to create a regional network for the support of a specific area of curriculum development in FE' (Further Education Unit, 1984, p. vi). These operated by means of what became known as 'curriculum-led staff development' using a 'cascade model' to 'train the trainers'.

It was becoming necessary to train the trainers in the further and technical education colleges because this area of educational provision was rapidly changing. Traditionally, further education supplied such training needs as employers could not provide themselves. It took over this role from various apprentice night-schools and from the technical schools when they became absorbed into the reformed comprehensives during the 1960s. As Andy Green (1986) pointed out, tertiary modern further education has always had three distinct tiers of students taught in three completely contrasted and isolated styles. Now traditional craft and clerical courses were being squeezed by academic courses above, and filled with students from decapitated comprehensive sixth forms and vastly expanded pre-vocational courses below. As youth unemployment rose and the expected numbers remaining at school to form a 'new sixth form' did not materialize, increasing numbers of unqualified youths gravitated towards further education. There they filled courses that grew out of and hugely augmented the previous traditional provision in the colleges for special school leavers with moderate or severe learning difficulties. There was then a proliferation of 'multiskills' workshops, where originally these special school groups were taught the skills that would help them to survive in the outside world, cooking, mending plugs, changing fuses and a little joinery, together with reiterated emphasis upon the core areas of literacy, numeracy and (with the aid of grants from the EEC Social Fund) some familiarity with computer keyboards. The FEU developed its own 'social and life skills' courses upon this foundation developed for special school leavers. As formulated by the MSC in its 'Instructional Guide to Social and Life Skills' 1984, this presumed that the lack of those 'basic day-to-day skills which most of us take for granted . . . all those abilities, bits of information, know-how and decision making which we need to get by in life' was responsible for the individual's lack of employment. 'One of the aims of Life Skills Training' therefore 'will be to adjust trainees to normal working conditions, giving attention to such matters as time-keeping, discipline and the maintenance of relations with others'.

The FEU also provided a behavioural philosophy within which to identify and assess these attitudes and habits now dignified as skills. 'Acquired skills' through 'experiential learning' 'transferred' to assure 'build up' in 'applied competencies' could be checklisted by 'profiled assessment'. To ensure that these 'skills and competencies' were 'work relevant' the FEU described for the wider benefit of trainers within further education and as an example to them the 'Coventry Lightbox Assembly'.

> Here trainees construct, wire and test equipment, then package it and write the accompanying advice notes. The organisation is tight and efficient, and a convincing assembly regime is produced. When the lightboxes reach their destination in the main College building they are dismantled and their components fed back for reassembly (FEU, 1978).

That this extraordinary modern version of digging holes and filling them in again took place in something calling itself a College shows how far the language and practice of vocationalism had already penetrated the further education sector even before the MSC took up and systematically popularized the pioneering activities of the FEU. It was with this language developed by the FEU and using the bridgehead which the Unit provided into the educational establishment of the DES that the MSC set about transforming the terms of educational debate.

Similarly the MSC was able to use the existing institutional arrangements for guiding the 'transition process', those provided by the local education authority controlled Careers Service. Formerly under the direction of the Ministry of Labour and still technically part of the Department of Employment which inspects it, the ambiguous situation of the Careers Service had more than once threatened its 3500 officers with absorption into the DES or the DE. It had been renamed three times since the war, which shows how bad things were! Perhaps the only reason why, as youth unemployment rose, it was not disbanded was that this would have been seen as an admission that there really were no careers left for young people. Under the MSC the Careers Service was preserved and given a new role. Especially with the introduction of the YTS as 'a permanent bridge between school and work', the Careers Service remained the major referral agency for young people onto schemes. Indeed at the launch of YTS in the autumn of 1983, a minister from the Department of Employment warned the annual conference of the Institute of Careers Officers that their service was on trial and its future depended upon how it handled the new scheme. So the ambiguous role of the Careers Service was sustained and it was used by the MSC to advise and inform about YTS in schools and colleges under local government authority where the MSC itself might not have received such a ready welcome or gained acceptance for the new scheme. In Northern Ireland, where it was still controlled directly by the DE, the service played a role in pioneering many of the developments in youth training that the MSC hoped to see extended to the UK as a whole.

There was nothing sinister in all this. The MSC merely sought to expand its own influence as an organization and to pursue the fundamental objectives which its leading officials believed were worthwhile, namely a comprehensive manpower planning framework for the economy. This could be achieved by beginning with the youngest entrants to the workforce and work towards the creation for them of a unified system of education and training. Some of those who came to believe in this goal and invested their efforts and their careers in pursuit of it imbued it with an almost missionary fervour. For it could be presented as a way to break down the invidious divide between academic education and technical training and would ensure them both a parity of esteem. Practical skills would then no longer be derided as second best but could compete on equal terms with academic qualifications. The new profiled assessments were not designed, like traditional examinations of literary manipulation and memory, to fail the majority of those who sat them. Instead everyone 'can do' at least some of the items on a list of profiled competencies and those that they cannot achieve in practice on one occasion they can come back and take on another. The new system might thus at last give credit where credit was due to a much larger range of attainments than those recognized by an increasingly irrelevant and antiquated educational hierarchy. And who could tell where such a fundamental transformation of social attitudes might end?

THE MINISTRY OF TRAINING

A unified system of education and training was now the shared goal of all those involved in the tripartite constitution of the quango. This was seen by the MSC itself as the way to secure its dominance over the area of vocational preparation that had become the largely accepted goal for educational endeavour. Education would then be subordinated to the end of comprehensive manpower planning which, the MSC had repeatedly stated, was the rational means to modernize the economy. For the government a restructuring of the workforce from the bottom up, beginning with its youngest entrants, was a contribution to Sir Keith Joseph's 'law-abiding free enterprise reconstruction of Britain's social relations of production'. In addition it would have the virtue of imbuing the rising generations with the values of enterprise culture. Accordingly, the 1984 White Paper 'Training for Jobs' now asked the MSC 'to expand its range of operations so as to be able to discharge the function of a national training authority' (para 44).

For industrialists, any help that they could get was always welcome in the artificially aggravated depression into which they had been plunged by the government's pursuit of arbitrary money supply targets. They particularly welcomed financial support for training, for in a recession this was always one of the first items of expenditure on which savings could be made. The fact that the new training allowances substantially lowered previous apprenticeship rates was also appreciated by them. Of course the trades unions could not be expected to go along with such an approach. However, they recognized that traditional apprenticeships and the favourable agreements they had secured for them were long gone and they appreciated their position on the MSC as a means of gaining the best possible deal that they could for young workers. In addition the leaders of Labour and the trades unions still believed that the MSC could be returned to what they saw as its proper role of extending the benefits of quality training to all school leavers and of reallocating manpower in a reconstructed economy. In the meantime therefore the quango should be preserved and protected for the increasingly distant eventuality of the return of a Labour government.

To all these combined influences only the entrenched interests of the educational establishment seemed opposed. In their second term of office, therefore, the Conservatives used the MSC directly to challenge and undermine the practices and procedures of the organization that in Britain had traditionally educated and trained the future workforce – the Department of Education and Science. To a growing extent this also meant marginalizing the local authorities, with whom the DES shared its responsibility for the schools and colleges. This was a happy coincidence for the government because, following the trades unions, it was the local councils, and particularly the socialist metropolitan authorities, which finally had to be abolished, who were the prime targets of the Conservatives' growing authoritarianism. 'Almost the only centre of power outside Parliament itself that can claim legitimacy on the basis of universal suffrage and a popular vote', the local state was also 'a major provider of collective welfare services and a substantial spender of public money – both seen by the Thatcher governments as basically inimical to national regeneration' (Duncan and Goodwin, 1988, pp. xii, xiii). Yet even though the Labour-controlled local authorities were also in continuing conflict with the government, both they and the DES were prepared to cooperate to a considerable degree with the MSC, particularly if they could be given responsibility for implementing the desired changes for themselves and were financed by MSC money. In this way the DES sought to preserve its own corner, and the rate-capped local authorities also welcomed any injection of scarce resources. Labour councils, like the TUC, also attempted to preserve the interests of young people and the unemployed on MSC schemes under their control as best they could by topping-up their allowances and providing what quality training with what assurances of employment after it they could manage.

David Young was instrumental in the government's new approach, both in his role as Chairman of the MSC and later when he was elevated to the House of Lords and to the Cabinet, of which, as Jackson (1986) said, 'he had long been virtually an undercover member' (p. 37). As head of the Enterprise Unit in the Cabinet Office, Lord Young was made the 'overlord' for enterprise, job creation and tourism. There he immediately began planning to coordinate the education, training and employment of the country's 14–18-year-olds. Later he was to be made Secretary of State for Employment. It was politically scandalous to the opposition that their MPs had no opportunity directly to cross-examine an unelected peer on the sensitive subject of unemployment. However, from the MSC's point of view, the move put a Minister with considerable experience of and interest in manpower issues into the Cabinet and at the heart of the Whitehall machine. Moreover, Young set the agenda for his successor as Chairman of the MSC, Bryan Nicholson. This former manager from Rank Xerox was greeted as 'The Man from Nowhere' by the *Times Educational Supplement* (26 October 1984), but to the MSC such an appointment in any case confirmed its high status in the new scheme of things. In place of the Young–Morrison axis, there was now the Nicholson–Young axis. In addition, the Overlord for Training and Enterprise enjoyed the confidence of the Prime Minister and shared the coordination of education and training with Sir Keith Joseph as Minister of Education, the man who had been her inspiration and who had been Young's original benefactor.

Young's public relations triumph in launching the YTS as a part of the government's successful election campaign paved the way not only for his own rise to power but also for his long-term goal of replacing traditional apprenticeships in British industry with a new and modernized apprenticeship system (interview 13 June 1985). Meanwhile, YTS continued to be judged by economists and the general public alike in terms of how successful it was in 'clearing the labour market'. Indeed, as seen, Young himself had accepted this criterion for the success of YTS when he had said that the Scheme would be judged by how many of its trainees graduated to employment. He therefore hailed as 'a highly encouraging start' the results of an MSC sampling of 3500 leaving YTS between April and July 1984 in nine areas of the country which showed 56 per cent going into jobs. These figures were denounced as 'a political fiddle' by the charity lobbying for young people, Youthaid, which alleged that 55 per cent of youngsters who had not gone on the YTS were also in jobs by this time. In 1985 the MSC was to admit that the placement rate had dropped below half to 48 per cent – just as YOP's placement rate fell as the programme expanded. Like the levels of take-up, the figures for placements were continuously disputed between the MSC and its critics. The fact that of 123,000 entrants to the YTS in its first year were unaccounted for at its end, and that the MSC admitted it did not know how many had left, where they had gone or whether they had been counted twice because they had moved from one scheme to another shows how confused things were. There were press accusations that for every person joining YTS two were leaving (*Times Educational Supplement* 30 March 1984) and that out of every four who joined one dropped out within six months (*The Guardian* 17 April 1984). Certainly those working on the ground with youngsters on schemes could confirm that chronic scheme changing had come to replace the frequent job changing that had always characterized a substantial section of the youth labour market. However, the real situation was obscured not only by the continuing high level of advertising hype for the scheme but also by the fact that the MSC changed its computer accounting method in 1984/85 which made comparisons with earlier years particularly difficult.

Running alongside the developing YTS were a series of youth labour market programmes. These were essentially Keynesian in nature, attempting to reduce the cost of employing young workers and damaged YTS by tarring it with the same brush. The Young Workers' Scheme, which had started the year before YTS in 1982, paid employers £15 a week each for every young person they took on whom they paid less than £45. Hardly the 'real jobs' that the government said it was bent upon creating! (There was a further anomaly in that the Department of Employment was thus subsidizing employers for paying below the national minimum wage that it was responsible for maintaining.) The YTS also encouraged employers to reduce permanent staff by replacing them with state-funded temporary trainees. In this way the YTS, as the Audit Commission suggested in 1985, actually contributed to increasing the level of unemployment. The YWS tended to function as the second year of YTS. With the numbers of young people on these schemes, together with older unemployed people on the Community Programme and other programmes that were also being rapidly expanded, the quango would soon find itself the indirect employer of up to a million low-paid workers subsidized through the state. This was an unprecedented extension of state control in a supposedly free labour market and was in complete contradiction to the ideology of free market capitalism to which the government had pledged itself. This contradiction has not gone unmarked in other areas of policy, where the commitment to 'rolling back the frontiers of the state' has accompanied measures of increasing centralization and control. To those who opposed 'Thatcherism' and all that it stood for, there seemed mounting 'evidence of the MSC as an increasingly sinister corporate creature' (Benn and Fairley, 1986). For these authors, and many others to the left of the Labour Party, the MSC had come to deserve 'its new street name: the Ministry of Social Control' (p. 1).

However, Benn and Fairley, and the trades unionists who continued to participate in the administration of MSC programmes nationally and locally through the Area Manpower Boards, persisted in their belief that the MSC could one day be returned to 'popular control'. In the meantime they imagined it could be restrained by their interventions – even though they were repeatedly overruled and ignored by the Boards. An internal MSC document relating to the Community Programme, but applying also to YTS, stated quite bluntly: 'We cannot allow trades unions to have a veto on projects'. If they did try to exercise their right of veto on approval of schemes by AMBs, the document advised that 'the sponsor should be invited to proceed without trade union approval'. Yet still Bill Keys was to be found at the 1983 TUC stating the view of the General Council that 'the MSC was the concept of the Congress and indeed we fought for it and we got it'. The TUC cited its success at raising Tebbit's original proposal for a £15 training allowance by £10 as an argument against those who, like the National Union of Mineworkers, urged a trades union boycott of the MSC. And the most left-wing of Labour Councils acted as agents for the MSC in managing their own training schemes, where they attempted to provide examples of good practice and increased rates of pay that they hoped would be followed elsewhere.

Only four major unions (the CPSA, UCW, POEU and NGA) opposed the YTS outright. The TGWU prevented the transformation of their existing agricultural apprenticeship into a YTS, while the Civil Service unions so effectively dragged their feet over its introduction into the Civil Service that it was to be many years before Lord Young could set the example that he had hoped of actually having youth trainees working directly under him. In other individual workplaces where trades unionists were strongly opposed, individual schemes were blocked whatever the attitudes of their national leaderships. But in most cases the continued support of the trades union leaders ensured that the YTS got off the ground. If the unions had opposed it initially the MSC would certainly never have been able to proceed with the scheme. Once it got going, however, even in the uncertain and imperfect form in which it did, the quango was later able to dispense with the TUC's support and advice.

Trades union attitudes were thus not the major obstacle that the quango faced in launching and sustaining the YTS. The sheer scale of the operation was what took most of the MSC's efforts. The flexible system of semi-independent private managing agents which it funded had its advantages but it was open to confusion and corruption. The 'training' provided by many of them was not of such a standard that it inspired public confidence in the new scheme. As Loney (1983) commented, 'many programmes were so badly organised . . . (they) succeeded, not in introducing young people to the world of work, but rather to a world of constant confusion' (p. 28). The MSC's civil servants were thus perpetually inspecting and chivvying individual schemes into the national shape that they hoped would eventually emerge for the YTS. In Bryan Nicholson's words, this would be 'an important, permanent part of national life which is seen and accepted by all as the sensible way of progressing from school to work' (*YTS News*, December 1985). Of course these arbitrary interventions from above were much resented by those struggling to do their best for the young people in their charge. An independent review by Income Data Services Ltd confirmed the feelings of many of these workers when it reported that MSC 'staff have neither the experience nor the time to monitor schemes adequately' (1984, p. 9). The accusations of racism and sexism that have dogged the YTS since its inception could not be dealt with save by statements of intent. Indeed, a scheme that made a virtue out of its adherence to market-led forces could not very easily counter the existing forces that relegated young women, ethnic minority youth and disabled young people to disadvantaged positions in the labour market. In addition the safety record of YTS was atrocious: in the year 1986/87 alone there were 9 fatalities, 315 major accidents (out of 315,300 trainees in that year) and 1728 reported minor accidents (Hansard 24 July 1987).

The MSC was sustained in its efforts to hold together a disparate and flawed YTS by one of the factors for which it was criticized by its opponents. Its undemocratic and unrepresentative nature made it, as Benn and Fairley (1986) alleged, 'see itself as a quango – that is, an organization intended to act independently of representative government and provided with accountability machinery to do so' (p. 7). The MSC, as Benn and Fairley said, acted on its own without any accountability save to the Minister.

> It is run entirely from the top down. All its boards – both national and local area boards – are created by appointment from overseeing bodies. . . . Its commands come not only from the top down, but from the centre outwards. Its objectives for work, education and unemployment require only that MSC orders are carried out. There is no need for feedback or discussion.

This autonomy did not make the quango into a monolith, however. Indeed, it was wracked with disagreements and misunderstandings at nearly every level of its organization, so that very often the right hand really did not know what the left hand was doing. Procedures and methods were changed rapidly in frequent reorganizations. However, the fact that the MSC was not directly accountable gave it the ability, especially when backed by the vast sums with which the government supplied it, to enforce its will. The quango was thus able to pursue not only the immediate aim of fire-fighting youth unemployment, with which it had been entrusted by government since the 1981 riots, but also its own ultimate goal of comprehensive manpower strategy to which its leading officials still remained committed and towards which they saw an improved YTS eventually leading.

For Lord Young, with his often repeated belief that the future for the British economy lay in the service sector, YTS could help to cultivate the enterprising attitudes that he approved of in the American economy. There, he opined, people were not ashamed to be waiters, for example. But one year of YTS was now considered insufficient to embody the modernized apprenticeship system that he believed was required – even though one of the original justifications for the Scheme had been that it eliminated the wasteful 'time serving' that had come to characterize the three and four years of the old industrial apprenticeships. The scheme would have to be extended upwards to remove all those under 18 years old from the labour market, as the MSC itself had long ago suggested (see p. 40). It would also need to reach downwards into the schools to bring about the required cultural revolution in habitual attitudes. By so doing the MSC would increase its influence over the education sector and move towards the integrated Ministry of Education and Training which Young saw himself as heading. He therefore initiated the Technical and Vocational Education Initiative for 14–18-year-olds. It was to begin in the schools and would coordinate with, if not eventually dovetail into, the YTS. This would fulfil the second objective of the New Training Initiative: to provide vocational education and training across the ability range for all 14–18-year-olds. The TVEI, Young considered, was by far the most important policy shift that he had had anything to do with. It would, he thought, finally move the bias of the British education system away from its pursuit of irrelevant academic excellence towards the world of work (interview 13 May 1986).

THE TVEI – A *FAIT ACCOMPLI*

The Technical and Vocational Education Initiative launched its first fourteen pilot projects in the autumn of 1983 at the same time as the MSC began recruiting for the first full year of YTS. Like YTS, 'the TVEI embodied the Government's policy that education should better equip young people for working life', as the White Paper 'Better Schools' (DES, 1985) put it. For the MSC, TVEI staked a claim to more than just vocational training after school but extended the quango's influence into the heart of secondary schooling. For David Young this was the real object of the changes that he hoped to bring about in Britain's education and training systems. More than the modernization of training which YTS would hopefully accomplish, this was the intervention that would lead to the transformation of attitudes necessary for the flourishing of an enterprise culture and so to economic regeneration. After all, Young argued, it was a change of mental attitude that was required; as he was reported in *Education* (1 February 1985), 'he did not believe youth unemployment had anything to do with the state of the economy. It had to do with the state of mind of young people leaving school, who lacked motivation and enterprise because their education had been too academic and unrelated to employment'. As well as this characteristic belief, TVEI also indicated Young's ambition for a unified Ministry of Education and Training as the project upon which the MSC was embarked.

The launch of TVEI also showed the cooperation between the 'Gang of Four' (Joseph, Thatcher, Tebbit and Young) who during the second Thatcher government came together to coordinate policy in the crucial area of education and training. It also illustrates their precipitate method of action from the centre, typically by-passing any of the conventional channels of procedure. McCulloch (1986) suggested that this was encouraged by victory in the war against Argentina, which emboldened Mrs Thatcher 'to give full reign to the rhetoric of change with which the Conservatives had swept to power in 1979' so that 'the scheme might be interpreted as a by-product of the "Falklands Factor" of 1982'. Certainly there was thereafter much talk of 'task forces' to take 'action' to deal with various problems from football hooliganism to the inner cities. In this context 'an "initiative" ', as Maurice Holt (1987) commented, 'appears to mean a unilateral decision taken without asking anyone who might object' (p. 61). Another factor contributing to the decision behind this particular Initiative, which McCulloch also noted, was the previous appointment by the Conservatives of a Minister for Information Technology (Kenneth Baker), who, for no very obvious reason and with no very clearly discernible effect, offered to place a computer in every primary school within the next five years. This, McCulloch (1986) said, 'probably fostered greater enthusiasm among Conservatives for technological education'.

Discussion within the 'Gang of Four' had been going on for some time on the matter, though significantly Sir Keith Joseph was not included in the details of the DE's implementation of the TVEI. The Organization for Rehabilitation and Training had, however, briefed Joseph, along with Norman Tebbit, Patrick Jenkin and Kenneth Baker, on the feasibility of introducing a technical–vocational stream into the 14–18 curriculum during the summer and autumn of 1982 (as recorded in the ORT's international magazine, vol. 3, No. 1, January 1983). DE lawyers had carefully checked that Section 5 of the Employment and Training Act enabled the MSC to provide education for school-age children.

The TVEI was then suddenly announced by the Prime Minister in answer to a parliamentary question planted by her friend Sir William von Straubenzee on Friday 12 November 1982. She told the House of Commons that £7 million would be made available immediately for a series of pilot projects 'to stimulate the provision of technical and vocational education' for the 14–18 age range. The initial idea was for 10,000 pupils to follow an entirely distinct curriculum in ten pilot projects, rather like the DES's later City Technology Colleges. The usual formal consultations with the educational interests involved were obviated by this parliamentary pronouncement, and the first that they heard of it was through the news media. 'The news burst on an unsuspecting educational establishment like a thunderbolt', Low (1988, p. 220) recounted.

> Nobody except the topmost officials in the DES and the Department of Employment had any inkling of what was afoot. The Director of the MSC, Geoffrey Holland, even claimed that he was first told about this invasion of sovereign educational territory at 4 pm on the Thursday afternoon (though not everybody believed this).

Similarly, Dale (1986) reported that 'the announcement came like a bolt from the blue to all the most directly interested parties. Neither the DES, the local education authority associations, nor even the MSC had been consulted before the announcement was made' (p. 43). As Young subsequently explained to *The Times* (22 November 1982):

> Supposing we had decided to launch a debate about technical education or the lack of it. We might have had a Royal Commission about it or it might have taken five years or even ten to get it off the ground. Now we have a pilot project due to start by September next year.

What it was exactly that was due to start in September was at first unclear. Young's perception of the TVEI was that it was aimed at 'the lower attainers' and would exclude 'the academically able'. This provoked an immediate reaction from the opposition and an educational establishment that still saw itself defending the comprehensive status quo. Technical and vocational education might be introduced into the system but not so as to recreate the tripartite divisions between technical schools and the rest. Despite the fact that Tebbit had declared that TVEI represented 'the rebirth of technical education', providing 'for those who do not fancy the rich, academic diet . . . a rather more nourishing technical diet' (*The Times* 13 November 1982), Young had quickly to backtrack and reassure everybody concerned that the TVEI would be open to all pupils, or at least the '15 to 85 percentiles of the ability range', as he told *Education* (19 December 1982), whatever that was supposed to mean! It was not clear, however, how TVEI could be open to a 'wide range' of academic ability since it seemed designed from the outset to be a selective programme. The fourteen Local Education Authorities selected to receive the £46 million of MSC money now available to them over the next five years to support their pilot projects were not permitted to generalize the TVEI to all of their pupils. The only authority that attempted to do this, Clwyd, was soon told by the MSC to restrict its spending to the 250 designated pupils in its five TVEI schools.

Like YTS, TVEI was intended as a 'pump priming' operation; once it had been demonstrated how successful it could be in practice it was expected that other schools and other authorities would wish to implement it and spread its benefits to as many of their pupils as possible. It would then be funded by local industrialists who would also come to appreciate its benefits. This was a common theme of MSC operations, as was the rather vague initial specification of goals. Typically, money was thrown at a situation in the hope that something would then develop which could be generalized and applied more widely. Moon (1983) had already noted the tendency of government pilot schemes in response to unemployment to become the basis for further policy developments. This caused a great deal of initial confusion until the pattern emerged and the situation became clear. Chitty and Worgan (1987) commented that:

> the apparently spontaneous conception of the TVEI may well account for the early confusion as to its nature and intent; for in the absence of documentation, a 'scheme' clearly did not exist; it was simply what Sir Keith Joseph, David Young or Margaret Thatcher said it was. Therefore, different conceptions of its true nature were not only advanced by each of them; but their view of what the scheme should be was continually shifting, not least in response to the reaction to their proposals (p. 22).

To a greater or lesser extent this confusion surrounded all of the initiatives launched by the MSC, especially under the determined and impulsive Lord Young. The TVEI was, therefore, as was said at the time, another 'experiment doomed for success'. Indeed, before the first year of the initial pilot experiments was even completed, an extension of the Initiative was announced.

The DES, the teacher unions and the whole of the education establishment, with the exception of course of the Minister for Education himself, were hostile to the TVEI at the start. It was widely seen as an attack upon the principle of comprehensive education for all. The TUC, even while it still continued to collaborate with the MSC, warned, in the words of Len Murray, that 'TVEI must strengthen comprehensive education, maintain the role of the public sector and ensure that vocational preparation does not mean early specialization and narrowing of study options' (*The Times* 16 December 1982). On the other hand, a leading TUC official confided that because of his patronage of TVEI, Sir Keith Joseph 'will go down in history as perhaps the most pioneering Secretary of State for Education since Butler'. If these somewhat schizophrenic attitudes continued to characterize the TUC, the *Times Educational Supplement* referred to the TVEI in its editorial of 19 November 1982 as 'a new imperialistic drive downwards into the secondary school' by the MSC. The local education authorities which shared the administration of education with the DES looked at TVEI in the same light. Indeed, it was not clear from the Prime Minister's statement, which mentioned collaboration 'where possible' and hinted at 'new institutional arrangements where not', whether they would have any choice in the matter. Lord Young, in an interview reported in the *Times Educational Supplement* (19 November 1982), said that the local authority associations were right to take the implied threat in the Prime Minister's announcement seriously. 'If in any of the regions there was no local authority prepared to mount a suitable project . . . the MSC would set up an establishment of its own.' He implied that if local education authorities did not cooperate then the MSC would set up its own technical high schools on inner city sites. He even proposed calling these 'Young Schools' (interview in *Education*, 19 November 1982)! However, the MSC itself had attempted to reassure LEAs in a press release (12 November 1982) that 'this is an invitation to the Local Education Authorities to work in partnership with us to further advance vocational education for young people'.

The DES was 'caught in a rather ambivalent position by the rapid turn of events', as *Education* commented at the time (26 December 1982).

> On the one hand, they were urging the local authorities to take part in the Initiative (which was supported by Sir Keith Joseph); on the other, they let it be known that they entirely understood and sympathized with the doubts the LEAs expressed about the constitutional propriety of the MSC administering and funding part of the service for which local authorities were responsible under the 1944 Act'.

Sir Keith had taken the view that, as the *Times Educational Supplement* editorial (19 November 1982) correctly surmised, 'given the existence of a large pot of gold, a lot of education authorities would be prepared to set up schemes of their own which would meet the MSC requirements'. This opinion proved to be correct, for soon the LEAs were falling over themselves to bid for the money to mount their own TVEIs. In fact the quango now earned the new nickname of 'Mad Scramble for Cash'. The MSC was in a position to reject for not very clearly apparent or consistent reasons the overwhelming majority of submissions that came before it by the spring of 1983. Despite the fact that Neil Kinnock and also Phillip Whitehead, the Labour Party spokesperson on further and higher education, called on the Labour-controlled LEAs to boycott the TVEI, only a very few LEAs refrained for principled reasons from joining the Gadarene rush for scarce resources. The ILEA was one authority that did for a time sustain a principled rejection of the TVEI and instead set up a working party chaired by Dr David Hargreaves to look at alternatives, but even it came round in the end.

The teacher unions were characteristically divided in their reactions to the initiative, for it represented a sudden influx of funds and equipment into some schools as well as promotion prospects for some of their members. On the other hand it was a further incursion by the training world in the shape of the MSC and it was also clearly an attack on the comprehensive principle they claimed to advance. However, an ex-president of the largest union, the NUT, had been recruited onto the national steering committee for TVEI along with Fred Jarvis, the Union's General Secretary. In 1985 he sent out instructions to the NUT's branch secretaries telling them not to include TVEI projects within the scope of the industrial action they were then taking aimed at gaining a pay increase. He justified this decision by arguing that the TVEI was an exemplary instance of curriculum development which was properly funded with smaller classes and improved prospects for teachers.

It was unclear initially what exactly the fourteen selected LEAs would be expected to do in return for the MSC's money. Young had specified the same criterion of success for the TVEI as for YTS: 'By the time they leave, our youngsters will be highly employable' (*Education* 19 November 1982). Clearly, one object of the TVEI was, as Young had confided in an interview (13 May 1985), to link up with the YTS. Like YTS, TVEI was a transitional programme, meant to bridge the gap between school and work. Pupils were thus expected to enroll at 14 years old for a four year programme of vocational training, work experience and relevant education to end at 18 years old. At the same time what they were signing on for was not at all clear, and varied between pilot projects. In some, TVEI could be made to supplement O and A level studies with practical experience of new technology and computing. In others, it seems that mainly 'sink' groups within schools were channelled into the TVEI as a way of sustaining their interest with work-relevant occupations that might possibly help them to get a job. Similarly the emphasis upon new technology training that was intended by the TVEI varied depending upon the local employers who could be persuaded into cooperating with it. The TVEI, like the YTS, did not emerge as a unified programme but varied from area to area. Of course this could be proclaimed as its strength or its weakness, but it did make it rather difficult to keep track of what exactly was going on. Especially when the TVEI was expanded in January 1984 with an additional £100 million for sixty-two authorities.

Roger Dale (1986) noted 'the very wide variation in TVEI schemes'. Similarly, *Education* (14 February 1986) stated that

> the number who have decided to stay on . . . fluctuates wildly from LEA to LEA and even from school to school. . . . In Birmingham 65 per cent stayed on, while in neighbouring Sandwell the figure is only 26 per cent. . . . There is no national picture to be drawn from the figures.

On average it seems, as the *Times Educational Supplement* (1 November 1985) reported, that 'In many cases the percentage of youngsters staying on appears to be little different from the normal average in their authority'. The TVEI became, as Holt (1987) concluded in a wide-ranging survey, 'not the sum of its parts, but a pot-pourri of separate efforts'. Thus 'Few, if any general conclusions are likely to emerge' (p. 76). He did, however, note one common factor, that no independent school ever showed any interest in adopting the TVEI and nor were any extra funds made available to them to do so. This is not surprising since the TVEI was not envisaged as appropriate for the élite of managers and executives in industry but for the technician-level operatives below them. As Young explained in *The Times* (4 December 1985):

> My idea is that, at the end of the decade, there is a world in which 15 per cent of our young go into higher education . . . roughly the same proportion as now. Another 30 to 35 per cent will stay on doing the TVEI, along with other courses, ending up with a

mixture of vocational and academic qualifications and skills. The remainder, about half, will go on to two-year YTS.

This may have been a modification of his original conception; however, it is consistent with his initial statement, which he was obliged to retract, that TVEI was a selective scheme. It seems, though, that he had abandoned his idea of linking the TVEI to the YTS.

The third phase of the TVEI extended it to all schools, again before the pilot second phase was complete. As Lord Young said at the press conference announcing the extension in July 1986, 'We cannot afford to wait to evaluate these schemes.' Having spent £200 million on the TVEI by the end of the pilot projects, an additional £90 million a year was now to be shared among all secondary schools to set up a national scheme. This money was not in addition to MSC's current expenditure but was found from the overspend on YTS caused by poor take-up of the scheme. It represented a drop of expenditure from £600 per pupil to £150 per pupil and was calculated by the teacher unions as being sufficient to supply only three-quarters of a technical teacher to each secondary school. Even though the national extension of TVEI was taken to mark the successful conclusion of the experiment there was still some confusion over who exactly would benefit from it. The new Minister for Education, Kenneth Baker, not yet adept at turning the niceties of educational phraseology, stated at the same press conference that TVEI was for 'children not terribly academically gifted'. Lord Young asserted, contrariwise, that it was aimed 'across the whole ability range'.

In one important respect the TVEI had in fact failed in its initial objective of involving employers in schools. Norman Tebbit had told the Institute of Directors to 'go into the schools and tell them what you need'. Despite the fact that this remark had been met with an enthusiastic stamping of feet, according to the *Daily Telegraph* report of the speech (19 March 1985), employers continued to show a stubborn resistance to actually going so far as to part with hard-earned ready cash to invest it in educational efforts which they did not regard as their responsibility and for which they could not see any very immediate benefit to themselves. This had already been seen as a problem facing the MSC in its administration of the YTS and it was to haunt Mr Baker in his efforts to establish a new type of technical and vocational education with the City Technology Colleges. These DES-initiated and, as it turned out, largely DES-funded colleges in fact signalled the failure of the TVEI in schools and were a product of a new situation in which the MSC suddenly found itself out of favour just before the 1987 General Election. To relate this unexpected turn in events at this stage, however, would be to anticipate the next chapter in our narration of the strange tale of the rise and fall of the MSC.

TWO-YEAR YTS – A GOAL ACHIEVED?

Meanwhile Nicholson's first task as Chairman of the MSC was to sustain the YTS, which had started its first full year in September 1983, and to guide its transformation into a two year programme. During the autumn of 1984 the MSC made moves to sound out support for an extension of YTS. According to Ken Atkinson, the Director of Youth Training at the MSC, discussions had been going on between the Cabinet

Office, the Department of Employment and the Commission throughout the summer. In his opinion they were spurred as usual by the uninterrupted rise in unemployment (interview 6 May 1985). Geoffrey Holland, the MSC's Director, made several representations to Number 10 in December but with Lord Young in the Cabinet, he did not have to knock very hard upon the door. Holland called for yet another 'new deal' to offer school leavers vocational education and training up to the age of 18. As reported by Finn (1986, p. 68), the aim would be to increase the supply of 'qualified workers' by giving young people the chance to participate in work-based and work-related training and further education. The scheme would be voluntary and would give school leavers a 'traineeship for today', involving the achievement of recognized competence in occupations or groups of occupations. It promised young people a new recognized 'trainee status', which was, Holland considered, 'not taking young people out of the labour market. It is putting them in, but putting them in on terms which secure their entry'. In March 1985, the Chancellor of the Exchequer, Nigel Lawson, committed funds for a two year scheme because he thought that the one year programme had already proved such a 'successful bridge between school and work' (quoted in Finn, 1986).

The proposals for two-year YTS basically repeated the arguments for the one-year scheme. One virtue of YTS as a 'modernised apprenticeship' that was now dropped, however, was the argument that one year of training would reduce the time-serving element of traditional apprenticeships. Now it was suggested that a certain amount of time-serving would in fact be necessary in order that, in the second year of the scheme, trainees could benefit from extended work experience, having laid the foundations for this in the first year. More time in work experience on employers' premises enhanced the role of employers in the scheme. The Mode A employer-based schemes were now bound to predominate even more over the second class Mode B provision in colleges and workshops in areas without large employers. 'To eradicate the false perception of first and second class trainees within the scheme' (MSC, 1985b), the MSC proposed abolishing the distinction between Modes but the quango had to keep on subsidizing 'premium' places in the old Mode B1 and B2 schemes. It later attempted to phase them out but this would immediately have led to the collapse of the scheme in many areas, particularly the most disadvantaged inner cities. Yet despite the increase in employer influence in the new YTS, there was now much less emphasis upon the expectation, which the government still entertained, that employers would contribute towards the cost of YTS.

Another difference with the original one year YTS was that there was now also less emphasis in its successor on universal provision for employed and unemployed alike. Instead, all school leavers if they were not in employment or further education were to be offered a 'guarantee' by the Christmas after they left school of quality training. As the White Paper (DES, 1985b) 'Education and Training for Young People' stated, this guarantee 'will constitute a major step towards our objective of ensuring that unemployment among young people under 18 becomes a thing of the past' (p. 7). The scheme was therefore accepted as very much more a programme for the young unemployed than in its original conception, though the long-term aim, cherished in the official ideology of the MSC, remained to include all those in as well as out of work and, beyond that, to offer training on an equal footing with academic education.

However, another problem was that there was still no recognized qualification of YTS completion. The 1985 White Paper proposed a 'recognized vocational qualification' for the two year YTS but the MSC Commissioners warned at the time that this would not be ready for 1986. The Certificate of Pre-Vocational Education which was being piloted by a consortium of examination boards within schools in England and Wales was also being piloted as the end certificate for the Youth Training Programme in Northern Ireland but nothing came of this. (It is significant that, with the higher levels of both unemployment and street violence in Ulster, the YTP was used as a test-bed for YTS, starting one year earlier there in 1982 and also moving on to a two year programme in 1985.) Two year YTS therefore continued, like the original one year programme, without any standard, national accreditation being offered to its trainees beyond a simple certificate of completion for the minority of trainees who stayed the course.

The new YTS would offer two years of training to all unemployed school leavers and one year to all 17-year-olds who signed on. This prolongation of social childhood and a state of dependence upon parents and/or the state also, incidentally, contradicted another of the original aims of YTS, which had been to maintain labour discipline in the absence of real work (see, for example, Sir Richard O'Brien's remarks on p. 57). The extra year implied that another 135,000 places were needed together with additional resources of £125 million for 1986 and £300 million promised for 1987/88. Much of this money came from the underspending on the one year YTS together with the saving on subsidies to employers through the Young Workers' Scheme, which the second year of YTS now superseded. The first year's allowance for trainees was set at £27.50, rising to £35 in the second year. Beyond this the Young Workers' Scheme was pushed up the age range and renamed the New Workers' Scheme to pay subsidies to employers who took on people between 18 and 25. YWS was originally known as the Walters scheme, after its architect, who was one of Mrs Thatcher's principal monetarist advisers. If it remained as it was it would only compete with YTS, so instead it would now subsidize low wage rates for YTS leavers. Lord Young could then claim that his employment criterion for YTS leavers was being met, even though trainees were in many cases only entering jobs subsidized by the state. A Department of Employment study was reported by *New Society* (12 August 1982) as showing that 'only one subsidy in 13 represents a new job created', so that 'the government is paying over £6,000 a year for every job (after accounting for savings in unemployment benefits and gains in tax)'.

The MSC also planned to expand the Community Programme for unemployed 18–25-year-olds by another 230,000 places, with '500,000 places being proposed in Whitehall' (*The Times* 15 February 1986). The CP had replaced the CEP (Community Enterprise Programme) in 1982 and was aimed at the long-term unemployed. At its introduction the government had followed Tebbit's ploy at the inauguration of YTS; they at first announced a 'benefits plus' scheme, the plus being £15 to £20 on top of Social Security entitlements. The TUC insisted on the rate for the job being paid to participants but, under the pressure of the original suggestion, settled for an average wage of £65. This compromise undermined the opposition of trades unionists involved in the programme and of the voluntary sector running it. The rate for participants in the programme thus fell from nearly £100 and the CP was left paying low wages for part-time work with no training. However, as Clare Short (1986) remarked: 'It is a measure of the success of the government strategy that a year or so later defenders of the long-term unemployed were calling for an expansion of the programme.'

Rather than retraining people for employment, this series of new programmes increasingly began to look like a succession of schemes for the unemployed, through two-year YTS to the New Workers' Scheme with graduation to the Community Programme and finally the Adult Programme at age 25. Moreover, the MSC's programmes were inconsistent in their stated aims and objectives: the YTS aspired towards a modernized apprenticeship training in flexible skills; NWS subsidized low wages in generally unskilled or semi-skilled jobs; the CP merely occupied the long-term unemployed for six months on such work as environmental improvement, tidying up canal paths and the like, before returning its participants to the dole queue; finally, Adult Training followed the completely different strategy of trying to meet the skill training requirements of the local economy; while Enterprise Allowances also introduced a new approach of trying to foster 'business in the community'. What the programmes had in common was the low wages or allowances on which they maintained a growing army of low-wage, reserve labour temporarily employed by the state.

The most vociferous opposition to this marginalization of the nation's youth and to the new YTS, with the implication in its 'guarantee' to all school leavers that it would be compulsory, came from intended trainees themselves. In April 1985 the promise in the Budget of compulsion for YTS in 1986 occasioned the largest school student strike in Britain's history when a quarter of a million pupils protested in towns and cities up and down the country. However, the Labour Party quickly reined-in its Militant youth section, which had called the strike, and carpeted the couple of MPs 'irresponsible' enough to have supported it. The Party's 'Charter for Youth' (1985) aimed to deflect the demonstrations against YTS into support for a 'socialist' YTS come the next Labour government. Similarly the joint Labour Party/TUC 'Plan for Training' (1984) was designed to deflect criticism from members of the trades union leadership's continuing participation in the MSC and Labour's support for that policy.

Finn (1986) recorded, 'As with YOP and YTS before it, another corporate consensus has been painstakingly constructed for a two year scheme, and the TUC has pledged support. . . [but] 'Not surprisingly, when the government's package emerged . . . it offered considerably less than the "new deal" portrayed earlier by the MSC's Director' (p. 68). This construction was in large part the work of Lord Young's successor as Chairman of the MSC, Bryan Nicholson. Although he had been regarded by the TUC as a typical Tory appointment from industry, he in fact lacked the abrasive personal style of David Young and proved a smooth manager of consensus. He had been left a situation in which Young had alienated nearly all of the elements with which the MSC still needed to cooperate. In fact, as Jackson (1986) wrote, 'Young disappeared . . . just at the point where he had got the Commission into a real mess' (p. 37). As has been seen, the MSC was by now exercising a profound influence over the colleges of further education, particularly in their provision of so-called non-advanced further education (NAFE). Encouraged by the success of his high-handed tactics in establishing the TVEI, Young had promulgated a similar decree from on high in the White Paper 'Training and Jobs' HMSO, 1984. From now on, this declared, the MSC would take over the direct funding of all NAFE in the colleges instead of the colleges' paying for this themselves out of the rate support grant that financed them through their local education authorities. The amount that would be lost to the authorities and their colleges and put under the quango's direct control was some £220 million. However, whereas funding for TVEI was welcomed by the local authorities because it had been provided by the MSC in addition to the increasingly straightened resources of the rate support grant, the quango now proposed to take away from the colleges and the local authorities money which had been theirs previously. Sensing the opposition that this latest proposal of Young's would provoke, even the MSC Commissioners refused to go along with it. The TUC representatives lined up with the educational interests on the MSC to block it until they were forced into agreement by Young's use of the Chairman's power of direction. He was supported by the then Employment Secretary, Tom King, who wrote a letter asking the MSC to fulfil the White Paper's request. 'There was a Directive', as the *Times Educational Supplement* (26 October 1984) noted. This was the closest the MSC ever came to actual formal Ministerial direction.

MSC officials accordingly began working on plans for a new bureaucracy to control all NAFE courses. The local authorities became increasingly hostile – the Labour-controlled Association of Metropolitan Authorities refused even to countenance the proposal, while the Tory equivalent Association of County Councils would only talk about it if they could still decide how to spend the money themselves. The fact that the MSC had ruled any discussion of general social and political issues beyond the scope of its Social and Life Skills classes in NAFE courses, which the colleges had accepted at the time, was now instanced by them as another example of totalitarian 'social control'. Young, however, still went around boasting that individual authorities would soon come around as they had done before. The two sides were therefore on a collision course, which was only prevented by Young's elevation to the peerage. It is curious that, despite the animosity this episode had aroused, the people most sorry to see Young go were the TUC Commissioners. It was they, and not the CBI representatives, who arranged his farewell dinner! And when he joined Lord Young in the Upper House, Lord Murray was 'glad to pay tribute to the noble Lord for what he did in his previous incarnation in the MSC . . . and for the drive which virtually brought together employers, trade unionists, and civil servants to help shape and fashion a better system of using the nation's manpower. . .' (House of Lords Debates, vol. 462, p. 243, 3 April 1985).

Nicholson meanwhile quickly patched up the rift by conceding that the local authorities could have their money for the coming year if they would join in discussions about the MSC's more limited role in planning and administering NAFE courses in the colleges. He was then able to turn his attention to the problems of two year YTS. However, he continued to take the trouble to give interviews in *New Society* (13 June 1985) and in union journals, where he appeared 'On the Side of the Angels' (*The Teacher* 31 March 1986). In fact, he even hedged his bets on the return of a Labour government so that in the strange period of artificial suspension which now intervened before the end of the government's term of office and the most opportune moment that it could find to call an election, Nicholson appeared, as Jackson (1986) shrewdly suggested as, 'the man who could restore the Commission's respectability in good time for the next election' (p. 39).

THE SKILL TRAINING PROBLEM

Despite a decade's involvement in British skill training policy, the MSC's record appeared far from positive compared with its work in vocational education and training. Expansion of the economy in the final year of the second Thatcher government was constrained as usual by skill shortages. The MSC's policy for skill training rested on the new ideas coming from the Training Division. The ITB system was a shadow of its former self, reduced, since Tebbit's hatchet job, to seven Boards. These seven still had statutory powers until 1991 to continue the levy/grant exemption scheme, but the non-statutory boards could only operate on a voluntary basis and soon withered away. Similarly, the skill centre programme was winding down. Prior to 1973 skill training was based on national considerations even though the ITB system was grounded in a sectoral approach. After 1973 Labour conducted a policy that emphasized national skill requirements operating to increase the national stock of skills and improve the supply of key skills to industry. This was supplemented by a skill centre programme which catered for skill demands in the locality and the ITB system which attempted to raise training at the level of the firm. The idea of the new Training Division was to concentrate its efforts on meeting skill shortages in the locality. Thus the Tories' skill training policy put aside national considerations and looked to other means apart from state-funded skill centres to supply local skill requirements.

The Adult Training Strategy launched in 1983 envisaged the Training Division acting as a catalyst for change in the local community and charged it with developing a framework for joint initiatives between firms and the suppliers of training. Many saw this as a direct attack on the existing further education colleges since each local college was the traditional fulcrum for local businessmen and educators to meet the training needs of the local economy.

In conjunction with the local economy approach the MSC embarked with government approval on a massive national advertising campaign. In reality this was little more than Robert Carr's complacent persuasion and exhortation policy of slapping industrialists on the back and asking them to keep up the good work. For the government the second arm of their strategy was a return to job creation but most observers were not blind to the real motive – a permanent level of unemployment around three million was a risky strategy to ensure victory in a third general election.

The Thatcher strategy was a new bout of scheme building, reminiscent of the early days under Labour. This propelled the MSC back into the field of job creation and retraining for the unemployed, now called Employment Training. However, the twin policy of local economy initiatives and massive unemployment retraining schemes ignored entirely the critical issue of skill shortages. The Tories systematically neglected the fact that skill shortages existed because British companies just did not train sufficiently. Some visionaries at the MSC and Sir Richard O'Brien, the former Chairman of the Commission, had suggested to the Treasury that companies should treat resources in human capital as on a par with plant and machinery for taxation purposes. Young maintained that a tax-based training investment system would merely cause over-training as managers simply trained for tax avoidance (interview 13 June 1985). In response, the Labour Party's joint document with the TUC returned to the old theme of a general training levy. So the MSC, directed by the government, adhered to a policy of merely persuading industry and commerce to train adequately. Peter Morrison had said back in 1984 that 'training means profit and profit means training'. This point was still being hammered home in May 1988, when managers were told in the MSC's magazine *Focus on Training* that the aim of training is 'to make money, so the idea of money making has to be at the heart of all training activity'.

Unfortunately, the MSC had an 'almost mystical respect' for employers (Collins, 1986). Collins further asserted that the MSC 'romanticised employers. They are depicted as forward looking, knowledgeable about training processes and ideal for managing new styles of training programmes'. He added, 'There are undoubtedly some fine examples of this type of employer, mainly among large companies. [But] The average employer offering little or no training has no long term plans and is in a survival situation rather than a position of regeneration' (p. 248). Employers were not, despite all their rhetoric, particularly interested in training. As always, they viewed it as the state's responsibility and wanted to have as little as possible to do with it themselves.

In 1985, nearly a decade after Callaghan's Ruskin speech had inaugurated the MSC's Training Revolution, an Industrial Society survey estimated that British companies spent less than 1 per cent of sales on training. It was part of the rhetoric of the Training Revolution that this limited investment compared poorly with the situation in competitor countries. As *The Economist* (20 December 1986) pointed out:

> Japanese firms do more than anybody else, followed by American corporations, and a long, long way behind come British firms. Overall, Britain plc is reckoned to have spent $2.8 billion on training last year. In America it is at least $40 billion, for a workforce only 4.3 times larger.

Similarly, the research by the MSC commissioned from Cooper's and Lybrand (MSC 1986) revealed that

> in the great majority of companies training is not a Board level matter. Most of the chief executives have a limited interest in what training is taking place in their company. . . . Expenditure on training is rarely seen or treated as an investment in any financial sense. It is not viewed in the same way as capital expenditure, or even like items such as advertising or building maintenance – either of which would often be Board level matters. . . . Training expenditure is not seen as an investment expected to lead to an identifiable income stream, but more as an overhead which can, like building maintenance, be reduced when times are hard (p. 248).

As for new technology, training in the higher-level skills that were created by the latest applications of cybernetics to industrial and commercial processes, the National Audit Office's 1987 Report (HMSO, 1987) on DE and MSC adult training strategy can only be described as a complete indictment of all the quango's much-vaunted efforts in this area. This government report detailed the incredible confusion that existed both about the amount of training that was actually given in industry and the skills possessed by the workforce: 'MSC has not so far devised any way of reliably measuring how much training, in total, was being provided by employers' (para. 7, 9); 'MSC has no national or local database recording the skills possessed by the working population and . . . has kept no inventory of the skills of the unemployed' (p. 23). Therefore 'it is difficult to see how the real requirement for MSC support for training can be determined accurately without a better balance sheet than exists at present of the supply of and demand for skills' (p. 24). As a result, the National Audit Office recorded that training may aim at the wrong job skills – skills that are not in fact required by employers – and was certainly duplicating training that was already given. New-technology training was especially in short supply and what was provided by the MSC was not of sufficient quality for employers' requirements. The idea of 'hands on' computer experience or 'computer literacy' as a component part of the YTS foundation course, while it had the virtue of attracting European Social Fund money to finance the scheme, had no very clear aim or results. Even such basic 'computer awareness' courses would not be available as part of the new Unified Adult Training Programme (later designated Employment Training).

Meanwhile, places where the MSC did actually provide new-technology training of the quality required, for instance on the National Computing Centre's Threshold Training Programme, which it funded, were continually cut in the interest of expanding low-level courses and work experience for the mass of the unemployed. The reason for this was not only government pressure upon the MSC but also of course the exorbitant cost of such training and the contradiction between the rhetoric of training everyone in new-technology skills and the small proportion of total vacancies in the area. The 176 ITeCs operating as a part of the YTS show the contradiction clearly. Because of the cost of equipping these centres, at first after 1981 in inner-city locations only, but subsequently expanded throughout the UK, and of the intensive training required, each trainee place is estimated to cost approximately £6,000 a year. Even though most ITeC trainees found employment with further training after one year, compared with the approximately half of YTS trainees and unemployed school leavers who did not in general go on to further training after their year on the scheme, the cost of ITeC training for all youth trainees is clearly prohibitive. In fact such specialization has already become a luxury the MSC can no longer afford. When two year YTS was introduced, both the ITeCs and Threshold were asked to spin out their one year courses to cover two years and at the same time to move towards the commercial marketing of their training facilities to adults and on a contractual basis for individual companies, so as to become self-financing. This is in fact the likely future for the small amount of real skills training the MSC ever did provide.

After nearly fifteen years (from 1973 to 1988) and an estimated £25 billion expenditure (at a conservative estimate) there was still a 'skills crisis' in the British economy. Indeed, skill training in British industry all but ceased. The result was that as soon as the economy picked up temporarily, as it did after passing through the trough of 1986, skill shortages became manifest and were said to be strangling industrial development. Consequently, 'Midlands engineering firms are heading for a disaster according to a survey carried out in Dudley' (*Birmingham Business Reporter*, March 1988), while a national survey of 2881 companies in manufacture and services by the Association of Chambers of Commerce reported that skills shortages in London, the Thames Valley and East Anglia had reached 'crisis levels'. In fact, in eight out of its twelve regions, the acute shortage of skilled and managerial staff was cited by firms as 'the main internal factor limiting output'.

> In the Thames Valley area, a staggering 92 per cent of firms recruiting reported difficulty in obtaining skilled manual labour and 85 per cent in finding suitable office staff. In the London area, some 67 per cent of manufacturing and 58 per cent of service respondents

are affected, in East Anglia, 53 per cent of manufacturers and 59 per cent of service firms, the West Midlands, 50 per cent of manufacturers and 57 per cent of service industry, and even Merseyside where 30 per cent of respondents reported skill shortages (ACC news release, 1988).

Almost a fifth of companies answering a National Computing Centre Survey said poaching was severely affecting them or even threatening their survival. Of the industrial sectors, engineering seems the worst affected; the Engineering Industry Training Board, which still survived Tebbit's axe in an attenuated form, told the House of Commons Select Committee on Employment in March 1987 that nothing had been done to avert the critical shortages in skilled engineers and that 'if anything, the level of training has fallen'. The situation is worse for the smaller firms which together make up the majority of employers. Although this is a growing sector of the economy, Storey and Johnson (1988) reported that 'the relative growth of the small firm sector constitutes a serious difficulty for governments attempting to introduce appropriate employment policies and to provide a skills training package for the unemployed' (p. 52).

Despite all the MSC's efforts, 'skills mismatch' was also held to account for the bottleneck that held back industrial advance and the full use of new technology. In the sunny Loseland (London and the South East) this phenomenon took on grotesque dimensions, as firms paid unusually high salaries to attract skilled staff. One insurance company even paid its employees a handsome premium if they could recruit their friends and relatives for office work. These shortages coexisted with the largest concentration of unemployed people in Europe and second in the world only to São Paulo and Mexico City. Instead of asking why, after all the money that had been spent by the MSC, the mass of London's unemployed had not been trained to occupy these vacant posts, or why they spurned low-paid work in the hotel and catering trade where vacancies also existed, the government as usual merely blamed the unemployed themselves for their laziness. The mismatches were used as an excuse to introduce benefit cuts for claimants who refused 'reasonable offers' of employment, thus preparing the way for national compulsory work for benefit programmes.

'Skill mismatch' was not only a consequence of inadequate training programmes but also another symptom of the hardening of the economic arteries of Thatcher's Britain. Not only did the overheating of some local economies, combined with the stagnation of others, explain the weird discontinuities of economic development, but the interaction of the jobs and housing markets trapped both middle-income earners and the poor in depressed regions of the country and in deprived districts within even the most prosperous areas. Wages and benefits for the poorest were forced remorselessly downwards, with new and invidious distinctions between the deserving and the undeserving poor being introduced by the 1988 implementation of the reform of social security. Meanwhile monetarism as a means of wage control proved inadequate to prevent real earnings for those in work rising every year since 1979, despite the most severe recession since the 1920s (when wages and prices both fell). Some have seen in this a deliberate political strategy to split the traditional Labour vote in successive elections and to marginalize a new underclass beyond the pale of society. The successive *ad hoc* programmes of the MSC in many ways contributed to the process. Like them, it can more safely be suggested that, rather than a deliberate conspiracy, this polarization was an unforeseen consequence of desperate crisis measures applied to a deteriorating and uncontrolled situation. In any case, government measures merely acted upon and exacerbated the already existing cleavages and interactions between discrete labour markets separated by age, gender, race and skill.

'Skill shortages' were supposedly an important factor holding back the British economy from catching up with its international competitors. Since 1976 the education system had been held responsible for the rise in youth unemployment that was said to be caused by the fact that school leavers were not equipped to deal with the increased demands that the applications of new technology now made upon entrants to the workforce. The YTS therefore promoted itself as an institutional 'bridge between school and work', while its one-time successor the Job Training Scheme for 19–20-year-olds advertised itself as 'bridging the skills gap'. Yet, for all its commitment to 'skill training', it was clear that chronic skill shortages continued to exist in British industry and that, with the destruction of the apprentice system which accompanied the MSC's provision of state training, training in industry was very much reduced overall.

SUMMARY

After 1983 Mrs Thatcher's government emphasized cultural more than purely monetarist solutions to Britain's persistent economic problems. The government used the MSC to bring about changes in education that it was not yet able to accomplish directly through the dual administration of the Department of Education and Science and the local-council-controlled education authorities. Advancing from the training empire it had already consolidated, the MSC had penetrated the further education colleges and, with the launch of the Technical and Vocational Education Initiative, it now laid siege to the heartland of secondary education, aiming to establish a unified Super-Ministry of Education and Training. TVEI in schools was intended to link up with YTS after school. The MSC also attempted to induce coherence into the succession of training, work experience and subsidized employment programmes it had initiated in response to the record rise in unemployment. Inconsistencies remained, however, between its adult and youth strategies. Also, despite all the MSC's training efforts, when at last the economy expanded somewhat from 1986 onwards, persistent skill shortages were immediately revealed in the labour market, together with a continuing 'skills gap' between Britain and its international competitors. These and other problems were hidden, however, in the run-up to the 1987 General Election. What was also hidden during this last phase of frantic activity was a complete reversal of the government's previous training and education policies. Only the election of a Labour government could have saved the MSC, and with the return of Mrs Thatcher for a third term its fate was sealed.

Chapter 5

The MSC under the Tories (1987–1988): The End of the Affair

THE QUANGO AT THE ZENITH

The year 1986 marked the Antonine age of the MSC. Its empire now comprehended, if not the fairest part of the earth, and the most civilized portion of mankind, then upwards of a million people directly or indirectly employed on its programmes. It was financed to the tune of over £2,000 million a year and more was to come. A total of £3,000 million was forecast for the quango's 1987/88 budget (more than twice the Exchequer grant to all UK universities). Half a million school leavers were anticipated on the two year YTS and another half million young unemployed were being talked about as the target for the Community Programme. The MSC also subsidized employed workers through the New Workers' Scheme and financed the non-advanced sector of further education in the colleges, as well as the gathering number of pilot schemes for the TVEI in the schools, for which it also supplied special teacher training. On its patronage depended a vast voluntary sector running multifarious programmes without which youth and community work would have collapsed in many areas. The MSC even sustained in being more than a hundred Centres for the Unemployed sponsored by the local authorities, churches and voluntary organizations, which claimed to organize the unwaged against unemployment. Adult training and Information Technology Centres were also included in its remit, as was enterprise training for budding entrepreneurs. In many places north of Watford the MSC was the biggest local employer. In others more and more statutory local authority services were coming to depend upon its support. Moreover, there was no end in sight to this continuing expansion. Lord Young's enthusiasm for urban regeneration through enterprise had linked the MSC to the Inner Cities Task Forces he announced in February 1986. New areas for MSC penetration persistently offered themselves: plans were laid for an expansion of YTS in the Civil Service and a new training scheme for nurses in the NHS. The MSC was also involved in pioneering various schemes of voluntary work, such as that piloted in Croydon hospitals and social services by Professor Marsland from Brunel University. Meanwhile the as yet virtually untouched higher education sector, where the MSC had helped to pilot only one or two shortened, two-year degree courses, promised a whole new field for rationalization and relation to employment. In 1987 a £100 million Enterprise in Higher Education Initiative was announced (see p. 111). There could surely be no end to the growth of this power and influence. Moon and Richardson (1984) contended that 'its growth has not been without criticism but there is no doubt that it had identified and exploited opportunities with great skill and as a result it is now a repository of a growing expertise in the fields of unemployment and training' (p. 100). Anderson and Fairley (1982) acknowledged 'it is a testimony to the ability of senior MSC staff that the Commission has through its youth policy largely re-written its objectives and won itself an expanding empire' (p. 206).

The MSC enjoyed not only ministerial patronage but also Opposition support. The Opposition political parties had no real alternative to the YTS or any of the other MSC programmes. They had to agree with Geoffrey Holland that 'If the two year YTS fails then we are at the end of the road. There is nowhere else to go' (*Times Educational Supplement* 3 September 1985). Indeed, Labour's only real difference with the Tories over YTS, as long as it was not compulsory, was that their government would legislate for employers to contribute to its costs. This was a position that the MSC was already moving towards urging upon the Conservative government, as it embarked in 1986 upon a two year inquiry into the funding of vocational education and training. This was another example of the way in which the MSC often preempted Labour attacks upon it by thinking up the opposition's policies in advance. Another example of this was the extension of YTS to two years which Labour had also advocated. Again, MSC supported the rationalization of qualifications which Labour too demanded. The unification of education and training was also a plank in Labour's programme which Lord Young himself used in his unsuccessful bid to succeed Sir Keith Joseph as Minister of Education and Training in a new Department of Enterprise that would fuse together Education and Employment.

The TUC, as has been seen, continued its participation in the tripartite MSC often over the opposition of individual unions and of many of its members. Ever since Congress had originally agreed to the YOP as part of the Social Contract with the Labour government, the argument that schemes create jobs had continued to influence trades union leaders who did not want to be accused of depriving youngsters of the chance to work. Similarly to many local authorities and voluntary organizations wanting to 'do something' about the deteriorating situation for young people, the trades unions had then found themselves embroiled in a structure within which they could do no more than legitimate the manipulation of the unemployment figures. The argument that YTS represented an extension of state educational provision was also favoured by the TUC. YTS could be presented as fulfilling the long-standing trades union policy of day-release for all young workers. The national training to agreed standards that YTS promised was also an old TUC demand. The MSC itself was also initially welcomed as the central statutory labour market body unions had long been requesting. By remaining involved in it, even when it was, as the TUC had it, hijacked by the Tories, the TUC representatives on the MSC could claim to have mitigated the worst excesses of the government. As seen, the improvement upon Tebbit's original proposal for a YTS training allowance of only £15 was held up as one example of such a concession that the movement had secured. So was the 'topping up' of allowances on Labour council controlled schemes.

Of course the MSC was not without its critics, even in the highest 'official' levels of government service. The Audit Commission performed this constitutional role and in a report (HMSO, 1985) on MSC programmes criticized the MSC for its 'inadequate accounting procedures' and its consequent waste of £55 million on unfilled youth training places. It also went so far as to suggest that 'YTS may have initially assisted the continuing decline in the number of permanent, employed training places in manufacturing industries' (para. 3, 13). Despite this admission that the YTS could actually be contributing to the unemployment problem it was supposed to alleviate and the continuing complaint that, despite all the MSC's efforts, skill shortages persisted within industry, the MSC dealt with all its critics in the same way. It either ignored them or conceded that there were teething problems which would soon be overcome. As Geoffrey Holland said, 'we learn as we go along.' This was its response to repeated allegations from the Commission for Racial Equality and the Equal Opportunities Commission of persistent racism and sexism within YTS.

For a long time the most effective and vociferous critic was Youthaid, the organization lobbying on behalf of young people. Its evidence to the House of Commons Employment Committee in 1985, for instance, criticized the confusion and disorganization that had existed over the actual implementation of YTS. As has been seen, Youthaid also challenged the government's often exaggerated claims for the success of MSC schemes. It also represented youth very differently from the feckless and idle stereotype of media and ministerial mythology. Where Lord Young had claimed that young people who did not want to go on YTS 'preferred to lie in bed all day', Youthaid presented evidence to show that some young people appreciated that entering YTS could in many instances actually reduce their chances of finding work. Similarly, it refuted Bryan Nicholson's claim in November 1986 that 'thousands and thousands' of young people were leaving school unable to read and write.

But such dissident voices were ignored and marginalized by a government which repeatedly ruled off the agenda any fundamental discussion of MSC programmes in general and of the YTS in particular – 'the jewel in the MSC's crown', as Finn (1986) had called it. The support of the opposition for many MSC measures lifted training above politics, so that Peter Morrison was able to declare, 'the YTS is all about the world of work and I don't want it to get a bad name if politics gets involved' (*Times Educational Supplement* 23 September 1983). Mrs Thatcher dismissed as 'professional moaners' anyone who criticized her policies, and at the same 1985 Conservative Party conference, Lord Young said that there was only one thing which made him see red and that was 'the left-wing wreckers in our society who run down the YTS'. Likewise, Bryan Nicholson told teachers on an in-service training course that teachers who communicated their opposition to the scheme to their pupils who were its potential recruits were 'a major threat to the scheme' (*Times Educational Supplement* 17 January 1986). Elsewhere he declared that the two year YTS 'will silence all but our most intransigent critics', who were 'knockers . . . out to sabotage the scheme' and thus Britain's economic recovery.

In fact these few 'enemies within' were all but submerged beneath a deluge of publicity from the MSC's chosen advertising agency, Saatchi and Saatchi. From £3 million spent in 1980/81 on combined press, TV, radio and poster publicity, the MSC's advertising expenditure soared to an estimated £16½ million during 1986/87

(*Hansard* 19 November 1986). This was nearly half of total government spending on advertising, which that year rose to pass the amount spent by any individual private company for the first time. As well as this, MSC press releases were dutifully relayed by an obliging media. When, for instance, John Pilger reported unfavourably on YTS for the *Daily Mirror*, the Employment Minister, Tom King, was given an inserted box to correct the 'misleading argument' of the article (February 1985).

With the shortage of funds for independent, academic research, the MSC financed the monitoring and assessment of many of its own projects, usually on a contracted-out basis to individual research institutes or departments within the universities and colleges. As in other areas of such government financed research, there were repeated complaints that the right to publication of findings was restricted. In addition, it was often specified in advance that research was to be of the 'action-research', or even 'action dissemination' type. This involved a commitment to the goals that were to be achieved by the action and was really only a measure of the particular means chosen to achieve them. Much of the assessment undertaken of local TVEI projects was of this type. For instance, the colourful 'information pack' printed by the MSC's TVEI Unit announcing the national research to be undertaken by the National Foundation for Educational Research and Leeds University, declared that 'evaluation . . . will help all young people to benefit from the Technical and Vocational Education Initiative.' Of course this assumed that a selective programme like the TVEI could actually benefit 'all young people', whereas its critics had suggested that, even if TVEI benefited the minority selected to go on the pilot programmes, it could do so only at the expense of the majority of pupils. In fact, as has been seen, TVEI was an experiment in name only, the outcome of which was in fact assumed in advance. Rather than independently assess the experiment, such 'research' was more like public relations for TVEI, particularly when it involved 'dissemination of findings'. The research effort was then more akin to the 'cascade' and 'trickle down' models of information and good practice that the Further Education Unit had introduced into the further education colleges. Moreover many potential critics of the MSC's efforts were caught up in the quango's machinery of administration. As researchers, lecturers, teachers and community workers, etc., their present prospects and future careers depended upon MSC money.

So the MSC remained the undisputed master of all that it surveyed, an empire growing without bounds upon which it seemed the sun would never set. And then something very peculiar happened. In the strange intervening period, well before the end of the normal five year term of the second Conservative government, in which, for a year and more, it seemed that the only business of government was to decide upon the most opportune moment to call an election that it could be certain of winning, whilst all the other functions of government seemed suspended, the political ground suddenly shifted from under the MSC's feet. First of all the Gang of Four, under whose protection the quango had grown to its pre-eminence over the whole education and training arena, disbanded. Sir Keith Joseph had led his Department into an impasse in the long-running dispute with the teachers which he was unable to resolve. He had virtually surrendered the independence of the DES to the strategic domination of Young and Tebbit at the Department of Employment. His own public presentation of policy became more uncertain and bizarre as he paused for apparently agonized and lengthening periods of thought during speeches and interviews (two minutes in one unbroadcastable videotape). Despite the fact that he was, as Mrs Thatcher acknowledged in her letter answering his resignation, 'more than anyone else . . . the architect who shaped the policies which led to victory in two elections', he appeared more and more, as Paul Johnson wrote, 'a tragic, bewildered figure'. He seemed 'overwhelmed by the magnitude of his problems and his own evident incapacity to surmount them . . . like a general after a catastrophic defeat' (*Times Educational Supplement* 11 April 1986). Partly his uncertainties and hesitations arose because for him the freedom of choice he wished to see extended throughout the schools system meant more than just a restoration of the grammar schools. He wanted the same freedom for the non-academic but could not see how it could be done. These uncertainties meant that he had to go. Then the other two members of the Gang, Tebbit and Young, fell out over the Chairmanship of the Conservative Party, which they both coveted. This led to prolonged feuding between them in which both vied for Mrs Thatcher's favour. Tebbit was carpeted for the lack-lustre election campaign he ran as Party Chairman, Lord Young being called in by the Prime Minister to supply a new advertising agency. Even Lord Young, the bringer of solutions and not problems, now fell from grace perhaps because of the resentments of his cabinet colleagues, who were happy to see him dispatched to the Department of Trade and Industry rather than become the overlord of a new super-Ministry of Education and Training as he had planned. There was then no one left to urge the virtues of a combined system of education and training as the means to bring about the cultural revolution necessary for the modernization of an enterprise society. The Prime Minister's ear was left open to the siren song of right-wing educational traditionalists who, meeting regularly at Number 10, began to sing her a new tune. Beneath the deceptive simplicity of its swelling strains the anthem of vocationalism to which the education and training world had been marching under the baton of the MSC since 1976 was soon all but forgotten. Rather than go forward to a modernized enterprise culture, education and training would now begin their reversion towards a new golden age of Victorian values.

ALL CHANGE AT THE DES

How exactly the Conservative government came to abandon the vocationalism which it had inherited and developed from Labour and how it entered the 1987 election with a completely new policy for education and training is beyond the scope of this narration of the rise and fall of the MSC. Clearly, though, what happened involved a complete turn-around by the government in the policies which it had supported at the MSC since 1981 and with which the MSC had been identified. There was also a reversal of the position taken over many years by the Department of Education and Science. Since the 1960s and the expansion of education at all levels together with the introduction of comprehensive schooling, the DES had supported these progressive policies under the general aim of widening 'equal opportunities' for all. The National Union of Teachers, as seen, had enjoyed a special relationship with the Department that was to their mutual benefit in enlarging their respective influence and membership. Even after the Great Debate, 'when', as Dale (1983) said, 'the NUT's national influence began to wane' (p. 40), the DES appeared as the defender of the educational establishment against the incursions from without of the MSC and DE. This led to growing friction between the two Departments of State and their inability to collaborate in pursuit of stated government aims (over Unified Vocational Preparation – see p. 39). It was Mrs Thatcher's own experience as Minister of Education which, it has been suggested, led her to use the MSC as a means of forcing change upon what she regarded as the entrenched educational interests of the DES. Of course this only increased the feeling in the educational world that it was under sustained attack from without. The DES therefore persisted, even under the contrary direction of Sir Keith Joseph, in preserving what it could of the old status quo and was largely hostile to what it regarded as outside interference by the MSC in its preserve. However, Sir Keith was only prepared to collaborate up to a point in allowing his Department to be used by Young and Tebbit at the MSC and DE to spread the ideas and practices of the enterprise revolution. When it came to the recasting of Tory education policy towards a complete free market model for the school system, he was unwilling to abandon the conception of a state education service that the DES had always provided. As he later made clear in his speech to the House of Lords opposing the Education Reform Bill (20 April 1988), his idea of state provision was not only for a selected, academic minority but also of technical education for the non-academic majority. This was, it has been argued, one reason why he had to go.

However, a change had patently taken place within the DES under the Conservatives. This was not so much that the older civil servants who had been identified with the reforming and expansionary educational policies of the past were gradually replaced by officials more open to new ideas. Many of the senior members of the Department, seeing which way the wind was blowing and that there would be no return of a Labour or even a centrist government in the foreseeable future of their careers, just changed their views. 'The speed of change in this area over the last three or four years has been remarkable', recorded Brian Simon (1988, p. 142). The result of this 'ideological cleansing' was described in the editorial of *The Teacher* in May 1988: 'The DES is now in thrall to the likes of the Hillgate Group and other assorted extreme right wing thinkers on education'.

Typical of the now openly expressed opinion was the senior DES official quoted by Ransom (1984) who considered that 'if we have a highly educated and idle population we may possibly anticipate more serious social conflict' (p. 241). Therefore, instead of further educational expansion, what was necessary was that 'people must be educated once more to know their place' (ibid.). This sort of élitist thinking had always had a place among the high mandarins of state, particularly that Department of state which saw as part of its concern the preservation of a national culture of élite values through education. The DES, for instance, continued to favour traditional adacemic excellence, demonstrated in largely written examinations over the new forms of experiential accreditation designed to test practical competencies. Traditional academic disciplines were justified by the theory of liberal education which the Department espoused. As most classically expressed by Hirst and Peters (1970), education is a process of initiation into the distinct disciplines which together make up the traditional humanist curriculum inherited through the Arnoldian tradition of public schooling. Such a traditional view of subject knowledge was expressed in the DES document (1980) 'Framework for the Curriculum'. It was a view that lagged far behind what had become accepted opinion among teachers and their colleges of education. Thus when 'Framework' was taken down off the shelf and dusted over to provide the basis for Kenneth Baker's 'new' national curriculum, it was described by Professor Ted Wragg of Exeter University School of Education as 'one of the worst DES papers ever produced' (*Times Educational Supplement* 25 September 1987).

The DES had initially produced 'Framework' in reaction to a characteristically more open interpretation of what should be taught in schools by HMI entitled 'A View of the Curriculum'. Her Majesty's Inspectors acted as intermediaries between the professional civil servants of the Department and the teaching force in the schools and colleges. Typically former teachers themselves, HMI leaned towards a more generous version of the traditional disciplines sustained by the DES (see Lawton and Gordon, 1987). In so far as the Inspectors had been prepared to support the innovations that the MSC had introduced into teaching, particularly through the TVEI, they did so because they saw in them a continuation of 'progressive' curricular reform. This had begun within the secondary modern schools and continued among the lower streams of those comprehensive schools that were not hopelessly attempting to prove themselves the equals of the grammar schools they had succeeded. Ideas of relevance to the lives of the pupils were stressed by teachers in an attempt to gain the interest and compliance of the lowest quartile of the school population. Curricular reforms of this kind that crossed subject boundaries and linked them in new and practical ways received a boost from the raising of the school leaving age in 1971/72. They were continued in bridging and link courses joining together the technical education of the colleges with the more academic approach of most secondary schools. As has been seen, the MSC, through the FEU in particular, appropriated these ideas of relevant and useful knowledge and transformed them into its own version of what became known as the new vocationalism.

The Inspectors, both local and national, played a role in disseminating across schools ideas that worked in the classroom. The experimental approach of Nuffield science, for instance, was spread to the state from the private schools that were also under the remit of the national Inspectorate. New approaches to what had been the particularly arid area of mathematics teaching were another instance of Inspectorial influence. The Inspectorate had also been instrumental in introducing the new, unitary GCSE examination that incorporated in its scope and methods many of the 'progressive' educational criticisms that had been made over the years of the divisive O level and CSE papers. Inspectors, while they are agents of central control over the teaching force by its employers, the DES and the LEAs, also therefore mediate between the schools and the educational authorities. Their attitude will be critical to the implementation of the Baker reforms of education, just as it had been to the schools' eventual acceptance of TVEI and to the changes teachers made in the Initiative as it spread to more, and ultimately all, schools. Thus Brian Simon (1988) predicted that 'Reports on the implementation of the "national curriculum" will be required from HMIs, although there is also a suggestion that LEA advisers may be hijacked into assisting in monitoring its "delivery" ' (p. 114). Indeed, this might go so far as the nineteenth century situation when teachers were paid by results, so that their wages 'depended directly on their aptitude in training pupils to hoodwink inspectors, who, in those days, conducted the examinations personally' (p. 128).

Within the DES as well as the élitist outlook of its leading officials, there was also an almost equally natural centralizing tendency. This had always been evident in the tension that existed in the peculiar English administration of education between the Ministry and the local education authorities. During the period of MSC predominance over education, to the extent that the new vocationalism endorsed élitist attitudes, the DES went along with the work-related curricula and assessments favoured also by government. These in any case only applied to the majority of pupils not destined for higher education via traditional exam success. However, the Department could not be expected to approve them fully while it was not entrusted with the funds to introduce the new vocational methods itself but was relegated to supporting their introduction from outside. Power might be taken by the MSC and DE from the local authorities but it was not being given instead to the DES. Now a new scheme of things was suggested to reinvest central authority with the DES itself.

Here entrenched educational interest met the insistent advocacy within the Conservative Party of the standards and values of traditional grammar school education. As already discussed (p. 52), this has been a constant theme in Conservative education policy. Mrs Thatcher herself expressed on more than one occasion this Conservative yearning for a return to the grammar school paradigm of educational excellence from which she considered she had herself benefited. The problem was how to effect such a restoration, for, as the former Conservative education spokesman Norman St John Stevas confided whilst in opposition, the reintroduction of grammar schools would benefit only a minority of the electorate (personal communication to the author). Or, as Lord Joseph put it, 'Parents flinch from the reintroduction of grammar schools . . . because they fear the reintroduction of secondary modern schools' (speech to the Lords 20 April 1988). Nevertheless the advantages of such a restoration continued to be urged upon Mrs Thatcher by the likes of Baroness Cox and Rhodes Boyson, who as former authors of the Black Papers spent much time and energy in feverishly devising complex voucher systems whereby the loss to the majority would be disguised. As seen, her ear was also bent by regular meetings at No. 10 of right wing, or 'libertarian right', lobbyists and academics without the government. The 'Radical Manifesto' of the Hillgate Group, for instance, declared that

> schools should be owned by individual trusts. Their survival should depend on their ability to satisfy their customers. And their principal customers are parents, who should therefore be free to place their custom where they wish, in order that educational institutions should be shaped, controlled and nourished by their demand (p. 7).

This would have the additional virtue of depriving 'the politicized local education authorities . . . of their major source of power, and of their standing ability to corrupt the minds and souls of the young' (p. 18). The Hillgate Group included among their number the ex-headmaster from Yorkshire, Ray Honeyford, who had been deposed by his local education authority for his alleged racism towards the Asian children in his charge. The Group's influence, John Quicke (1988) considered, 'can be clearly seen in the flood of consultative documents on education produced by the incoming Conservative government in its first few months of office'.

However, Kenneth Baker, the new Minister of Education, was not of this mould and his not so private differences with the Prime Minister over education policy were repeatedly seized upon by the government's opponents. Indeed, at one stage during the 1987 Election, DES officials were directed not to listen to Baker but to take their instructions direct from the Cabinet Office! Yet Baker's overweening ambition had been noted by observers of all political persuasions and it was a commonplace of Sunday supplement commentary that the Ministry of Education was a suitable springboard from which to make a bid for the eventual succession to the premiership, just as both the leaders of government and opposition had previously been their parties' education spokespersons. It was similarly generally considered that Baker's commitment to what he began by calling his Great Reform of education was plainly subordinate to his primary commitment to his own political future.

Moreover, immediately upon assuming office, Baker embarked upon an aggravation of the long-running dispute between the teachers and their ultimate employer, the DES. The origins of this conflict lay in the determination of the teachers to stop 'the reduction of teachers to hourly-paid workers', as the NUT's President told his union's 1986 Conference. It was a rearguard action that teachers had been fighting ever since the end of educational expansion, signalled by the 1976 Great Debate, threatened to deprive them of a precarious professional status. Baker brought matters to a head and changed the character of the dispute by depriving the teacher unions of their negotiating rights. He thus opened the way to scrapping the nationally negotiated rate for the job, not only because this accorded with the government's general preference for plant by plant wage bargaining, but also because it could lead to different rates for the job of teaching in the different types of schools to which he hoped his reform of education would lead. Baker announced the first of these new types of school, the City Technology Colleges, at his first Party Conference as Minister of Education. They were intended as 'a halfway house' between the independent and the state sector and, as he later told the *Times Educational Supplement* (3 April 1987), 'I would like to see many more halfway houses'. The idea for this particular means of restoring selective schools has been credited (especially by himself) to Professor Brian Griffiths, monetarist head of the Downing Street Policy Unit. He certainly had a large hand in drafting the 1987 Conservative election manifesto, especially its education sections. These, Mrs Thatcher said in an interview a few hours after announcing the election date, 'are going much further with education than we had ever thought of going before'.

The announcement of the CTCs by the DES appropriated not only the substance of the MSC's approach to technical and vocational education and training but also its style. As aptly described by John Clare in *The Listener* (23 October 1986), the DES's own glossy brochure *A New Choice of School* (October 1986) is 'a City Prospectus. It even boasts a corporate logo: CTC, for City Technology College, the T bent into an arrowhead, thrusting hopefully upwards'. Inside,

> 16 shiny, tastefully designed pages illustrated with technicolour pie-charts, flow-charts, maps and diagrams, all decorated with friendly drawings carefully showing black children as well as white and, in the approved manner, boys passively looking on while girls do things on work-benches, computer terminals and rock faces.

This was a style that Lord Young had made his own at the MSC and was to go on to apply to the revamped DTI, renamed on his arrival the Enterprise Department (or Starship Enterprise, as it became known among its junior civil servants).

More ominous for the MSC was the fact that with the CTC announcement the DES had at last recaptured the initiative in the technical and vocational area of education. Of course it was obvious that 20 CTCs, with only 750 to 1000 pupils each, as proposed in the prospectus, could not do anything in themselves to alter the outcomes of education for the mass of Britain's school population, let alone provide the trained technicians for the future workforce as they apparently intended. Even the Conservative Party's own Education Association had declared them 'irrelevant'. But they clearly represented an alternative to the MSC's own Technical and Vocational Education Initiative, which critics had alleged was likely to be equally ineffective and was certainly not producing any very clear or concrete results. Most worrying for the MSC, CTCs were a much cheaper alternative to TVEI. Baker's brochure estimated establishing the new schools for only a million pounds each, and some of this was supposed to come from industry. Even if this proposed contribution were to prove as illusory and difficult to extract from the pockets of the nation's entrepreneurs as the funds the MSC had once supposed they would donate to YTS and TVEI, a new tier of technical schooling for only £20 million was cheap compared with the £90 million a White Paper had announced that same year the MSC would spend on extending the virtues of TVEI to all schools. This latest sum was on top of the £200 million the MSC had already lavished on the 'experimental' pilot projects. While this latest extension of TVEI brought the MSC into contact with all secondary schools in the country and thus widened its influence considerably, that influence was now spread so thinly as to make little difference in practice. Rather than spread scarce resources so widely, the CTCs intended to concentrate them in a few inner city centres.

In another respect the CTCs indicated that the days of the MSC's dominance over education were numbered, and the action (and money, limited though it was) had moved elsewhere to give back to the DES the initiative it had lost for so long. As Baker said on 'Weekend World' in December 1986, CTCs were 'prototypes' for the development of schools in the future. This commitment was written into Clause 80 of the Educational Reform Act, demonstrating the government's determination, in Brian Simon's (1988) words, 'to bring into being the "variety" of semi-independent schools Baker favours' (p. 55). It was a prototype that the DES had copied directly from the MSC itself, for, as has been seen, the quango had gained much of its credibility with the government from the speed at which it had been able to mount huge operations to contain unemployment, such as YOP and YTS. The flexibility of these efforts in response to local conditions had been achieved largely through the system of semi-private managing agents which the MSC had elaborated from the rather *ad hoc* arrangements for YOP and which it had refined somewhat to deliver YTS. The DES now utilized the same mechanism of grant-aiding independent managers for every trainee/pupil that they enrolled in return for which they would deliver the education/training that was required in the new CTCs. The annual grant per pupil that the DES would contribute would, it was stated, be equivalent to what was provided by LEAs for maintained schools serving similar catchment areas. At these rates, Chitty (1988) estimated that the true costs of the CTCs would be between £35 and £40 million a year, much more than the million pounds each that had been announced as needed to set up twenty of them. The government's own estimates for the 10 colleges for which it was subsequently able to find sites and at least some sponsorship rose from £86 million in September 1988 to £126.3 million by June 1989. This was matched by only £17.25 million of private tax-free donations from various contributors to Conservative Party funds. Other companies, such as ICI and BP, declined to support the venture. These independent trusts were to be granted chari- table status and would therefore be unable actually to run at a profit but the same principle need not apply when the system came to be generalized to all the nation's schools. Self-management on grants supplied per pupil from the LEA was already being piloted in secondary schools in Cambridgeshire and once all state schools were allowed the possibility of opting out of LEA control in return for support from the DES, success in a competitive system would be measured in terms of which schools attracted most pupils and thereby most resources.

The CTCs involved some of the same interests and individuals who had supported the TVEI. The Director General of the Organization for Rehabilitation through Training was on the Council set up to administer the CTC Trust and described by Claire Holmes in *The Teacher* (8 June 1987) as 'not so much a line-up of the great and the good but of the rich and the right'. Dan Sharon, the Technical Director of ORT, has also been active in supporting the CTCs. Following his suggestions, it is proposed that CTC pupils will be selected through aptitude tests and then separated into three distinct streams of ability. Lessons will be replaced by 'educational events' conducted at 'work stations' by 'area managers' (or teachers) following 'learning parameters and procedures' (a lesson plan). ORT will also be involved in training the teachers for the CTCs. This influence 'is not altogether surprising', as the *Times Educational Supplement* editorial (22 May 1987) stated, since 'ORT's technical sec- ondary schools have long been admired by Sir Keith Joseph and Lord Young'. The experience that TVEI had provided was also acknowledged in the CTC prospectus (p. 3). However, when it came to the publication of the DES's 'National Curriculum 5–16' in July 1987 (DES, 1987), TVEI gained only two passing mentions: as an 'example' of 'curriculum development . . . to build on the framework offered by the national curriculum and to take forward its objectives' (para. 27); and 'For the final two years of compulsory schooling, the national extension of TVEI will also help LEAs in the development and establishment of the national curriculum' (para. 85). Nevertheless, Geoffrey Holland defiantly declared that, thanks to the TVEI, a broad- based education for all young people was now in sight, 'no matter what is on the front of the Education Bill' (speech to Institute of Personnel Management, 22 October 1987).

TOWARDS WORKFARE

The DES was not the only Department of State at which profound changes in policy were being put into effect. A review of social security spending had been going on for some time at the DHSS under Norman Fowler. It was similarly intended that, as the Green Paper summarizing progress stated, 'The social security system must be consistent with the government's overall objectives for the economy' ('Reform of Social Security', vol. 1, para. 1.12). It was the government's plainly stated policy that there was an 'inescapable connection . . . between public spending and the taxes required to finance it', as another Green Paper on 'The Next Ten Years: public expenditure and taxation into the 1990s' put it (HMSO, 1984, p. 43). So to achieve its goal of cutting taxes public expenditure would have to be reduced. However, even though spending on social security had risen under the impact of mass unemployment to one-third of government expenditure, unlike the parallel review of the housing benefit system, the Fowler Review, as it was called, was not intended to make overall savings in the social security budget. Rather, the aim was to retarget benefits to 'those most in need', the deserving and not the undeserving poor. Means-tested benefits would therefore be targeted on the 'working poor', particularly those with children. The rest, the idle but able-bodied poor, were to be set to work to earn their maintenance on publicly provided benefits, until they too developed the qualities of enterprise and initiative which would enable them to break from their dependence upon the state's subsistence. The reform of social security was therefore intended to provide further inducements to the unemployed to take jobs. This was consistent with the government's view that unemployment was caused by the poor attitudes of job seekers and not because of a lack of jobs.

Here the reforms ran contrary to the spirit of the MSC's efforts which had begun as a process of job creation, though they had gone on through a series of schemes to subsidize existing low-paid jobs. The Young Workers' Scheme, which ran from 1982 to 1986, for instance, provided employment mainly for YOP and one year YTS leavers. Although it had the effect of reducing average youth wages by £2.40 to £40 per week, it was claimed that YWS also created more permanent jobs than the number of workers on higher wages that it displaced. Also, YWS was supposed to involve at least some training. After all, training was the whole *raison d'être* of the MSC. It was to lengthen the training period and to raise its quality as well as its quantity that the MSC introduced two year YTS, shifting YWS up the age range to become NWS (see page 88). The MSC's strategy always was a change of attitudes towards training and towards working life from the bottom up. By starting with the youngest entrants to the workforce, the flexible attitudes required by a rapidly changing economy were to be introduced through YTS as 'a modernised apprenticeship for all'. At the same time it was intended that employers would come to appreciate the value for them of the training revolution. The voluntary principle was of cardinal importance in this process, not only to sustain its credibility and the support of the trades unions who were necessary to get the schemes started, but also because forced training was clearly impossible (though forced labour was not).

The government, however, was coming to take an opposite view. Jeffrey Archer, whilst he was the Deputy Chairman of the Conservative Party, expressed the traditional prejudice towards the unemployed as 'scroungers' when he described young people to the 1985 Tory Party Conference as 'finding it very convenient to collect every single benefit God can give'. A few months later he was repeating on BBC Radio's 'World This Weekend' that 'the truth is . . . they are quite unwilling to put in a day's work. It's no use saying that the figures are three million. I suspect there's a vast amount in there who could work if they wanted to.' Lord Young, though he could be equally crude on occasion (e.g. see page 98), more subtly attacked the 'exaggeration of the [unemployment] numbers for political motives' (quoted in *Youthaid Bulletin* November 1985). Over the next year his priority became to lower the dole total in the run-up to a General Election. Indeed, one of the many calculations in deciding upon the most opportune moment at which to call what was fast becoming an exercise in the media manipulation of public perceptions was when exactly it was that it could be claimed unemployment had fallen below an arbitrarily defined total.

The MSC was thus increasingly drawn into the redefinition and recounting of unemployment. And again, while this was certainly contrary to the quango's long-term aims and intentions, it was to its immediate advantage. The MSC's original expertise in fire-fighting unemployment was now called upon to create a whole series of schemes that could claim to have removed large numbers of people from the dole queue.

The government was aided in its efforts by the fact that unemployment actually peaked, at least temporarily, during 1986. However, it became increasingly difficult to disentangle the real fall from the redefinition of employment and unemployment that was also going on. Lord Young, visiting an unemployment blackspot in Newcastle that September, asked reporters in a widely quoted remark to 'please stop talking about unemployment and start talking about employment'. He went on: 'The way people talk, you would think we still had a recession. We don't. We have a strong and sustained recovery in the economy, but with high unemployment'. This may not have been an expression of his usual ebullient optimism but, just possibly, a considered statement on the problems of 'jobless growth'. Whatever it was, it still gave him 'real hope that we are now over the worst in long-term unemployment' (19 September 1986). Clearly, though, the problem of the long-term unemployed themselves remained, and attention now increasingly turned to the 'hard core' of the estimated 1.4 million long-term unemployed. The MSC thus became involved in the Restart programme of supplementary Benefit Office interviews and the 'availability for work' test of those unemployed for more than six months. These tests and interviews were designed to 'shake out' those who claimed benefits whilst participating in the black economy and to offer to those genuinely in search of work the facilities of the MSC's Job Clubs and the new Job Training Scheme. If claimants could be removed, even if only for six months, from the unemployment register, it could be claimed that the total of the long-term unemployed was being reduced because they would return to the dole queue as fresh claims who were no longer part of the 'hard core' of 'real' unemployment – as opposed to the 'millions' whom Lord Young claimed were just changing jobs or retraining.

Lord Young, contrary to his earlier assurances that there was 'no short-cut to reducing unemployment', now committed the DE to paying out £20 a week to unemployed people who accepted jobs at less than £80 per week. There was no training element involved in this Job Start Scheme (as opposed to Restart). In addition, employers merely reduced their wages to take account of the subsidy and then took on a new batch of low-paid labour when the six month support ran out. There was a similar dishonesty involved in dressing up the Restart interviews as some friendly advice from the local benefit office as opposed to the reality of putting the frighteners on the long-term unemployed. Out of more than four million interviews, *The Observer* (10 April 1988) reported, a mere 0.5 per cent had found work. The most unreal of these various programmes, however, was the new Job Training Scheme, again with absolutely no training element involved. This was the first of the MSC's many schemes actually to have more reality on a video than in real life. Piloted in ten areas since late 1986, JTS was planned to expand nationwide for 110,000 long-term unemployed 18–25-year-olds. For the first time an MSC programme offered work experience and training at an income level tied to its participants' Supplementary Benefits. The principle of the rate for the job that had been established with the Community Programme, or of training allowance as for YTS, was thus effectively breached. Moreover, no additional resources were made available to the MSC for this planned expansion. It was to be financed out of the shortfall on expenditure for YTS, together with hastily implemented cuts in places that did provide skill training to 10,000 employed and unemployed adults.

The trades unions and even their representatives on the MSC were becoming increasingly restive over these moves to massage the unemployment figures prior to an election. They also resented the increasing pressure upon the unemployed, especially the work for benefits regime of JTS. New terms of reference reduced the powers of trades unionists on the local Area Manpower Boards to approve or reject programmes. At the central MSC, although the TUC's representatives argued for substantial trades union input to the scheme, in practice virtually all responsibilities under JTS now devolved to its Managing Agents. This showed the direction in which the government intended the MSC to move, towards a privatization in which more managing agencies took on the functions previously undertaken by the MSC itself. The other MSC Commissioners were also unhappy about the turn towards compulsion presented by the JTS, even though Lord Young gave assurances that nobody would lose benefit for refusing to take up a place on the new scheme. The MSC appeared to be dragging its feet about introducing JTS as fast as the government would have liked. Bryan Nicholson had said that he would like to see the scheme introduced into every workplace in the land eventually but that the speed with which this goal was achieved would be subject to the need to create 'a quality scheme'. In a letter Nicholson warned Lord Young that the Commissioners 'are determined not to be rushed into anything and to take decisions in a measured way' (22 January 1987). Nicholson was also known to be unhappy with the Conservatives' inclusion of a commitment in their election manifesto to prevent any young person claiming benefit who 'unreasonably refused' the offer of a place on YTS.

For, although the rapid expansion of programmes for the adult unemployed might, if they could be infused with some real training elements, put the MSC back on its original track of skill training and job creation for the working population, it was at the same time becoming divorced from its youth training base. In fact Nigel Collins (1986) presciently considered that 'the very things which made the MSC so powerful in the 1980s would be its undoing in the 1990s' (p. 236). Despite the expansion of the Community Programme, the launch of JTS, the increase in the New Young Workers' Scheme and the boosting of the Enterprise Allowance Scheme, Collins' prediction was already being fulfilled. The pressure on the two year YTS was reduced by the easing in the bulge of school leavers, a demographic factor that also added to the government's luck in reducing unemployment during 1986. From a peak of 3.7 million in 1983 the population of 16–19-year-olds fell to 3.5 million in 1987 and is anticipated to bottom out at 2.6 million in 1994. School leaver unemployment in September 1987 was thus at its lowest level since 1974. In addition, compulsory training for school leavers after 1987 would effectively remove unemployed 16 and 17-year-olds from the real concerns of the Department of Employment and place them in the position of claimants working for their benefits. As Kenneth Clarke told the House of Commons (28 January 1987), 'for the first time from this Easter there need be no unemployment under 18 and anyone under that age who remains unemployed will have chosen to remain unemployed'. Nor would the process necessarily cease at age 18, for the Fowler Review of Social Security had raised the age of majority to 25. Below this it was expected that young people would be dependent upon their parents or the state. As the Green Paper on 'The Reform of Social Security' had put it (Vol. 2, para. 2.7.3): 'It is clear that at the age of 18 the majority of claimants are not fully independent and that the great majority above 25 are . . . the government has concluded that an appropriate dividing line in age is 25'. Considering that many women get married around their twenty-third year and many young people are not living or no longer wish to live with their parents up to 25, this seems not only unclear but a completely arbitrary division below which a second-class level of benefit – £5 a week less than anyone else's – will be paid because the government thinks young people should get money from their parents. This could only add to the growing problem of youth homelessness. Meanwhile (in 1988) the government split the benefit functions of the DHSS from responsibility for the Health Service by dividing the Ministry in two.

The rapid boost to its programmes in the prolonged lead-up to the 1987 General Election was to be the MSC's last gasp. As with a great whale swimming for too long close to the shore, the turn of the tide left it stranded on the beach. The MSC as it was had outlived its usefulness to the government, being no longer required either to contain the threatening rise in unemployment or to imbue the young with the values of enterprise culture. For the social security system this implied discrimination between the deserving poor and the undeserving poor. The undeserving were defined as young and childless. Like 'the able bodied poor' before them they must be 'put to work' to earn their maintenance from the state. This workhouse dole was now to be the function of YTS for 16- and 17-year-olds and of the Job Training Scheme, or the Employment Training scheme that came to replace it, for those aged 18 to 25. This was plainly not the attempt to retrain the entire workforce for a new industrial revolution that had been heralded by the New Training Initiative at the beginning of the decade. All this was clearly signalled by the Conservatives in the months leading up to the June election.

At the same time that such measures indicated the MSC would no longer have anything to do with real training, the Education Reform Act signalled the end of vocationalism in schools and colleges. Careers education did not even figure as a foundation subject in the national curriculum, while it has been predicted that the testing of pupils will result in a competition for academic success that will render vocational and pre-vocational qualifications completely irrelevant. This, after teachers, abetted by the MSC, had spent the last eleven years since Ruskin trying to put together the rudiments of a vocationally relevant schooling for the majority of pupils who would not progress to higher education. No wonder so many in both education and training found it hard to appreciate that such a turnaround had really occurred. The Inner London Education Authority, for example, had been desperately trying to prove its vocational credentials to a government that was no longer interested in it or them. ILEA's belated embrace of the TVEI, which it had previously rejected, was ignored. So too were the authority's efforts to team up with local employers and even to make promises of employment for pupils conditional upon their improved performance in schools. In fact, soon after agreeing to the abolition of the London-wide authority, the government announced the extension of the 'Compact' scheme nationwide without at first acknowledging that it had been piloted in London schools.

The fact that the £17 million to do this was given to the MSC rather than the DES was interpreted by the *Times Educational Supplement* (11 March 1988) more as a slap on the wrist for Mr Baker than a sign that the MSC was back in favour. In fact, this was the usual feud breaking out again between the DE and the DES, the latter now trying to gain control of NAFE as the DE cut back on it and to use the DE-funded TVEI in support of the national curriculum. Until recently TVEI and other MSC programmes had been regarded by educationalists as hostile incursions into their territory. Now they suddenly seemed to offer the only source of innovation and support in face of their subjection to the narrow traditionalism that the Education Reform Act represented. There was, however, little point in rallying around the 'new vocationalism' as the only credible opposition because, as John Quicke (1988) demonstrated, 'the "new right" seems to be willing and able to accommodate this movement, despite its difference with it'. In the now dominant new right view of education, instrumental vocationalism for the majority was quite compatible with traditional academic pursuit of education for its own sake by an innately intelligent minority. This had certainly always been Sir Keith, now Lord, Joseph's view, as he made clear in an interview (24 June 1989).

The MSC too saw a hope for itself and its vocational approach in the schools and colleges as it desperately tried to prove it still had a place in Mr Baker's new order. Sir John Munn, who succeeded Bryan Nicholson as Chairman of the MSC, in his first speech urged professional bodies to get involved with the TVEI, which the MSC still hoped to save. He proposed to arrange that in return teachers would spend some time working in industry. However, the commitment to give all teachers such work experience for two weeks in every five years was soon undertaken not by the MSC but by Lord Young's DTI/Enterprise Department. Not that it is ever likely to happen given the chronic and persistent shortages of teachers. Meanwhile Anne Jones, the Director of the MSC's Education Programmes, claimed that testing at 7, 11, 14 and 16 was quite compatible with the practical assessment of experientially acquired competencies long advocated by the MSC. The profiles that educationalists once looked at with scepticism might now, she suggested, offer a painless way of administering the required tests. The well-publicized differences between the Prime Minister and her Education Secretary over these tests gave both teachers and the MSC, who now suddenly found themselves strangely allied with their former foes, hope that such a vocational approach could yet predominate over Mrs Thatcher's clear preference for the Victorian values of traditional testing for the three Rs. Already, however, the MSC's jargon looked jaded.

Somewhat desperately in 1987 the MSC launched a £100m Enterprise in Higher Education Initiative, inviting ten institutions, individually or in consortia, to bid for £200,000 each over the next five years in return for which they would undertake 'to develop competencies and aptitudes relevant to enterprise' in all their students. The next year a further ten bids would be accepted and so on in a rolling programme until Enterprise reached all HE colleges. Notwithstanding the fact that for a long time most people in the universities and colleges thought MSC was a postgraduate degree, the Commission had long had its eye on higher education. What seemed to it over-long and irrelevant courses appeared ripe for the rationalization and relation to industry that it had imposed upon secondary and further education. It had already been involved in the piloting of two year degree courses over the objections of the

University Grants Committee, which refused to endorse the experiment. But now higher education also saw itself under attack from the new Education Act and was increasingly short of funds, so bids for the tranche of MSC money went ahead. 'Enterprise' was at first defined in an entrepreneurial sense of business skills but this narrow approach soon broadened into ideas of encouraging work placements and project work in economic environments. Definition of enterprise then settled upon an emphasis upon personal transferable skills, so the initiative had all the hallmarks of the MSC's usual approach of throwing in money (saved from cuts elsewhere) with no very clear end in view, to see what might develop. Anne Jones spoke of the needs for the projects, work experience, new styles of learning and teaching with records of achievement and profiled assessment for all students — familiar MSC fare. 'The core skills of an enterprising person that lie at the heart of an enterprising culture . . . [are] ability to innovate, recognise and take opportunities, work in a team, take risks and respond to challenges, communicate effectively and be computer literate', as publicity for the EHE explained.

The Enterprise Initiative was announced by the MSC as TVEI for higher education. Like TVEI, the MSC's money was intended only as pump-priming. It would be provided for five years to get schemes off the ground. After that enterprise programmes should be self-financing, or rather financed by enterprise itself in the shape of local authorities. For this reason bids for the first hand-out included 'a requirement for a contribution from employers in cash or in kind equivalent to at least 25 per cent of the MSC contribution over the first two years and rising to a substantial proportion for the third year of the programme'. 'In cash or in kind' might seem a let-out for the local employers whom colleges hurried to approach, but it was no more likely that they would end up funding an education initiative for which they had no real use than that they would ever contribute to the costs of TVEI, the YTS or the DES's City Technology Colleges. It was extraordinary that the agonized discussions that now took place in the universities and colleges repeated the same arguments over whether or not to accept the MSC's money as had occurred ten years previously in the staffrooms of schools and further education colleges. Then too voices were raised to defend independence and then too they were overruled by the need to secure jobs and gain funding. The Enterprise Initiative in Higher Education was in fact just another effort by the MSC to prove that it was still needed. It had, however, no plans to extend the activities of its newly founded education unit beyond the Initiative. But here again the powers which Baker had taken over higher education, particularly contract funding, were quite sufficient to ensure the compliance of the sector and to enforce upon it the savings required by the government.

THE DEATH OF THE QUANGO

The attitude of the third Thatcher government to the Manpower Services Commission contrasted sharply with the administration that preceded it and had a great deal in common with Mrs Thatcher's first period in office. After seven years the marriage that had seemed so perfect was staring divorce in the face. The Conservative manifesto argued for a new manpower authority specifically responsible for 'training' and nothing else. The abolition of the tripartite MSC was an expression of Mrs Thatcher's determination to break any remaining links with Britain's corporatist past. The decision to increase the number of employer representatives on the newly constituted training board reflected the ideological commitment of the new Tory government to put those who benefited most from training, and in the long run those who would have to pay the greater part of its costs, in overall control.

The proposed changes followed swiftly after the election victory. Lord Young, scenting a change in the air, or because for him too the MSC had fulfilled its purposes, transferred to the DTI, which he renamed and endowed with a new logo to bring enterprise to the inner cities. From there he was moved sideways into the Tory Party as Deputy Chairman to Kenneth Baker. As anticipated, Norman Fowler transferred to the DE from the DHSS and Bryan Nicholson did not renew his Chairmanship of the MSC when his three year contract ended in September. He moved to the Post Office, where his conciliatory attitudes helped to avert a Christmas mail strike. He had always been opposed to the principle of compulsory entry onto MSC programmes but had been overruled in the case of JTS before the election, while the Conservative mandate now committed the government to compulsory YTS beginning in September 1988. An exchange of letters between the new Secretary of State and the MSC had detailed the Commissioners' objections to the government's proposals for the MSC and its new Unified Training Programme as it was then called. These were duly noted by the Secretary of State, who then instructed the Commission to get on with preparations anyway.

Decisions to reduce the overall funding, the first reductions in MSC grant-in-aid since 1981, were already taken but the quango was also stripped of its employment functions so that it could be pruned into a National Training Authority. The MSC lost its Job Centres and the Enterprise Allowance Scheme to the DE. Additionally the Restart Initiative and disability services went the same way, and so did the Careers and Occupational Information Centre, which was transferred to the Careers Service Branch of the DE. Fowler's move to the DE indicated that 'training and job creation' would from now on be more closely tied to the DSS, where his review of the social security system resulted in changes that came into force from April 1988 onwards. However, the first priority for Norman Fowler was to find personnel to lead the quango in a period of dramatic change.

A temporary replacement for Bryan Nicholson was found in the form of the Chairman of the MSC in Scotland, Sir James Munn. The fact that he was appointed only as a caretaker Chairman for a six month period indicated the uncertainty that now hung over the quango's future. Geoffrey Holland left his position of Director for a Permanent Secretaryship in the DE, and in exchange Roger Dawe, who brought his expertise with special employment measures in the 1970s, was imported from the DE as Director-General. This upgrading indicated that the next and permanent Chairman of the quango would only be a part-time appointment, as the TUC had feared would happen in the case of Sir Richard O'Brien's original appointment to the Chairmanship. This was indeed the case with Brian Wolfson's appointment to a part-time chairmanship in July 1988.

The 1987 Employment Act formally proposed the establishment of the new Training Commission. Suddenly and unexpectedly, it seemed quite possible, as Sam Whitbread — an employer whose family firm had been particularly committed to staff (especially youth) training — had predicted, the whole training movement could 'simply fade away over the years' (*Times Educational Supplement* 17 July 1987). Two careers officers writing in the same paper asked in bewilderment 'Whatever happened to the Training Partnership?' (15 January 1988). The editorial could now see the YTS as having been nothing more than 'a quick and impoverished fix for mass unemployment' (15 April 1988). The new magazine for managing agents, *Training Tomorrow*, also questioned whether the MSC still had any future (December 1987) and whether the YTS did (March 1988). The Training Commission's creation marked a watershed in British training history primarily because training and unemployment were no longer entwined. Geoffrey Holland in his new post stuck to the old ideology when he told the leaders of the training community: 'The new MSC is a national authority. It has a significant contribution to improving the UK's business competitiveness at home and abroad' (*Focus on Training*, May 1987). Yet ironically in just over a year, Holland, who, with Cassels, had largely been the imaginative driving force behind the MSC, was overseeing the reabsorption of the quango into its parent Ministry. Despite the reiteration of the importance of training over the past decade and more, the cooperative effort of employers, government and unions had been abandoned and training was back in the hands of Whitehall.

And yet the proposed creation of the new employer-dominated Training Commission was not the overriding reason for the abolition of joint responsibility for training — a central tenet of the MSC's birth fifteen years earlier. Even at this stage the Training Commission had the token support of the TUC but it was the introduction of Employment Training that sounded the death knell for the Training Commission and the final links with the Manpower Services Commission.

Indeed, the TUC even 'brushed under the carpet' the government's insistence upon making YTS compulsory. For the government the move fulfilled the long-standing aim of raising the age of entry into the labour market for those without a job. Once more the unemployment total was reduced 'at a stroke'. Clearly delighted at his ingenuity John Moore, the new DHSS Minister, declared to the House of Commons that 'unemployment for young people need no longer exist' (2 November 1987) and the removal of the right to benefit would take care of those youths 'who deliberately choose to ignore this opportunity'. 'This guarantee [of high-quality training leading to a recognized qualification] is unequalled by any of our principal competitors', Kenneth Clarke added (28 January 1988), ignoring the fact that training quality was still uneven, to say the least, and that no agreed qualification had ever been accepted except the worthless YTS leaving certificate.

The TUC also 'gritted its teeth' when the government implemented changes that reconstituted the Area Manpower Boards (AMBs) to reflect the predominance of employers in their nominally tripartite structure. Their membership, which might be expected to overlap with the Local Employer Networks based on Chambers of Commerce, would be determined by chairmen appointed by the Secretary of State. At the MSC's suggestion, the AMBs were to be renamed Labour Advisory Bodies, again showing the more marginal training role the MSC from now on would have to be satisfied with. Arguing that local labour markets and employer links had changed considerably in the four years since the AMBs were first established, the Commission recommended that the new bodies take on the role of strategic planning coordination and quality assurance. They would therefore no longer be concerned with the approvals for individual projects or renewal applications.

All this considerably reduced trades union influence on the MSC and then the Training Commission. Whether the unions withdrew mattered very little since the schemes could continue without their collaboration, though many of them would not have started without union cooperation. What broke the camel's back was the introduction of ET. In September 1987 the TUC called upon the government to make significant modifications to the Employment Training scheme, but after much typical fudging and confusion the Economic Committee of the TUC finally agreed to boycott ET. This gave government an excuse finally to abolish the Commission. Abolition came in September 1988 after only ten days of existence. The previously semi-autonomous MSC, whose creators had aspired to transform it into a new super-Ministry of Education and Training, was now relegated to the ignominious position of a Training Agency within the Department of Employment.

Thus for all its efforts the MSC was out in the cold after the 1987 general election, and after a short-lived reincarnation was eventually discarded. However, Roger Dawe, the Director-General of the Training Commission and in turn DG of the Training Agency, soon recognized the change in the political climate, telling the annual conference of the Association of Colleges of Further and Higher Education that the years ahead were 'going to be quite different from the early '80s when our money was increasing every year. The days of the MSC being the all-provider have gone' (*Times Educational Supplement* 18 March 1989). The MSC was left scraping around desperately searching for a new *raison d'être*. The fall in the number of school leavers and the temporary upturn in the economy had also lessened the MSC's more obvious importance to government. Its original ideas of transforming Britain's industrial landscape by comprehensive manpower training from the bottom up had been hopelessly compromised.

THE TRAINING AGENCY AND THE COMING OF TECS

Policy making in vocational education and training had come full circle. The Training Agency was an exact replica of the Training Services Agency that was created in 1973. In fact the new Training Agency was to have less direct responsibility for the administration of national training programmes than its predecessor because responsibility for managing the national training budget was to be devolved to local-employer-dominated Training Enterprise Councils. The ghost of Robert Carr's conception of a national training authority, limited in scope and primarily setting training standards, had been resurrected a decade and a half later to possess the training community.

The new Training Agency had two central tasks; on the one hand it had to continue to improve YTS and on the other it had to launch nationwide Employment Training. There should have been very few difficulties with YTS, if for no other reason than that the main principles of youth training had been firmly established and what the training community expected was a step-by-step improvement in quality of YTS and not any major policy reversals. To the bitter disappointment of many, YTS was changed beyond recognition.

Sir Bryan Nicholson concluded his chairmanship by saying that the climate of hostility which greeted the introduction of YTS had disappeared and the scheme provided Britain with a 'thoroughly respectable model'. Improvement in the quality of training would take at least another decade to materialize fully but while it was right to expect improvements he asked the training community to moderate its demands, stressing 'YTS is fundamental; it gives people the right start.' However, the problem still remained of how managers would change their attitudes to spending more of their own cash on skills training and how YTS could help reshape their attitudes. This was more than just scapegoating the schools for the failure of the economy and for failing to deliver the progress to social equality the comprehensive reform had promised in the 1960s (see Ainley, 1988). By the mid-1980s the state had been advocating vocational education and training for a decade but now the so-called training problem could plainly be seen as a management issue. A poor skill training tradition and the lack of manpower planning in industry were a direct outcome of the less than total commitment to youth training. As Shirley Williams (1986) stated, 'The main reason why YTS is not yet a satisfactory bridge from school to work is that employers do not see it as an essential preparation for all workers. Their attitudes remain ambivalent between viewing the scheme as an essential basic training like the first year of the West German apprenticeship and as a lifeboat for the young unemployed which incidentally provides employers with cheap labour' (p. 180).

Under Lord Young's stewardship it seemed that the two distinct areas of provision for 16–19-year-olds and skill training might be linked more closely together because it had been recognized that YTS had largely replaced the traditional apprenticeship. In an interview (13 June 1985) Young said he saw the long-run objective of YTS as being to act as a shock treatment to employers' attitudes and be in the vanguard of Britain's skill training effort. The aim was presumably to ensure that all managers at whatever level of enterprise grasped that 'the ultimate difference between education and training is that the latter is about making money pure and simple' (*Focus on Training*, May 1988).

However, the Training Agency reversed what had taken a decade to achieve. Fowler placed his faith in a 'market YTS' (Lucy Ball, 'What future YTS?', *Unemployment Bulletin*, Summer 1989) that was responsive to the local needs of employers. In practice the 'training element' was to be seriously affected and the new flexible YTS was a shadow of the two-year scheme adopted under the New Training Initiative. It was as though the government was wantonly undoing what had taken over a decade to achieve: a youth training scheme with a degree of credibility and ready to be extended in coverage to include more and more young people in employment who had found jobs. The higher demand for young people coupled with the absurd decision to move towards a 'market YTS' would only reinforce the incentive for new labour market entrants to find jobs with employers where no provision for training existed.

The second task of the Training Agency was to publicize and promote Employment Training. The scheme was to have a throughput of 625,000 adults annually (an increase of 200,000 over initial estimates) and cost the Exchequer £1345 million a year. It mixed together elements of all the MSC's schemes into a flat rate of benefits plus £10 (including £5 to cover the costs of travel to work). This YTS for grown-ups replaced the Community Programme and the Job Training Scheme. It promised a 'guarantee' similar to the Christmas offer school leavers would be unable to refuse. In this case 18- to 25-year-olds unemployed for six months were to be given from six to twelve months' training and practical experience with employers and on CP-type projects. The proposed funding structure for the scheme indicated that the government was looking to statutory and private-sector employers to run most of the places. Employer-based schemes meant that people on benefits plus £10 would work alongside waged workers and this would lead to wholesale job substitution.

Employment Training also 'aimed' to include long-term unemployed adults up to 50 years old, once its 'guarantee' to the under-25s had been fulfilled. The Training Agency fooled no one with its slick advertising campaign into believing that ET was a skill training programme. The suggestion that ET was a scheme 'training the workers without jobs for the jobs without workers' deluded only Training Agency officials and their DE masters. If anything, ET was a programme that fell into the government's general neoclassical thinking on unemployment by suggesting that it was caused by the poor attitudes of job seekers, including poor attitudes to training, and not by the lack of jobs. In fact the point could be made that if ET was a skill training programme why was it that the state was once again subsidizing what was a legitimate function of industry? The true purpose of the scheme was to spread the idea that unemployment no longer existed because everyone not in employment had the offer of training or retraining. Indeed in Tory circles it became unpatriotic to mention the word 'unemployment' at all! However, independent research by the Institute of Manpower Studies in June 1989 suggested that only one in three employers had heard of ET and that the programme had only 165,000 places filled by October 1989.

Although ET was not an 'approved' scheme in the sense that benefit could be stopped if a person decided against joining the scheme, participation on it automatically reduced the unemployment count. The determination of the government to bring the official unemployment total down at any cost was shown by the introduction of what was considered by many to be one of the most pernicious Tory Bills ever to receive the royal assent. The 1989 Social Security Act made it encumbent on the unemployed to 'actively seek work'. This redefinition of the responsibilities of the unemployed individual to the state in respect of receiving benefit served only to discredit ET. In short, if ET was seen by the long-term unemployed as a credible training and retraining programme they would actively seek retraining as a legitimate exit menu from the dole queue. It was as though the government was committing the same mistake as it did with YTS. In a desperate attempt to reduce official unemployment YTS was always followed by a scheme to reduce the cost of employing young workers. Here again the government was trying to coerce the adult unemployed onto a low-quality programme to retain their social security benefits. Lamentably, it seemed that training would always be associated with managing and massaging that unemployment.

Meanwhile Norman Fowler presented a government White Paper entitled 'Employment for the 1990s' (HMSO, 1988) which proposed ending the statutory status of the remaining seven Industrial Training Boards by 1991 and privatizing the whole national training programme. The Training Agency was to oversee a multitude of Training Enterprise Councils. These were to be employer dominated and focus the delivery of national training programmes to the needs of local labour markets. How TEC consortia would ensure total geographical coverage was a problem to be resolved but clearly the Secretary of State was playing a high-risk game in handing the national training budget to employers. It was clear that Fowler hoped that this was the best method of achieving the long-term objective of passing on the full cost of training to industry and individual employers. But, as Corney (1989) argued, 'If past experience is anything to go by these reforms are bound to foster the dependency culture which the Tories are so determined to seek out and destroy elsewhere. Under the new TECs, industry will be in a powerful position to resist cuts in State support — especially if the long-term trend in unemployment continues to fall in the 1990s — while at the same time allocating taxpayers' money in an area where employers' contributions should be much greater.'

What was clear was that the current wave of interest in training by employers was a response to the predicted shortage in the supply of labour, not a change of heart in their attitudes towards the level of skill of their labour force. The next recession will witness the traditional cutbacks in training expenditure, but with their influence on TECs employers are better placed than ever to ensure that the state will continue to provide subsidized training to industry. What Fowler failed to realize and his chief officials at the Training Agency continued to overlook was that Britain's firms lacked a pro-training culture.

SUMMARY

It was ironic that the MSC was absolved of all responsibility for training at a time when academic researchers, economists and policy makers were beginning to realize more and more the strategic value of human capital to national economic performance. In practice the sweeping changes of direction at both the DES and the DSS transformed the policy context in which the quango operated. The place of the new 'vocationalism' which the MSC had introduced into education was overtaken by a reborn 'old academicism', while the review of social security funding removed even further the training/retraining rationale from MSC programmes, associating training firmly with 'workfare'. Training policy had come full circle with the creation of the Training Agency but the government had put the issue of training on course for a brand new adventure with the formation of TECs. A British government had finally handed local responsibility for the state's training effort to the group that had persistently underinvested in training — Britain's employers. The 'partnership approach' to training, which had done so much to put training on the political agenda, was rejected and national control was again in the hands of mandarins both in Whitehall and the Training Agency. Viewing the history of the MSC dispassionately, it is fair to conclude that the quango had created many enemies, stamped on many toes, but a powerful Civil Service headed by a tripartite Commission looked a better prospect than the one that had replaced it. The last chapter of this history of the rise and fall of the MSC examines what, if any, was its permanent legacy.

Chapter 6

Conclusion: The Legacy of the MSC

CHANGING THE BRITISH SOUL

The Manpower Services Commission had embarked on an attempt to remake the entire basis of Britain's education and training system. This plan was directed at transforming industrial society and with it the nation's soul. The MSC disseminated a set of ideas that linked education and training to reverse Britain's seemingly inevitable industrial decline. Paramount in the thought of policy makers at the MSC was the connection between the country's outdated attitudes towards wealth creation and what had been called the 'British disease'. By explicitly connecting cultural values with economic regeneration, the MSC secured the elevation of training on the political agenda. It acted as a catalyst to persuade politicians and industrialists to re-evaluate training and its place in the modernization of the British economy. However, whilst technology was seen as fundamental to this modernization, it required a concomitant training revolution. Britain's education/training problem was rooted deep in the nation's past, as Perry (1976) had argued:

> The training problem is part of a larger education problem, and this in turn part of a social attitude based upon Britain's prosperity and leadership in the nineteenth century, which generated a feeling of effortless superiority in the service of the church, state and the professions, rather than in industry and commerce. It was largely this social climate that created the dichotomy between education and training which caused it to be more deeply entrenched than elsewhere (p. 312).

Thus success for the MSC was dependent upon the unification of education and training to end the anti-industrial values permeating Britain's education system. As such, training in its wider, sociological definition was both a cause of and solution to industrial decline.

This ideology was the basis of the MSC's policies and was derived from a cultural explanation of Britain's economic demise. Martin Weiner (1980), read widely at the MSC, argued that the 'British disease' was 'rooted deep in the nation's social structure and mental climate. The more closely Britain's twentieth century economic decline is examined, the more social and psychological elements are found to be intertwined with economic factors' (p. 5). At the heart of the MSC's philosophy was the goal of explaining to the workforce 'the way in which wealth is produced and used in society' (MSC, 1975a, p. 1). On the one hand this explanation was in terms of enterprise and efficiency and so emphasized the role of entrepreneurial activity in opening up new markets and business activities. On the other, it elevated labour as a factor of production and saw investment in human capital as critical for economic performance.

Essentially the MSC claimed ideas that were part of a larger body of social and economic thought. The cultural thesis had as its starting point the relative positions of the fathers of sociology, Karl Marx and Max Weber. Morishima (1982) conveniently expressed the divergence in their relative views:

> Whereas Marx contended that ideology and ethics were no more than reflections of underlying material conditions, Weber made the case for quite the reverse relationship. He considered that it is the ethic that is given and any type of economy which necessitated the people possessing an ethos incompatible with that ethic will not develop (p. 3).

Another prominent academic supporting the cultural thesis and hence the view that Britain lacked a social ethic suitable for modern economic development was Professor Ralph Dahrendorf, former Director of the London School of Economics. Dahrendorf was convinced that a connection existed between economic success and cultural attitudes and called upon future British governments to ground their economic strategies within the 'cultural sphere' (*The Listener* 14 October 1976). The MSC's governing ideology cannot be divorced from the background of these ideas. So it is within this wider and deeper ideological tradition that a proper historical perspective of the Commission's activities emerges.

If wealth creation was important to the thinking of the MSC, so was the production process and the world of work. Manpower policy 'is essentially about work. It views people as a factor of production, a means towards the end of producing goods or providing services' (MSC, 1976, p. 12). It was through the provision of state-funded training and unemployment programmes that the MSC attempted to implant its ideology into the hearts and minds of Britain's workforce. This point was especially emphasized by neo-Marxist commentators. While Markhall and Gregory (1982), for example, argued that the MSC 'supplied the seeds of a work ethic whilst simultaneously denying access to it' (p. 68), they also fully appreciated the MSC's real purposes, even if they vehemently opposed them. As they observed:

> It is at this point that we can see that the MSC cannot simply be understood as an unemployment palliative. It is not simply absorbing or distracting the young unemployed, it is also actively and increasingly intervening in the cultural and material processes of the young unemployed.

From both the perspectives of Weiner and Dahrendorf, who emphasized cultural factors, and from the positions of Markhall and Gregory, whose analysis began from the material conditions of society, culture and values were seen as critical in explaining the history of education and training in Britain. Weiner, in particular, said it was the uncertain position of industry within education that stood out. While Finn (1982) reflected 'the distinction between education and vocational training has been a marked feature of Britain's education system' (p. 42). Markhall and Gregory (1982) also concluded that 'the reappearance of mass youth unemployment has reopened the profoundly political purpose of education and training' (p. 68). At the same time what was mistaken in their perceptions was that they seemed to think education alone could sufficiently prepare young people for working life. Thus Finn (1987), for example, exalted existing programmes in schools in the early 1970s which prepared school leavers for work. This led him to conclude that the role of the MSC had been merely to 'persuade public opinion that the young working class now need longer periods of training before they can even enter the labour market' and to see that the MSC as part of the state 'has come to assume a greater central and direct role in the economic management of capital' (p. 174). However, what the MSC aimed to do was formalize vocational preparation. This was intended to be for all pupils and was to form the basis of a new education and training system. However, Marxist interpretations of education in capitalist economies, and particularly those by English writers attached to the Labour Party, are generally unable to reconcile the contradiction that education is seen as enhancing labour power in terms of skill but at the same time makes labour more malleable to the needs of capitalist production. Thus any process which strengthened closer links with the ideology of work and wage labour, such as replacing liberal education with a more vocational approach, implied for them a stronger bond to capitalism.

Therefore Marxists tended to view the MSC as an integral part of the Welfare State. Gough argued that the primary function of the Welfare State was to 'modify the reproduction of labour power and maintain the non-working population' (1979, p. 44). Consequently the role of the MSC was to maintain the unemployed population and it could hence have no part to play in skill training. But why, asked Perry (1976), had it taken mass unemployment to force a debate on vocational education and training? How could anyone overlook the gulf between education and training which Sir Peter Venables so cryptically commented upon:

> I have an education, he has training. I have a degree or diploma, he has a certificate. One is a professional, the other vocational. I am a teacher, he is an instructor. We have a syllabus, they have a programme. Ours is a preparation for life, theirs a rescue operation (quoted in Perry, 1976, p. 293).

John Wellens (1963) warned, 'We shut our eyes to the causal relationship between the educational system and the work situation' (p. 23). More than twenty years later Maurice Kaufman (1986) concluded that the existence of the MSC had only deepened the dichotomy between education and training. 'A major fundamental problem arose', he wrote, 'from the contradiction between the essential unity or identity of education and training . . . the divisions between education and training systems at all levels have been obstructive, frustrating and harmful' (p. 140). Nevertheless the weight of the evidence suggests that this peculiarly British problem had deep roots well before the MSC came on the scene. Moreover, even some of the MSC's most hostile adversaries concluded that education and training needed to be integrated in recognition that 'the best preparation for any job is a high level of general education and that all jobs should involve a high quality of training' (Benn and Fairley, 1986, p. 23). But of course from their point of view this would also instil 'bourgeois values' in working-class youth (Byrne and Padfield, 1986, p. 204).

In short, the MSC had been seen as a refashioner of attitudes, involved in sustaining and reinforcing basic cultural values. However, other commentators denied the case that in the wider context Britain's business and public institutions were anti-enterprise, for example Gamble (1983). The real question was not whether Britain's establishment was anti-enterprise, but whether Britain's workforce held sufficiently pro-industrial values. The MSC obviously thought not. It contributed to debates that had raged since the mid-1970s. Then the end of the Keynesian economic era was marked by Callaghan's speech to the 1976 Labour Party conference in which he said that Britain could 'no longer spend her way out of recession'. The eclipse of Keynes paved the way for the economic doctrine of monetarism. Assessments of the rise to power of monetarist thinking, including that of Keegan (1984), missed what was critical to the new monetarism. Bosanquet (1983) noted that far from being a dry and technical theory of macro-economics, monetarism contained assumptions directly connected with changing the behaviour of economic agents. Moreover, Callaghan's 1976 Ruskin College speech on education had far more visionary zeal than his Conference speech of the same year. Benefiting from the collapse of the Keynesian system through a massive injection of public funds to manage unemployment, the MSC found a permanent niche in the wake of the Ruskin revolution. The gospel of the MSC was for all political persuasions. In the event it was transformed under Thatcherism.

As the Thatcher crusade proceeded, the cultural revolution solution to Britain's economic crisis became more explicit as training gave way to 'enterprise'. The MSC prospered in an economic and social debate focused on 'how successful methods like lowering marginal tax rates and restricting the money supply would be in affecting cultural values formed over many years' (Weiner, 1980, p. 82). Sometime earlier Sir Keith Joseph, the man above all who inspired and advised the 'Iron Lady', argued that monetarism would not be enough (1976) and suggested ideas for freeing up both product and labour markets. Later Joseph (1978) was publicly to support social inequality because it acted as a major drive for material advance. Restructuring the social welfare system was to become the main object of Mrs Thatcher's third term, but working in tandem with these policy choices were the very keen and reconditioning forces of technological change and the fear of unemployment. The return of mass unemployment led Theo Nicholls (1986) to see that unemployment itself may change attitudes among those in employment: 'Those in employment are not an undifferentiated mass; they experience different opportunities, but whatever the Thatcherites think about how "unemployment works" those who are working are most likely to feel threatened by unemployment when it is their own jobs that are endangered' (p. 42). Hirsch (1978) argued that generally policy makers in capitalist countries faced even greater difficulties in economic management because of the depletion of what he called 'social morality'. Although the social allegiance to work and wealth creation constituted only one aspect of social morality, there was a possibility that those citizens denied a place in the process of wealth production might form alternative cultures. The MSC provided the state with a very strong arm of intervention, acting as a direct lever on the expectations and attitudes of Britain's workforce, employed and unemployed alike.

THE STATE, TRAINING AND MODERNIZATION

As long ago as 1963 Wellens had argued that Britain needed a 'training revolution from the shopfloor to the boardroom'. He called for 'a new culture, a new attitude and a new awareness', since the task ahead was none other than retraining the entire workforce. For the MSC a long-term objective, a matter of decades rather than years, was to shift attitudes to training and to elevate it on the political agenda. Advertising the significance of the proposed revolution, the MSC explained that 'manpower is the key resource, perhaps the country's most valuable asset and it should be in the forefront of the government, industry and company strategy, and not as a residual factor as so often happens at present' (MSC, 1976, p. 12). The document continued: 'The Commission's job is to make this clear in every possible way'. Leading the cause of training, the MSC certainly had prominent supporters. Sir Monty Finniston (1982), one of the country's leading industrialists, implored policy makers to realize that 'a country which is poor in natural wealth can only meet its needs when the skills and talents of its people translate ideas and concepts into products and services' (p. vii).

Critical to the training debate was whether resources channelled into training constituted investment in a commercial and economic sense. A major obstacle was the lack of a distinction between human capital and physical assets. Coates and Hilliard (1986), for example, confirmed and continued an unfortunate tradition by not differentiating between investment in physical assets and personnel. William Keegan (1985) stated that it was difficult to envisage how the contemporary investment shortage could be met if the economy was not stimulated in some way in the short run. He also argued that 'A lack of stimulation should not mean the postponement of a reconstruction of the capital stock in the longer run, which could only accelerate the problems of a "Britain without Oil" ' (p. 106). How human capital was to fit into the regeneration process was not clear. Pollard (1983) was convinced that critics of economic policy had not grasped the central idea that 'future prosperity depends upon providing sophisticated capital machinery for a workforce, not only highly skilled but trained to be forward looking and flexible' (p. 412). This recognition was not widely shared, however, for what distinguished British training policy from the history of other industrial countries, according to Sheldrake and Vickerstaff (1987), was an ambiguity by policy makers and corporate managers towards the contribution training could make to improved national economic performance and enhanced internal manpower management.

Vital to this state of affairs was the negative impact of economists and their thinking on the training issue. Where economists had a theory of human capital to elucidate the potential benefits of training, they largely forgot its application to manpower. Economists produced volumes on its relevance to education but, with few exceptions (e.g. Manley and McCormick, 1967; Lees and Chiplin, 1970), ignored its relevance for training. Most empirical studies confined themselves to the rate of return on university graduates. Hirsch (1978) summarized the new perspective on education that human capital theory provided as follows: 'The product of education was not limited to culture and humanism. Education in this approach produced investment in human beings with direct returns equivalent to those direct economic returns on investment in physical assets' (p. 48). Educational policy makers, however, continued to look at education mainly in terms of 'culture and humanism'. Although the 1964 Robbins Report on higher education began with 'instruction in skills. . . . We put this first, not because we regard it as the most important, but because we think that it is sometimes ignored or undervalued' (para 25). Similarly, the 1959 Crowther Report on 15–18-year-olds described them as 'the technicians and craftsmen of the future' (p. 34). Yet while it urged teachers to 'experiment' in the 'no man's land between school and work' (p. 197), the Report was chiefly instrumental in regularizing an examination system that only served to emphasize traditional, literary, academic skills. Newsom's was the other major report which instigated the expansion of education at nearly all levels that was to follow. Although concerned with the 'below average' ('the Browns and the Robinsons', as the Report called them), who were then considered to be wasting not only their own but the nation's resource, Newsom's main consequence was a belated raising of the school leaving age in 1971/72.

In fact, British training policy was anchored to social objectives. Roy Hattersley argued that Britain 'neither thinks, nor describes training as investment' (*The Observer* 25 September 1986). Sir Richard O'Brien, the second Chairman of the MSC, asserted that 'We in Britain have over the years consistently underinvested in human capital' (1982, p. 55). Even when the state did place resources in training the economic case was secondary. Colvin (1985) remarked: 'After training, the individual concerned faces the market again in an effort, it is hoped, to succeed in employing new skills. The question at issue is what return can be expected from the state-subsidised investment in human capital?' (p. 73). Crossley (1974) defined manpower policy as 'concerned with making public investments to maximise the present value of human capital embodied in the labour force' (p. 13). However, Colvin notes that British training and retraining policy was not seen in this light, because policy was based on social objectives, including improving the opportunities of disadvantaged individuals in the labour market. At best economists comprehended training in terms of the bottleneck simile. As expressed by Andrew, later Lord, Shonfield, this argued that 'again and again during the 1940s and 1950s and the 1960s British industrial rejuvenation came up against a series of bottlenecks caused by the shortage of skilled manpower' (1976, p. 118). Hugh Clegg, a leading expert in the field of industrial relations, maintained that the role of an active manpower policy was to 'ensure that new skill requirements were met and industrialists have the opportunity to meet the changing needs of the economy' (1971, p. 23). In this concept manpower policy was seen as a passive policy response, meeting the whims of industrial and technological change.

Thus the discussion of manpower issues was clouded and confused by the attachment of policy makers to physical forms of investment. Bacon and Eltis (1976) in their book *Britain's Economic Problem: Too Few Producers*, which was so well received by the Labour government of the day, suggested to the Chancellor, Denis Healey, that he should 'get more people in the factories', thereby assuming that labour was an easily malleable factor in production, ready to be moulded to any productive process. It is not surprising therefore to see industrial policy dominating manpower planning especially in the 1960s and 1970s.

Yet human capital theory suggested that resources invested in labour would produce positive rates of economic return. Economists, however, were too preoccupied with macro-economic issues. This overemphasis was in part a consequence of the

Keynesian revolution and resulted in what Professor Allen described as 'a partial understanding of the *modus operandi* of the modern economic system' (1978, p. 3). But the rise of monetarism only perpetuated the Cinderella status of training. There was no mention of training's contribution to economic growth in Friedman's analysis and, moreover, no reference to training reducing the so-called natural rate of unemployment. Friedman (1968) argued that there was a contribution to be made by improving labour mobility and reducing friction inside the labour market, within, naturally, a tight budgetary policy. Patrick Minford (1983) similarly dismissed training. The main thrust of his argument was that for labour markets to clear there would have to be lower wages and this would only come about through debilitating unionized relative to non-unionized labour. Other monetarist suggestions included adjustments to the benefit system forcing the unemployed to do community work, raising tax thresholds in order to remove the poverty and unemployment traps, raising council house rents and introducing a regional employment subsidy. In this comprehensive list, training was nowhere to be seen.

What is fascinating about the effect of the monetarist revolution on the training debate is the fact that economists put to one side the case for investment in labour power in making unemployed workers more employable. This was because, as Sanderson (1985) stated, the primary aim was to ensure that labour markets cleared. This, he said, 'has been the intention of job creation schemes and wage subsidies which have been targeted at young people'. In the short term 'These measures also reduced unemployment by postponing their entry into the labour market' (p. 212). The fact that programmes administered by the MSC cut wage rates, improved the employability of young people and in many ways postponed their entry to the labour market all contributed to a set of major hurdles against the promotion of training and retraining in Britain. Alan Walters, the chief economic adviser to Mrs Thatcher, explained that the main purpose of labour market measures introduced under her government was to put 'some downward pressure on real wages' and to ensure that policies worked with market forces rather than against them (1986, p. 183). A consequence of working with the market was that wage subsidies would kill off the regular labour market. This possibility led to the conclusion that youth training policies were short-term measures that would be dispensed with when the upturn of the economy materialized and cast aside the role of training in economic development. Tomlinson (1986) suggested that although MSC schemes 'may be seen partly as a form of cheap labour, they should predominantly be seen as ways of trying to reduce the numbers on the unemployment register' (p. 17). This link with unemployment bedevilled training policy but had its origins in the mass unemployment of the 1920s and 1930s. Managing the mass unemployment crisis was an extreme form of the social service provided by training. Hill (1981) agreed that the theme of social responsibility was inherent in manpower policy 'which need not be examined in terms of its contribution either to full employment or economic efficiency. It may be evaluated in terms of its contribution to the relief of the suffering experienced by the casualties of the economic system' (p. 57). In the 1970s these casualties were increasingly the unemployed, and the bond between training and unemployment symbolized manpower's social, as opposed to its economic, role.

The connection between unemployment and training had a long history well before the MSC came on the scene. It had been suggested quite erroneously that the

Industrial Training Act of 1964 was designed with industrial modernization in mind, but it was in fact motivated by the fear of rising youth unemployment (Perry, 1976). Modern training policy may be traced back to the regional aid programmes of the inter-war years when training centres were established to keep the young unemployed off the streets. That the able-bodied poor be put to work lest the devil find other occupation for their idle hands was a constant theme from workhouse days. It was repeated more or less subtly in official reports ever since Victorian times. Beveridge (1909), for example, called for 'good and wholesome discipline for the un- and under-employed' (p. 233). These ideas materialized in the form of 200 Junior Instruction Centres situated in the depressed areas. Training in its latest incarnation thus took over where regional aid had left off. The halcyon days of British regional policy were coming to an end by the late 1960s and deep cuts in the funding of regional aid during the following decade focused attention on the alternative provided by the MSC.

Parsons' study (1984) of the political economy of regional policy argued that political expediency rather than economic efficiency was the prime mover in the development of regional policy. This political bent naturally spilled over into discussion of training, both academic and at the policy level. Sir John Hoskyns, a chief policy adviser to Mrs Thatcher, summarized the Tories' initial feelings about MSC schemes when he admitted there was no prospect of getting unemployment down to acceptable levels but the government had to be seen 'doing something'. This approach had all the hallmarks of crisis management. Moon and Richardson (1984) argued that MSC schemes have enabled governments, especially the Conservatives since 1979, 'to escape the accusation that nothing had been done for the unemployed' (p. 125). Moreover the disproportionate emphasis on the young, in Britain as in other industrial countries, attempted to contain concern about a 'lost generation'. The MSC took part in operations that removed the potential explosiveness of mass unemployment, so that Moon and Richardson concluded Britain had managed the unemployment crisis quite successfully and predicted that 'if social unrest on a significant scale is likely to occur then the political system is likely to respond with new schemes and new money' (p. 186). Such a process might incidentally create a better-trained and more efficient workforce.

The MSC's desire to create a new attitude towards training implied a complete restructuring of Britain's education and training systems. However, this ambitious plan was tempered by the knowledge that the training–unemployment link had to be broken. Few supported its ideas and the MSC attempted to manipulate the unemployment crisis in order to achieve its objectives. Hawkins (1978) saw the quango as 'an ambulance service for the unemployed' (p. 116). Moon (1983) similarly perceived it as a 'holding mechanism', constraining expectations and controlling social unrest, enabling socialist and Conservative governments alike to pursue politically sensitive and economically painful industrial and social strategies. Managing the unemployment problem was the responsibility of ever-expanding, ever-changing and ever-proliferating Special Employment Measures. The MSC, said Sinfield (1981), was not diverted but subverted by unemployment. Benn and Fairley (1986) agreed with him:

Labour governments from 1974 to 1979, thrown off any Socialist course by successive crises, alternated between using the MSC as a training agency, and using it to cover unemployment. The MSC's change in role began during this period of Labour's embarrassment at rising unemployment when the MSC palliatives were a cheap way of concealing reality. . . . Conservatives had no such embarrassment or hesitation when they decided to keep the MSC in 1981. They used it single-mindedly in the service of Monetarism (p. 3).

Clearly, the Conservatives, like the Labour government before them, had little idea about the role of training in Britain's economic development. However, this version of events argued that the MSC was only sustained by the wicked Tories to establish schemes for the unemployed. Benn and Fairley accepted that the MSC did not actually create mass unemployment. This was a consequence of the internal contradictions of international capitalism. The moral of the tale was that if only the MSC could be recaptured by a reforming Labour government it could again fulfil its true purpose of allocating and training manpower for the socialist reconstruction of the capitalist order.

What was certain was that the training issue was highly political in nature and if it were to be removed from the predominant concerns of unemployment the MSC had to build a consensus of opinion that highlighted the economic case for investment in human capital. The state had to transform its understanding of human capital if the economy was to regenerate. Reich (1983) argued that

the only way industrialized nations can increase living standards in the future is to . . . keep world leadership in new industries based on advanced technologies. Japan understands this future. So to a lesser extent do West Germany and France. . . . Governments and businessmen in these countries are therefore racing to gain sophistication in these new sectors and to prepare their labour forces – their stores of human capital – to participate in them' (p. 231).

The whole effort of the MSC was quite simply to make Britain and her government and industry understand this futurology.

RE-EVALUATING THE TRAINING PROBLEM

If the task of the MSC was to explain the importance of human capital to the process of economic development it had to rid the training issue of certain myths and shibboleths. The MSC began the long haul of dissociating training from unemployment, but it was unable to disengage training from the obsession public policy had with the so-called 'skill shortage' problem. Unfortunately the definition of the 'training problem' did untold harm to the conduct of post-war training policy. Policy makers all too often confined the 'training problem' to the number of shortages reported by firms and the number of skilled vacancies at job centres. This definition of the problem forestalled a wider evaluation of Britain's training malaise.

As has been seen, the 'politics' of managing mass unemployment rather than the 'economics' of human capital was the crucial input into the post-war debate on vocational education and training (VET). The objectives of training policy throughout the lifetime of the MSC were often confused and muddled, to such an extent that even when a policy was genuinely designed to improve national economic development, most measures were seen by the training community and society at large as unemployment palliatives. In part, the answer to the confusion generated rested on the failure of policy makers to be explicit about how investment in VET affected the economy. Essentially policy makers did not distinguish between three types of initiative: reforms designed to raise the rate of productivity growth by upgrading the nation's stock of skills; reforms improving the inflation/unemployment trade-off through reducing short-term skill shortages; and reforms providing a more equitable distribution of job opportunities by means of job creation for the long-term unemployed. In practice VET initiatives by the MSC were simply lumped together under the political panacea of 'training'. Thus, the effects of directing resources to vocational education and training to the productive potential of the economy became horribly blurred. However, when statistical analysis of the state's investment programme in VET indicated that it had at last reached international standards during the mid-1980s (MSC, 1985a), no one was in any doubt that the prime mover had been mass unemployment.

An important insight into the state's failure to devote adequate resources before the mid-1980s was the fact that there was little hard economic evidence connecting investment in training with national economic development. For example, the Training Services Agency (1973) argued that there seemed no apparent reason for the state to invest in training for young people despite the fact that such an investment would raise the 'whole potential of the workforce' (p. 14). The TSA concluded that it was less easy to demonstrate the economic case in readily identifiable ways because the failure to provide vocational preparation does not immediately result in shortages of workers lacking clearly defined 'packages of skills'.

From the outset, then, the MSC was put on the defensive. It appeared that from the view of economic efficiency, state action was only valid where shortages of precisely defined packages of skills could be detected. Hence the commitment of public resources for a comprehensive youth training programme had to be argued initially on the grounds of social justice (i.e. asking the state to spend as much on young people in employment as on the academic élite in further and higher education), and later on the basis of the more dangerous political issue of the collapse of the youth labour market. However, the emphasis on skill shortages was the main parameter guiding the training debate even before the MSC's creation. British policy throughout the post-war decades was obsessed with identifying skill shortages and attempting to eradicate them.

By looking at the training issue as a problem of skill shortages within a market context, the policy response was to be judged successful if the quantity of training undertaken in the labour market was increased. It never occurred to British policy makers that the training problem within British industry was more deep rooted, and as much a problem of the attitudes of British management as a question of the cost of training. Unwittingly, by thinking about the training problem as primarily an external labour market issue, policy makers assumed that intervention was supplementing the training effort of employers, whereas in fact state intervention bolstered industry's arrogant and ignorant attitude towards manpower. Put bluntly, the training problem was like an apple rotten to the core and the effect of such market-orientated thinking was to cause the MSC and successive governments to misjudge the nature of the intervention required and degree of state investment needed.

It is not, however, very difficult to explain the reasons why British policy makers in the 1960s and 1970s saw the training problem as a market issue. On the one hand, the market concept is central to mainstream economics. On the other hand, the types of economic problem which economists have attempted to solve have also been an important factor. The failure of economists to get to the root of the training problem reflects the profession's deep concern with providing answers to the twin evils of creeping inflation and rising unemployment, or what has been commonly called stagflation. Short-term skill shortages had an important role in economists' assessment of the causes and cures of stagflation. Skill shortages, so the argument went, would in the immediate term cause employers to bid up wages in order to attract skilled workers, which in turn would increase the likelihood of wage inflation; in the long run British goods would be more expensive, sales would fall and reduced production and more unemployment would follow. Alternatively, in a non-inflationary environment skill shortages create bottlenecks in the economy that result in lost orders, lost production and eventually industrial layoffs. Either way the economy suffers.

Thus for labour economists it was essential to remove these structural rigidities in the economic system, so that the labour market could function more efficiently. Regulation or direct provision of training by the state could therefore, in a period of stagflation, reduce short-term skill shortages and improve the inflation/unemployment trade-off. Moreover, during the down-phase of the business cycle state training programmes could improve the nation's 'stock of skills' in readiness for the upturn in the economy, and job creation policies could help the long-term unemployed by redistributing the existing opportunities in the labour market. In sum, state-administered programmes would ensure that the labour market cleared. An effective labour market policy would therefore reduce the 'mismatch' of skills in the labour market and improve the 'employability' of the jobless through better training and retraining.

From this perspective the solution to industry's skill shortages was a matter of tailoring state training and retraining programmes to the needs of industry. However, from this perspective little or no attention was given to the question of raising the quantity of training and improving manpower planning at the level of the firm. Moreover, an active labour market policy presumed that industry was training sufficiently to meet its own needs.

To determine the responsibilities for training at the level of the firm policy makers applied human capital theory to explain why short-term skill shortages arose and analyse the best forms of intervention to cure the problem. Granted, human capital theorists began by analysing the reasons why a firm did not train, but the solution they proposed emphasized increasing the total supply of skilled labour within the labour market and not specifically improving the internal manpower practices of each firm.

The basic Becker (1964) model argued that the responsibility for the provision of specific skills to the firm rested with the employer. Responsibility for the cost of general skills that were transferable within an industry were to be shared between the employer and the individual. Theoretically the employer would pay a wage that equated the level of output the employee achieved whilst training and the individual would pay the remaining training costs. Under conditions of perfect competition Manley and McCormick (1967) and Lees and Chiplin (1970) argued that state intervention was not necessary as each firm would supply its own manpower needs. This model, as Jones (1988) notes, allowed no room for poachers since firms providing general training would not incur any net costs during the training period. Market failure in the generation of general skills could occur, however, as a consequence of the fact that individual workers could not always raise the necessary finance to invest in general skills training, or did not have the inclination to do so. Equally important to market failure was the fact that it might be difficult for an individual to judge the type of general training to undertake because of imperfect information of the labour market.

Clearly the appropriate policy response was to improve the workings of the capital market (Hartley, 1977) and inculcate a risk-taking culture within individuals to invest in training. If an additional role existed for the state then it was limited to providing more information about occupational training and in deciding whether the finance of loans for training should come from the private or public sector.

However, there were other grounds to support state intervention. For smaller firms and medium-sized industrial concerns, the short-run costs of investing in specific skills could be prohibitive with the further implication that the cost of investment in general skills would be even greater. The alternative for small and medium-size enterprises to training to meet their own needs was to increase marginal wage rates and poach skilled labour from the market. Supporters of the levy-grant system (Hughes, 1973) argued that poaching was not only 'unfair' but likely in the long run to prove self-defeating since the providers of training would eventually cease to do so. However, supporters of the levy-grant system did not specify why poaching 'should have inhibited training for general skills not only in Britain but also in any other countries with employer-based systems' (Jones, 1988, p. 58).

In the short term, to circumvent poaching in the labour market the appropriate response by each employer would have been to stop recently trained workers leaving the firm that sponsored them by imposing a legal requirement for the trainee to remain for a given period. More generally, to make investment in specific and non-specific training more attractive for small and medium-sized firms the policy response should have been to reduce rather than redistribute the cost of training. On the one hand firms could have been encouraged to pool training resources and collaborate with other local firms. On the other hand, specific grants to individual firms and methods of reducing the cost of employing a trainee could have been undertaken, either by lowering employers' national insurance contributions, or by devising schemes to reduce the wages of young trainees. Equally, tax incentives could have been applied to help all firms, irrespective of their size, to take an interest in training.

In the event policy makers from the 1960s onwards plumped for a system that redistributed the costs of training throughout industry via the levy-grant mechanism. What proponents of the levy-grant system failed to do, however, was to 'provide any alternative perspective on Britain's failure to train' (Jones, 1988, p. 58). In short, whilst, for example, Japanese and West German employers focused on the relationship between manpower planning, training, company profitability and corporate growth, British policy makers, in a response to persistent skill shortages, attempted to raise the quantity of training in the labour market rather than increasing the opportunities for each enterprise to train to meet its own needs. Policy makers forgot that the best institution to solve the short-term skill shortage problem and raise the skill level of each enterprise was not an intricate administrative device but the firm itself.

Between 1964 and 1982 the training tax under the Industrial Training Board system provided a regulatory approach to skill training. Effectively the system was built on a national legislative framework but control remained with industry. The Industrial Training Act 1964 placed a levy on all firms within a given industrial sector. If a firm trained well then it received the bulk of the levy back in grant and if it trained above its needs then it received the levy paid in by firms that did not train. Between 1971 and 1972 it was found that the bulk of the levy, from most of the 23 ITBs that had been established, was being channelled back to the same firms that had been charged the training tax. Though this was the main reason behind the reform of the 1964 Industrial Training Act, it should not have surprised policy makers since the levy did not place any incentives for managers to change their attitudes towards training and re-evaluate their practice, but simply to underwrite the levy as a cost of production.

However, the 1973 Employment and Training Act introduced a levy grant exemption scheme whereby, if a firm had historically trained to meet its skill needs, it would be exempt from the training tax. A further weakening of the system came about under the 1982 Employment and Training Act, which removed the statutory status of all but seven of the ITBs. The government's approach was that if each industry wanted an ITB (with or without a levy scheme), employers would have to agree voluntarily to keep a training board. In the event many folded. Now the government is preparing the complete abolition of the statutory system. Its reason is that once again the preponderance of the levy is being paid back in the form of grant to the same companies. What the government fails to appreciate is that if the policing role of the levy grant exemption apparatus is removed, training by industry collapses, especially in a cyclical recession. In other words the current Conservative government has misread what is the mark of the ITBs' success, namely the fact that the levy grant exemption system keeps employers on their toes.

Yet the focus upon raising the total quantity of skilled manpower as a means of solving the short-term skill shortage problem implied a much wider role for state intervention. As Metcalf (1987) argued, there was a social role for state intervention on the grounds that society would be giving up nothing while an unemployed worker was getting trained or retrained. Equally, there was a state role to re-equip and retrain workers in a period of structural change. Yet all these proposals to increase the stock of skills in the economy were outside the specific needs of employers and geared more or less to what policy makers thought employers wanted to find in applicants when applying for existing jobs.

Obviously the social role of training was important, but the concept of state provision could only work in an environment where employers themselves believed in training and respected state provision. The return of high unemployment levels in the 1970s and 1980s resulted in the growing politicization of manpower policy with the consequence that employers saw state provision as outside their needs. Policy makers in Britain failed to take on board the effect of mass state provision on the attitudes of employers. The evil of mass unemployment and the use of training to manage it created a high degree of scepticism from employers about the value and relevance of state-administered training programmes. This unconscious effect of the massive injection of public money illustrated how the actions of the state adversely altered the attitudes of industry on this vital economic issue. On the other hand, the attitudes of employers also influenced policy makers and their perceptions of the training problem. For example, employers often blamed the state, as in the case of the education and training of young people, for Britain's poor training performance. The interaction between state and industry is therefore fundamental to understanding Britain's so-called training problem. For instance, if within industry a positive affinity to training was already in place then state-funded training facilities would have been seen to be complementary to the training effort of employers and therefore important in meeting short-term skill shortages in industry. In addition, employers who took the training and retraining of their own workforces seriously would recognize the value of, rather than despising, state job creation programmes and the provision of skill centres for the long-term unemployed, in order to increase the stock of skills in the economy. Yet, without a strong commitment to training, state action has been seen as peripheral by employers to their needs and in many ways as a social service for the unemployed.

If it could be argued that the state was at last fulfilling its role in investing in VET comparable to Britain's international competitors by the time of the MSC's abolition, research indicated that industry's problem remained largely unsolved. How could chronic skill shortages persist in an age of mass unemployment, the critics of the quango asked? Certainly this was the greatest indictment of the fifteen year history of the Manpower Services Commission. The extent of the training problem within industry was made clear to the MSC by the publication of two surveys. In 1984 the Industrial Society published a pioneering if somewhat crude survey of employer expenditure on training. It estimated that British firms spent less than 1 per cent of sales on the training and retraining of their workforce. Shortly afterwards, *Competence and Competition* (MSC, 1985a) stated that in West Germany and the USA employers spent 3 per cent and in Japan the figure averaged 5 per cent. This proved that an international skills gap existed between what employers in other countries spent on training and what British firms paid out.

More information on the state of training in industry came in an MSC-sponsored survey conducted in 1984 by accountants Coopers and Lybrand. They found that on the whole employers in Britain treated training as a cost of production and not as an investment in the wellbeing of their enterprises. The authors of *A Challenge to Complacency* (MSC, 1986) also argued that Britain's employers should treat training as an investment that would have a recognizable income stream comparable to any other investment. Yet even this would represent only a first step in radically challenging the attitudes of employers, so that they would end their 'almost fanatical concern for their machinery and equipment' (Robinson, 1985).

Indubitably historical factors influenced the decision of employers to invest in training, including the attitudes of Britain's unions and the low levels of company profitability in the 1970s. Britain's training problem was indeed compounded by the attitudes of the nation's trades unions. Hall and Miller (1975) argued that 'irrespective of the definition of skill in terms of human capital, the determination of skill was in the hands of those groups that held power in society' (p. 3). In particular, they were alluding to the power of the craft unions, which controlled the supply of skilled labour at the workplace through the apprenticeship system.

In addition to the control of labour, this outdated form of training conferred other powers such as union demarcation, duration of training and wage remuneration between the skilled and the unskilled, as well as holding back training practice in other areas. Wellens (1963) complained bitterly that the apprenticeship system adversely affected training: 'However unsatisfactory the arrangements for "initial training", our arrangements for "promotional" training and "retraining" of established workers are far more defective' (p. 20). Wellens argued that the apprenticeship system simply divided young workers into two camps: those who received training and those who did not. The fear that the craft unions might be swamped was the paramount consideration in the minds of their leaders throughout the 1960s and 1970s. In reality, the system was an anachronism with more to do with job preservation than industrial efficiency. Lord Shonfield (1976) claimed that these attitudes reflected 'an outdated ideology based on circumstances when jobs were scarce and cheap labour plentiful' (p. 118). Perry (1976) concurred, adding that the 'attitude of the British Trade Union movement was ambiguous . . . Recognition of the need for reform of the apprenticeship system was marked by the traumatic and deeply ingrained experience of mass unemployment' (p. 167).

The level of company profitability has also been important in shaping the minds of employers. Benn and Fairley's (1986) accusation that 'despite billions of pounds poured into their pockets, many employers are no more capable of investing in new skills in their workforce than . . . investing in old or new technology' (p. 19) needs Aldcroft's (1982) qualification that 'it has been a favourite pastime . . . to castigate managers, to regard them as the villain in the piece, becoming the convenient scapegoat when things go wrong, or wicked Capitalists when profits are too high' (p. 52). However, after a sustained period of economic growth between 1983 and 1989 many critics assumed that employers would spend more on training.

For employers the rate of return on resources invested in training was critical. Page (1967) admitted that 'Unfortunately in the long run there is not always a clear cut pay-off . . . and (training) makes a less attractive form of investment than most to the businessmen' (p. 17). Similarly, Robinson (1985) echoed these sentiments, conceding that managers saw training as 'a greater financial risk than other options for investment of an organisation's scarce resources' (p. 20). A partial explanation of the lack of financial systems to measure the rate of return on human capital is that those advising corporate managers and entrepreneurs — managerial economists, personnel managers and above all accountants — have neglected the relationship between manpower planning and corporate growth. Bridge (1978) has argued that manpower planning at the level of the enterprise has been secondary to financial control. Indeed, in most corporate planning and personnel management courses manpower planning was hardly touched upon and, whilst accountants readily treated plant and machinery as assets, they did not treat a firm's workforce in the same light.

Nevertheless, the lack of an adequate means to show the rate of return on human capital is a far from convincing explanation of why overseas employers train and Britain's employers do not, since it begs the question as to whether employers in other countries find it as difficult to quantify profits from investment in training as they evidently do in Britain. It could be the case, however, that German and Japanese employers mirror their own governments' intuitive grasp of the role of investment in training and manpower planning. Kaufman (1986) was indeed correct in stating that the skill shortage problem was created by 'the general lack of a training tradition in Britain and the unwillingness of most companies to spend money on it' (p. 143); but, as Hawkins (1976) argued, 'it would be naive to regard the easing of skill shortages in terms of providing more government facilities. The root of the problem lies in the casual attitude of managements' use of resources' (p. 127). Fundamentally employers had to change their attitude to training from the boardroom to the shop floor and it was the role of the MSC to devise policies to attack this cancer upon industry.

The MSC had to ensure that human capital had an equal footing with physical forms of capital in industry and commerce. Rather than persuade employers to keep to a cautious and essentially empirical view of the benefits of training, the MSC should have been in the vanguard of obtaining an acceptance by industry of the intuitive claim of training's relevance to company profitability, productivity and corporate growth as adhered to by Britain's premier competitors. Some employers were beginning to become more forward-looking in this respect; one company manager explained, 'We are now in a position where training is a central part of our culture. We don't have to quantify it. It is essential' (*Training in Focus*, February 1988). Yet evidence of such a general shift in employer attitudes was scant and on the whole the MSC failed miserably in devising a training strategy that attempted to change the behaviour of industry.

Of course, the attitude of government was also important in shaping the behaviour of industry. Finegold and Soskice (1988) argue that the relationship between investment in VET and national economic development is as much a self-evident economic truth as a matter for empirical measurement; either government believed in the connection or it did not. At the very least British experience suggests that if past governments were aware of the connection between VET and national economic performance they were not committed to the same extent as the Japanese and the West Germans. It is reasonable to ask why British policy makers had taken so long to analyse this commitment that guided so much of the thinking of the Japanese and the Germans. The answer was that policy makers at the MSC and elsewhere were simultaneously too busy dealing with other, more pressing problems, most notably unemployment, and on the whole viewed the training problem from the competely different intellectual perspective of 'crisis management' and 'labour market efficiency'.

If policy makers are to learn from the MSC's failures then they must 'be prepared to put public expenditure into supporting within-enterprise training rather than training for the market, a shift foreshadowed in the MSC's NTI but without much apparent subsequent impact on policy' (Jones, 1988, p. 80). Future policy must directly bear on attitudes and at the same time reduce the cost of training to individual firms. In an endeavour to improve the stock of skills within the firm, future public policy should bear in mind the size of enterprises, the type of training undertaken and the appropriate financial incentives relating to the particular training under discussion. A two-tier policy between small and large firms thus needs to be developed. Hence for large firms training for specific skills, policy makers need to extend the levy grant exemption system and re-establish a wider network of ITBs. The levy grant exemption system should be limited in scope to the finance of training for strategic skills specific to the firm.

In order to raise the general standard of training within small and large firms and to finance the retraining of the whole workforce in a period of structural change, the system needs to be supplemented by other policies that will change the attitudes of employers to training. A guiding principle is that new policies should work with the trends of profitability and enterprise and not against them. Therefore to supplement the statutory system a generous but limited tax incentive should be made available. In this way a firm will not be coerced into training without a commitment to it by managers who see the investment in training as in their own self-interest. Policy makers should also encourage major enterprises to change the current wage/profit sharing principle that is taking hold in industry and encourage the provision of a wage/profit/retraining package, especially during a period of major internal restructuring. Also, since it has been found that 'trainee' costs in Britain are substantially higher than in other countries, government should also consider reducing the employer national insurance surcharge to reduce the total cost of retraining for established workers. All these measures should be backed up by an extensive consultancy service in a much expanded Business Growth Training Scheme. The setting up of Training Committees on similar lines to those of Health and Safety Committees should also be recommended.

To conclude, there is a battery of alternatives on offer to the failed *laisser-faire* approach to skills training of the current government and the old-style training tax that is supported by opposition parties. The alternatives are also compatible with Finegold and Soskice's (1988) general conclusion that 'rather than incentives being used to increase the amount of training as such, they can more effectively be used to increase a company's training capacity by giving companies an incentive to train and produce a stake in training as a company activity' (p. 50). Nevertheless, given the magnitude of the existing problem within industry, a move over to a German type of dual system is perhaps the best possible solution to Britain's training dilemma. In some respects this would be going against the current trend in the development of VET systems in other countries. Policy makers in Japan, the USA and Sweden all acknowledge that 16–19-year-olds should be encouraged to stay on, either in full-time or part-time further education, or receive training off and on the job whilst in employment. The staying-on rate for these countries is on average over 75 per cent, whereas in Britain the figure has only just crept over 50 per cent for the first time in 1988/9. The key difference in Japan, the USA and Sweden is that employers actively support the objective of restricting the entry of young people onto the labour market. Moreover, since employers train effectively for their own workforces and have a pro-training culture in place they are not too worried about the types of institution that provide VET. There is no bias against state provision of training as there is in Britain.

In contrast, provision for 16–19-year-olds in West Germany is employer based with 90 per cent of the cost of youth training paid for by employers. This employer-led model indicates quite strikingly that employer commitment to young workers is the basis for employers' willingness to pay for training and retraining of established workers. Consequently employers use the dual system as the backbone of their internal manpower strategies for the workforce as a whole. In many ways there is a strong case that YTS in Britain should be used as a Trojan horse in the state's endeavour to come to grips once and for all with British employers' reluctance to train.

What is certain, however, is that Britain lacks a credible training strategy at the level of the firm. If the Trojan horse approach is not undertaken then TECs require a fresh focus for their policies. The management of the national training budget is not their primary priority. The first priority is to get those they represent to pay more for training. It is quite apparent that a conflict of interest exists in the TEC model. For, as Frank Coffield (1989) remarks, 'To entrust the future of training in this country to a group whose commitment, goodwill and track record in this field are an international joke shows the triumph of political preferment over experience.' Therefore policy makers need to think again about bringing back a national training authority based on the 'partnership' approach so that training does not once again become the Cinderella of British economic policy.

GOVERNMENT BY QUANGO

The MSC had a direct influence upon the future management of the Civil Service. Generally the favourable impression the MSC made on Tory ministers reflected their desire to systematically hive-off wholesale sections of the state machine. The relation of the MSC to the DE foreshadowed the recommendations of the Ibbs Report for the hiving-off of Civil Service departments into a host of new agencies which was proposed by the 1987 Thatcher government. Just as the government trimmed the size of the MSC in 1979 and did not allow it to expand in line with the extension of its programmes, so the Civil Service staff level as a whole has been reduced by 139,000 since 1979 and stood at 593,000 in 1988, the lowest figure for decades. The further reductions which the government intends, and the autonomous operation and eventual privatization of the parts of the whole state bureaucracy which it proposes, will not therefore necessarily reduce central state control. If the precedent set by the MSC is followed, it can be expected that control by the centre will be increased. In fact, power will be concentrated within a new and smaller élite.

This is 'a government and above all a Prime Minister, that now believes it can break any convention, dispatch any sacred cow to the abattoir, with absolute impunity', so that 'change and reform have now become ends in themselves and the rhetoric of dynamism has become the touchstone of party purity', as Ben Pimlott wrote in the *New Statesman* (11 March 1988: 'Thatcherism in Its Maoist Phase'). According to the Ibbs Report, the relation of these independent Civil Service organizations to the government will be 'that heads of executive agencies would have delegated authority from their Minister for operations of the agencies within the framework of policy directives and resource allocations prescribed by Ministers' (quoted in *The Guardian* 29 February 1988). This revives the suggestions of the Fulton Committee and Heath's Businessman Team, which were critical in the original decision to establish the MSC (see p. 17).

A clear advantage of government by quango is that the government can retain firm control of policy development but distance itself from the detailed day-to-day management of programmes. Additionally, Civil Service bureaucracies can be expanded and disbanded 'to task', according to the exigencies that arise. If Job Centres can be shifted so easily from the Department of Employment to the MSC and back again, then why not despatch them to the DSS, or (more immediately likely) privatize those job placement functions that can be made profitable? The Department of Employment itself could then just as easily be disbanded, while the

Department of Energy may also privatize itself out of existence, once British Coal has followed gas, oil and electricity into the market place. This new flexibility of response has allowed government to by-pass and eradicate the remnants of Britain's corporatist and tri-partite past. The history of the MSC shows how initially a consensus of opinion and support from large interest groups, including local government, the TUC and CBI, was needed. Once it was established however the quango could afford to ignore these bodies and required only lip-service from them. The TUC's influence could then be further marginalized by reconstituting the MSC to increase employers' representation and finally to abolish the quango, leaving training back in the hands of industry.

Control by government was always powerful. As Ridley (1984) noted, the hiving-off process for the MSC 'has not made the organisation anything like as free in its procedures, as say the nationalised industries' (p. 62). Its parent Department of Employment always retained important responsibilities for controlling the expenditure of the MSC at a general level and formally sanctioned all MSC plans and policy documents. Not least, the MSC's resources emanated from the Treasury in the form of grant-in-aid via the Department of Employment. The Chairman of the MSC was thus the chief accounting officer and responsible directly to the Secretary of State for Employment. He was technically under the 'direction' of the Minister, though this power was not invoked save in the case of Tom King's instruction to a reluctant MSC to assume command of £200 million worth of non-advanced further education in 1984. Even then the DE denied that a directive had been issued (see pp. 89–90). In addition, the Minister had the authority to nominate the Chairman of the Commission for a three year term. This second power was very important in recent years, for a change of Chairman could, because of a distinctive personality and political outlook, alter the ethos and direction of what the MSC was attempting to achieve, or indeed, bring it into opposition to the government. Such a change, with concomitant changes in direction, occurred when Sir Richard O'Brien was replaced by David Young. Finally, the related nature of the DE's and MSC's work meant that civil servants at all levels interchanged considerably. Originally the Employment and Training Act stipulated that officials would be employed directly by the MSC but, under pressure from Civil Service unions, the then Secretary of State for Employment, Michael Foot, reinstated Civil Service status for all the MSC's employees. Thus, as Moon and Richardson (1984) recorded, 'Whilst the MSC has undoubtedly become the main vehicle for government policy in the field of unemployment and to a considerable degree has seized the initiative in this formulation of policy ideas the DE of course retains important powers and responsibilities' (p. 91).

The growth of the MSC was allowed by the 1973 Employment and Training Act, section 5 of which empowered the Minister temporarily to employ British citizens. However, the Act did not give specific responsibility to the MSC itself. On the contrary, the MSC had to prove to successive governments through its fire-fighting activities that it could manage the unemployment crisis. Ridley (1984) remarked on 'the uncharacteristic speed with which new ideas were taken up' (p. 60). Typically, traditional Civil Service practices of custom and seniority were ignored. As Sir Richard O'Brien recalled: 'Unlike other Whitehall departments, the MSC was a body where rapid promotion could take place and the civil servants responded to this fact' (interview, 23 June 1985). Most notably, the egregious Lord Young was helicoptered in from outside the system. The MSC pioneered the promotion of meritocratic former middle managers within Civil Service departments. They have largely replaced the old public school boys at the top of the Civil Service, as shown by the fact that twenty-four out of the twenty-seven Permanent Secretaries have resigned or retired since 1979.

Another reason for the MSC's apparent success in rapid scheme building was the way the quango could by-pass traditional policy making circles. The process was particularly marked in the major local government service, education. Here it has been seen how the MSC was used by the government to subvert the conventionally decentralized and shared processes of educational decision making in the interests of direct central control. Traditional notions of local representation and democratic accountability were thus devalued. Moreover, the formal democracy of consumer choice with which Thatcherism attempted to replace the old conventions of public life, antiquated and unsatisfactory as they were, reduced the real choice of the public, redefined as consumers. An example is the 'parent power', advanced as one justification of the 1988 Education Reform Act. This in fact masks an unprecedented concentration of central state power over the administration of schools and colleges, which had previously been shared with locally elected authorities.

The regional and local dimensions of MSC operations were critical to its growth. Very quickly the two sister bodies, the Scottish MSC and the Welsh MSC, had been established with responsibility divided between the Ministers for these areas and the Secretary of State for Employment. The corporate and tripartite model corresponded with the original MSC but each had a powerful regional and local delivery service. Regional offices of MSC divisions, here as elsewhere, supervised the sponsoring activities of the local offices. On the original Canadian model (p. 31), the local offices were responsible for finding the sponsors to carry out training and issued them with grants. In many localities large unemployment industries emerged where managing agents were set up outside industry, commerce or the public sector. Howells (1980) illustrated this powerful 'centre–periphery' relationship exhibited in MSC policy. Criteria for training standards and periodic inspections were internal to the MSC and hence local officers rewarded those managing agents who met MSC criteria and refused funding to those who failed to comply. Agents who caused the MSC head-aches were closed down since the power of funding was vested solely with the MSC and on a fixed-term basis. Many fine projects, especially in the voluntary sector, were wound up over the years owing to the changing criteria of MSC guidelines. Despite this, the centre–periphery model tapped the power of the locality, for without the commitment from within the locality, the crisis management measures would have faltered. To this extent the MSC was a 'multi-partite' body buying the goodwill of the local community. The powerful re-routing that the MSC could achieve was highly regarded by the government and because the MSC was the sole organization with spare financial resources (saved from savage pruning elsewhere), it could by-pass entrenched interests at the DES, in the LEAs and in local government generally.

'At one time,' wrote Byrne and Padfield in 1986,

> it was assumed that local goverment would be safe from excessive interference because ultimately central government depends on local government for the delivery of national environmental, economic and social services. This safeguard is now much less certain as central government's commitment to such service provision diminishes. Central govern-

ment does not need the cooperation and goodwill of local authorities to the same extent as before since it is no longer concerned about the delivery of rate services, and those programmes which the government does seek to protect or fashion may be passed into the hands of more pliant quangos such as the MSC (p. 223).

The conflict between a reduced but strengthened and more flexible core central state civil service in the shape of the MSC and the local state bureaucracy subject to local authority control has been recorded throughout this narration of the MSC's activities. It is particularly apparent in the selective targeting of central government resources through the ending of regional aid and its replacement by the Inner Cities Initiative led by Lord Young from his renamed Enterprise Department. Here again, the MSC was instrumental in undermining local government services that were already struggling against the effects of rate-capping and other cuts. The logical end of this process came when new quangos were set up to take over the running of services after the abolition of the GLC and Metropolitan Counties. The abolition of the MSC itself followed when it too had served the government's purpose.

The centre–periphery model encapsulated much of the new-right thinking on local government. The Tories increasingly saw each authority operating only as a holding company to act as a resource for financial control and the distribution of grants. In this new order there would be no role for locally elected bodies save as rubber-stamping machines. Duncan and Goodwin (1988) even predict that the final solution to what the government sees as 'the local government problem' is for it to impose regional administrative structures beyond the reach of any local democratic account-ability and control. The MSC was a forerunner of all this and hence it is quite correct for many to fear the anti-democratic tendencies of the MSC model. Notwithstanding that many local council services have come to depend upon the MSC as the only remaining source of funds and even, in the case of the education service generally, now look upon it as a saviour from the return to academic competition intended by the 1988 Education Reform Act, there remains a deeply held suspicion of the MSC within local government. Leisha Fullick (1986), a local councillor, reflected bitterly: 'The MSC has been a very effective means of maintaining the local labour market but it has played a key role in pursuing other objectives of the Thatcherite political project' (in Benn and Fairley p. 230). Moon and Richardson (1984) also recorded the feeling that the MSC acted without sensitivity to established local government practice and without taking due account of existing local expertise, 'notably its desire to bring solutions from outside without seeking change from within the existing system' (p. 114).

This sort of intrusion into other departments at both local and national level has aroused deepening resentment. There is a sense that collective democratic freedoms are being deliberately eroded in the name of individual market freedom. Trevor Smith (1986) commented that

No one would deny the need to do everything possible to develop policies and programmes designed to improve the prospects of the unemployed to find work but a genuine concern for them should not blind us to the need to subject the MSC and its agencies to a reasonable degree of scrutiny (p. 52).

However, as Heald (1984) argued, 'the purpose behind the establishment of the MSC was to move away from cautious Civil Service style administration towards more innovative management' and thus there has been a willingness at the MSC 'to cut corners' (p. 171). One function of the MSC has been to reward agencies that fit the Thatcherites' thinking and impose sanctions by withdrawing funding to those that do not. The MSC set the example for 'privatizing' the education system and was instrumental in pioneering the restructuring of the Civil Service. Privatization of training was to be extended into hiving-off the schools, hospitals and entire sections of the Civil Service.

The Thatcher model of government combines the politics of Hobbes at the authoritarian centre with the libertarianism of Adam Smith in the economy. This central state intervention has been accomplished not merely by legislative means under central government direction but by the semi-independent activities of government departments. In pursuit of these ends the MSC proves once again that 'necessity breeds invention' but, more importantly perhaps, it bears witness to the fact that economic freedom in a highly competitive international environment is mutually incompatible with traditional forms of consensual democracy. Economic advance has its democratic price.

SUMMARY

This book has chronicled the historical development of the MSC and traced the far-reaching influences of its ideas and policies. The MSC aimed to integrate mental and manual labour in a new system of vocational education. It raised the issue of training in relation to the demands of new technology for a modernized economy. The MSC sharpened the focus on a fundamental choice within British political, economic and social life – if Britain wanted to remain a prominent economic power and a major player in the world economy, then it not only had to have a highly skilled workforce but also a highly motivated one. However, it has been difficult to realize this vision in practice. The New Training Initiative was never comprehensive: it never applied, as was intended, to the employed as well as the unemployed and to those who remained in schools and colleges as well as to school leavers. In fact it became solely for unemployed school leavers. Nor did industry take the MSC's advocacy of training seriously enough ever to pay for either the YTS after school or the TVEI within schools, as was also the intention. In general, the MSC's training tended to narrow the range of skills of its trainees to the performance of itemized competencies in isolated and subdivided tasks. It did not aim at comprehensive theoretical understanding of whole systems within which to integrate their associated practical skills. In addition, the adult strategy became divorced from youth training.

All this was hardly surprising for, as has been seen, British industry had for long considered the training problem illusory. On the one hand, employers did not invest in training even when they invested in physical plant and machinery within the country rather than engaged in financial speculation abroad. On the other, unions feared the consequences of new technology applied so as to de-skill their members and they therefore stubbornly retained defensive demarcations between obsolete trades together with anachronistic apprenticeships to them. Further, the education system contributed to this rigid division of labour. Its latest reversion to type through the 1988 Education Reform Act merely swings it back towards a narrow academicism on the old grammar school model after a decade and more in pursuit of an equally narrow 'work-relevant' practicalism. Economic policy makers also had a wholly negative effect on training initiatives because they were more concerned with physical than human capital. Above all, government has manipulated the MSC for its own purposes. Labour diverted the quango into mopping up unemployment. The Conservatives continued this but also tied the MSC to popularizing enterprise culture, subverting local authorities, undermining trades unions and quangoizing the Civil Service. The MSC was thus forced to take a more active role than it ever intended in directly combating unemployment through programmes which it attempted to infuse with a training element, rather than through its original goal of comprehensive manpower planning to sustain full employment.

And yet the MSC broke the bond between unemployment and training, in theory if not in practice. It connected, in the minds of policy makers at least, training with wealth creation. Economic modernization in terms of the Thatcher government is about the pursuit of wealth creation for its own sake – surplus value to produce more surplus value. The market system is ethically and economically self-perpetuating, where alternative models of economic regeneration pursued wealth creation not for its own sake but for the sake of wealth redistribution. Before Thatcher politics had been about the distribution of wealth. Now, even though many still consider wealth creation a dirty phrase, it emerges as the unspoken principle underpinning much of contemporary economic and social debate.

In this sense, Mrs Thatcher's governments have been a cultural rather than an economic experiment and in this respect she has indeed changed the British soul. Yet, ironically, contemporary Britain has many parallels with other disastrous cultural revolutions. 'In the Soviet Union, Mao observed, the Bolsheviks had taken power, eliminated their enemies, extended their hold over the country, and placed the means of production under state control. Yet Stalin had neglected to transform the Russian "soul" ' (Karnow, 1984, p. 10). Mrs Thatcher had aggravated mass unemployment, wasted North Sea oil, freed markets, allowed competition and privatization and partially dismantled the Welfare State in a successful attempt to transform the British 'soul' at the cost of deindustrializing the economy. Britain now has the motivation, energy and drive, but no longer the tools for the job of economic modernization. The MSC played no small part in this process of transforming industrial society.

Bibliography

Ainley, P. (1988) *From School to YTS. Education and Training in England and Wales 1944–1987*. Milton Keynes: Open University Press.

Aldcroft, D. (1982) 'Britain's economic decline'. In Roderick, G. and Stevens, M. (eds) *The British Malaise*. Falmer: Brighton.

Allen, G. (1978) *British Industry and Economic Policy*. London: Macmillan.

Anderson, M. and Fairley, J. (eds) (1982) *The Politics of Industrial Training*. Conference papers. Edinburgh: University Centre for European Governmental Studies.

Ashton, D. (1986) *Unemployment under Capitalism*. Brighton: Falmer.

Atkins, P. (1986) 'MSC, TVEI and education in perspective'. *Political Quarterly*, **Summer**.

Bacon, R. and Eltis, W. (1976) *Britain's Economic Problem: Too Few Producers*. London: Macmillan.

Bain, G. (ed) (1983) *Industrial Relations in Britain*. Oxford: Blackwell.

Ball, L. (1989) 'What future YTS?' *Unemployment Bulletin*, Summer 1989.

Barnes, D. (1976) 'The reorganisation of manpower services'. *British Labour Review*, **January/February**.

Barnett, C. (1979) 'Technology, education and industrial and economic strength'. *Journal of the Royal Society of Arts*. **February**.

Barnett, J. (1982) *Inside the Treasury*. London: Deutsch.

Barton, L. and Walker, S. (eds) *Youth Unemployment and Schooling*. Milton Keynes: Open University Press.

Becker, G. (1964) *Human Capital*. New York: Columbia Press.

Benn, C. and Fairley, J. (eds) (1986) *Challenging the MSC on Jobs, Training and Education*. London: Pluto.

Berg, I. (1971) *Education and Jobs: The Great Training Robbery*. Boston, MA: Beacon Press.

Beveridge, W. (1909) *Unemployment: A Problem of Industry*. London: Longmans.

Birmingham Trades Council Union Resource Centre (1984) 'The Great Training Robbery. An interim report on the role of private agencies within the Youth Training Scheme in the Birmingham and Solihull Area'.

Birmingham Trades Council Union Resource Centre (1987) 'National labour movement inquiry into youth unemployment and training'.

Bosanquet, N. (1983) *After the New Right*. London: Gower.

Bridge, J. *Economics in Personnel Management*. London: Institute of Personnel Management.

Brittan, S. (1977) *The Economic Consequences of Democracy*. London: Temple Smith.

Broadfoot, P. (ed) (1984) *Selection, Certification and Control: Social Issues in Educational Assessment*. Brighton: Falmer.

Byrne, T. and Padfield, C. (1986) *Social Services Made Simple*. London: Allen.

Central Policy Review Staff (1980) *Education, Training and Industrial Performance*. London: HMSO.

Chitty, C. and Lawton, D. (1988) 'The national curriculum'. *Bedford Way Paper* No. 33.

Institute of Education, London University.

Chitty, C. and Worgan, J. (1987) 'TVEI: origins and transformation'. In Chitty, C. (ed) *Aspects of Vocationalism*. Occasional paper. Post-16 Educational Centre.

Clegg, H. (1971) *How to Run an Incomes Policy and How We Made Such a Mess of the Last One*. London: Heinemann.

Coates, D. (1980) *Labour in Power. A Study of the Labour Government 1974–1979*. London: Longman.

Coates, D. and Hilliard, J. (eds) (1986) *The Economic Revival of Modern Britain: The Debate Between Left and Right*. London: Elgar.

Coates, K. and Topham, T. (1986) *Trades Unions and Politics*. Oxford: Blackwell.

Cockburn, C. (1987) *Two Track Training: Sex Inequalities and the Youth Training Scheme*. London: Macmillan.

Coffield, F. (1989) 'Hunting the heffalump: the rise of the enterprise movement (unpublished paper).

Collins, N. (1986) 'MSC and the education of young people', *Political Quarterly*, **Summer**.

Colvin, P. (1985) *The Economic Ideal in British Government. Calculating Costs and Benefits in the 1970s*. Manchester: Manchester University Press.

Commission for Racial Equality (1984) *Racial Equality and the Youth Training Scheme*, London: CRE.

Corney, M. (1988) 'The politics of training: a study of the Manpower Services Commission 1974–1987', *M. Phil. thesis*, London University.

Corney, M. (1989) 'The wrong option', *Training Tomorrow*, May 1989.

Cotgrove, S. (1958) *Technical Education and Social Change*. London: Allen & Unwin.

Crosland, S. (1982) *Tony Crosland*. London: Cape.

Crossley, J. (1970) 'Theory and methods of national manpower policy'. In Robertson, D. and Hunter, L. (eds). *Labour Market Issues in the 1970s*. Edinburgh: Oliver and Boyd.

Dahrendorf, R. (1984) *On Britain*. London: BBC publications.

Dale, R. (1983) 'You ain't seen nothing yet: the prospects for education'. In Wolpe, A. and Donald, J. (eds) *Is There Anyone There from Education? Education after Thatcher*. London: Pluto.

Dale, R. (1985) 'Examining the gift horse's teeth, a tentative analysis of TVEI'. In Barton, L. and Walker, J. (eds) *Youth Unemployment and Schooling*. Milton Keynes: Open University Press.

Danniel, W. (1975) *Whatever Happened to Workers in Woolwich?*. London: PEP.

DES (1959) *15 to 18 (The Crowther Report)*. London: HMSO.

DES (1963) *Half Our Future (The Newsom Report)*. London: HMSO.

DES (1963) *Higher Education (The Robbins Report)*. London: HMSO.

DES (1976) *A Framework for Expansion*. London: HMSO.

DES (1976) *Getting Ready for Work*. Conference Report. London: HMSO.

DES (1979) *16–18: Education and Training for 16 to 18 year olds, a consultative paper*. London: HMSO.

DES (1980) *Framework for the Curriculum*. London: HMSO.

DES (1985a) *Better Schools*. Cmnd. 9469. London: HMSO.

DES (1985b) *Education and Training for Young People*. Cmnd. 9482. London: HMSO.

DES (1986) *A New Choice of School*. London: HMSO.

DES (1987) *The National Curriculum 5–16*. London: HMSO.

Duncan, S. and Goodwin, M. (1988) *The Local State and Uneven Development: Behind the Local Government Crisis*. London: Polity Press.

Eversley, J. (1986) 'Trade union responses to the MSC'. In Benn, C. and Fairley, J. (eds) *Challenging the MSC on Jobs, Training and Education*. London: Pluto.

Fiddy, R. (ed.) (1983) *In Place of Work: Policy and Provision for the Young Unemployed*. Brighton: Falmer.

Finegold, D. and Soskice, D. (1988) 'The failure of training in Britain: analysis and prescription'. *Oxford Review of Economic Policy*, **4** (3).

Finn, D. (1982) 'Whose needs? Schooling and the "needs" of industry'. In Atkinson, P. and Rees, T. (eds) *Youth Unemployment and State Intervention*. London: Routledge.

Finn, D. (1986) 'YTS, the jewel in the MSC's crown?' In Benn, C. and Fairley, J. (eds) *Challenging the MSC on Jobs, Training and Education*. London: Pluto.

Finn, D. (1987) *Training without Jobs: New Deals and Broken Promises*. London: Macmillan.

Finn, D. and Markhall, G. (1981) *Young People and the Labour Market: A Case Study*. London: Department of the Environment.

Finniston, M. (1982) Foreword to Roderick, G. and Stevens, M. (eds). *The British Malaise*. Brighton: Falmer.

Foot, M. (1983) *Another Heart and Other Pulses*. London: Collins.

Friedman, M. (1968) 'The role of monetary policy'. *American Economic Review*, **58** (1).

Fullick, L. (1986) 'The MSC and the local community'. In Benn, C. and Fairley, J. (eds) *Challenging the MSC on Jobs, Training and Education*. London: Pluto.

Further Education Unit (1978) *Experience, Reflection, Learning: Suggestions for Organisers of Schemes of UVP*. London: DES.

Further Education Unit (1980) *Day Release – A Desk Study*. London: DES.

Further Education Unit (1984) *Evaluation of FE Contribution to the YTS 1983–1984*. London: DES.

Further Education Unit (1984) *Instructional Guide to Social and Life Skills*. London: DES.

Gamble, A. (1983) *Britain in Decline: Economic Policy, Political Strategy and the British State*. London: Macmillan.

Gamble, A. (1988) *The Free Economy and the Strong State; The Politics of Thatcherism*. London: Macmillan.

Gilmour, I. (1982) *Britain Can Work*. Oxford: Robertson.

Gleeson, D. (ed.) (1983) *Youth Training and the Search for Work*. London: Routledge.

Gough, I. (1979) *The Political Economy of the Welfare State*. London: Macmillan.

Grant, R. and Shaw, G. (1975) *Current Issues in Economic Policy*. London: Allen.

Green, A. (1986) 'The MSC and the three-tier structure of further education'. In Benn, C. and Fairley, J. (eds) *Challenging the MSC on Jobs, Training and Education*. London: Pluto.

Gregory, D. and Noble, C. (1982) 'Trades unions and the special measures for the young unemployed'. In Atkinson, P. and Rees, T. (eds) *Youth Unemployment and State Intervention*. London: Routledge.

Grosch, P. (1987) 'The new Sophists: the work and assumptions of the FEU'. In Holt, M. (ed) *Skills and Vocationalism: The Easy Answer*. Milton Keynes: Open University Press.

Hall, K. and Miller, I. (1975) *Retraining and Tradition: The Skilled Worker in an Era of Change*. London: Allen and Unwin.

Hall, S. (1983) Introduction to Wolpe, A. and Donald, J. (eds) *Is There Anyone There from Education? Education after Thatcher*. London: Pluto.

Halsey, A., Heath, A. and Ridge, J. (1980) *Origins and Destinations: Family, Class and Education in Modern Britain*. Oxford: Oxford University Press.

Harrison, P. (1983) *Inside the Inner City: Life under the Cutting Edge*. London: Penguin.

Hartley, K. (1975) 'Industry, labour and public policy' In Grant, R. and Shaw, G. (eds) *Current Issues in Economic Policy*. London: Allen.

Hartley, K. (1977) 'Training and retraining in industry'. In *Fiscal Policy and Labour Supply*. London: Institute of Fiscal Studies, 1977.

Hawkins, K. (1976) *Handbook of Industrial Relations Practice*. London: Kogan Page.

Hawkins, K. (1978) *Unemployment*. London: Penguin.

Hayek, F. (1984) '1980s Unemployment and the Unions', *Hobart Paper 87*, 2nd edition. London: Institute of Economic Affairs.

Hayes, C. *et al.* (1982) *Foundation Training Issues*. MSC/Institute of Manpower Studies, Brighton.

Hayes, C. *et al.* (1983) *Training for Skill Ownership in the Youth Training Scheme*. MSC/Institute of Manpower Studies, Brighton.

Hayward, J. and Norton, P. (eds) (1986) *The Political Science of British Politics*. London: Wheatsheaf Books.

Heald, D. (1984) *Public Expenditure: Its Defence and Reform*. Oxford: Blackwell.

HMI (1980) 'A view of the curriculum'. London: HMSO.

HMSO (1944) *Employment Policy*.

HMSO (1958) *Training for Skill (the Carr Report)*.
HMSO (1965) *The National Plan* (Cmnd. 2764).
HMSO (1971) *Small Firms: report of the committee on small firms* (Cmnd. 4811).
HMSO (1972) *Training and the Future. A Plan for Discussion*.
HMSO (1974) *The Regeneration of British Industry* (Cmnd. 6315).
HMSO (1975) *A New Approach to Industrial Strategy* (Cmnd. 1710).
HMSO (1977) *Education in Schools: a consultative document* (Cmnd. 6869).
HMSO (1980) *Report on Non-Departmental Public Bodies* (Cmnd. 7797).
HMSO (1981) *The Youth Training Scheme* (Cmnd. 8455).
HMSO (1984) *Public Expenditure: the Next Ten Years* (Green paper).
HMSO (1984) *Training and Jobs* (White Paper).
HMSO (1985) *Employment, the Challenge for the Nation* (Cmnd. 9474).
HMSO (1985) *Vocational Education and Training for Young People*. Report by the Comptroller and Auditor General (Cmnd. 9823).
HMSO (1987) *The Reform of Social Security* (Green paper).
HMSO (1987) *Department of Employment and Manpower Services Commission Adult Training Strategy*. Report by the Comptroller and Auditor General.
HMSO (1988) *Employment in the 1990s* (White Paper).
Heron, F. (1975) *Labour Markets in Crisis*. London: PEP.
Hill, M. (1981) 'Unemployment and government manpower policy'. In Showler, B. and Sinfield, A. (eds) *The Workless State: Studies in Unemployment*. London: Robertson.
Hilliard, J. (1986) 'Thatcherism in decline'. In Coates, D. and Hilliard, J. (eds) *The Economic Revival of Modern Britain: The Debate Between Left and Right*. London: Elgar.
Hirsch, F. (1978) *Social Limits to Growth*. London: Routledge.
Hirst, P. and Peters, R. (1970) *The Logic of Education*. London: Routledge.
Holland, S. (1975) *The Socialist Challenge*. London: Quartet.
Holmes, M. (1985a) *The Labour Government 1974–1979: Political Aims and Economic Reality*. London: Macmillan.
Holmes, M. (1985b) *The First Thatcher Government 1979–83: Contemporary Conservatism and Economic Change*. London: Wheatsheaf.
Holt, M. (1987) *Skills and Vocationalism: The Easy Answer*. Milton Keynes: Open University Press.
Howells, D. (1980) 'The Manpower Services Commission: the first five years'. *Public Administration*. **Autumn**.
Hughes, J. (1973) 'In defence of the Industrial Training Act'. *Journal of Industrial Economics*, **April**.
Hughes, J. and Pearlman, R. (1978) *The Economics of Employment*. London: London School of Economics.
Income Data Services Ltd (1985) *Youth Training Scheme*, Study 293, July.
Jackson, M. (1986) 'A seat at the table?' In Benn, C. and Fairley, J. (eds) *Challenging the MSC on Jobs, Training and Education*. London: Pluto.
Johnson, P. and Thomas, B. (eds) (1985) *Economic Perspectives on Key Issues* Oxford: Blackwell.
Jones, K. (1983) *Beyond Progressive Education*. London: Macmillan.
Jones, K. (1989) *Right Turn: The Conservative Revolution in Education*. London: Hutchinson Radius.
Jones, P. (1988) 'An evaluation of YTS'. *Oxford Review of Economic Policy*, **4** (3).
Joseph, K. (1976) *Monetarism Is Not Enough*. London: CPC.
Joseph, K. (1978) *Conditions for Fuller Employment*. London: CPC.
Joseph, K. and Sumpton, K. (1978) *Inequality*. London: Unwin.
Karnow, S. (1984) *Mao and China*. London: Penguin.
Kaufman, M. (1986) 'The MSC and a new national training system'. In Benn, C. and Fairley, J. (eds) *Challenging the MSC on Jobs, Training and Education*. London: Pluto.
Keegan, W. (1984) *Mrs Thatcher's Economic Experiment*. London: Penguin.
Keegan, W. (1985) *Britain without Oil: What Lies Ahead*. London: Penguin.

Kenny, J. and Reid, M. (1985) *Training Interventions*. London: Institute for Personnel Management.

Keynes, J. (1936) *The General Theory of Employment, Interest and Money*. London: Macmillan.

Kumar, K. (1978) *Prophecy and Progress: The Sociology of Industrial and Post-Industrial Society*. London: Penguin.

Labour Party (1985) *Charter for Youth*. London.

Labour Party/TUC (1984) *Plan for Training*, London.

Labour Party/TUC (1984) *Training for the Future*. London.

Landes, D. (1969) *The Unbound Prometheus: Technical Change and Industrial Development in Western Europe from 1750 to the Present*. Cambridge: Cambridge University Press.

Lawson, N. (1984) 'The British Experiment', the Fifth Mais lecture, 18 June 1984.

Lawton, D. and Gordon, P. (1987) *HMI*. London: Routledge.

Lees, D. and Chiplin, R. (1970) 'The economics of industrial training'. *Lloyds Bank Review*, **April**.

Lewis, D. and Wallace, H. (eds) (1984) *Politics into Practice*. London: Gower.

Lindley, R. (1983) 'Active manpower policy'. In Bain, G. (ed) *Industrial Relations in Britain*. Oxford: Blackwell.

Lockwood, J. (1979) 'The MSC, an opportunity missed'. *Industrial and Commercial Training*, pp. 467–71.

Lodge, P. and Blackstone, T. (1983) *Education Policy and Economic Inequality*. Oxford: Robertson.

Loney, M. (1983) 'The YOP, requiem or rebirth?' In Fiddy, R. (ed) *In Place of Work: Policy and Provision for the Young Unemployed*. Brighton: Falmer.

Low, G. (1988) 'The MSC: a failure of democracy'. In Morris, M. and Griggs, C. (eds) *Education: the Wasted Years? 1973–1986*. Brighton: Falmer.

Lucie-Smith, E. (1981) *The Story of Craft*. Oxford: Phaedon.

McArthur, A. and McGregor, A. (1986) 'Training and economic development'. *Political Quarterly*, **Summer**.

McCulloch, G. (1986) 'Policy, politics and education – TVEI'. *Journal of Educational Policy* **1** (1).

Manley, P. and McCormick, B. (1967) 'The Industrial Training Act'. *Westminster Bank Review*, **June**.

Markhall, G. (1982) 'The Job Creation Programme: some reflections on its passing'. In Rees, T. L. and Atkinson, P. (eds) *Youth Unemployment and State Intervention*. London: Routledge.

Markhall, G. and Gregory, G. (1982) 'Who cares? The MSC interventions – full of Easter promise'. In Rees, T. and Atkinson, P. (eds) *Youth Unemployment and State Intervention*. London: Routledge.

Metcalf, D. (1982) 'Special employment measures'. *Midland Bank Review*, **Winter**.

Metcalf, D. (1987) 'Labour market flexibility and jobs', Centre for Labour Economics, LSE, Discussion Paper 254.

Miller, R. and Wood, B. (1984) *What Price Unemployment? An Alternative Approach*, London: Institute of Economic Affairs.

Minford, P. (1983) *Unemployment: Cause and Cure*. Oxford: Blackwell.

Moon, J. (1983) 'Policy change in direct government responses to UK unemployment'. *Journal of Public Policy*, **Spring**, No. 3, part 3.

Moon, J. and Richardson, J. (1984) 'Policy making with a difference, the technical and vocational education initiative'. *Public Administration*, **Spring**.

Moon, J. and Richardson, J. (1985) *Unemployment in the UK: Politics and Policies*. London: Gower.

Morishima, M. (1982) *Why Has Japan 'Succeeded'?: Western Technology and the Japanese Ethos*. Cambridge: Cambridge University Press.

Morris, M. and Griggs, C. (1988) *Education: the Wasted Years? 1973–1986*. Brighton: Falmer.

Morrison, J. (1982) *Youth Training: Principles and Practice*. London: Hutchinson.

MSC (1974) *There's Work to Be Done*. Sheffield.

MSC (1975) *Annual Report, 1974/5*. Sheffield.
MSC (1975) *Vocational Preparation for Young People*. London.
MSC (1976) *Towards a Comprehensive Manpower Policy*. Sheffield.
MSC (1977) *Young People and Work*. Sheffield.
MSC (1978) *Review and Plan*. Sheffield.
MSC (1980) *Outlook on Training, A Review of the 1973 Employment and Training Act*. Sheffield.
MSC (1981a) *A New Training Initiative: A Consultative Document*. Sheffield.
MSC (1981b) *A New Training Initiative: An Agenda for Action*. (Cmnd. 8455).
MSC (1984a) *Instructional Guide to Social and Life Skills*. Sheffield.
MSC (1984b) *Report on YTS Leavers Survey*. Sheffield.
MSC (1985a) *Competence and Competition* (with NEDC). London.
MSC (1985b) *Development of the Youth Training Scheme,* Sheffield.
MSC (1986) *A Challenge to Complacency*. Sheffield.
Mukherjee, S. (1974) *What Needs to Be Done*. Sheffield: MSC.
Nicholls, T. (1986) *The British Worker Question: A New Look at Workers and Productivity in Manufacturing*. London: Routledge.
O'Brien, R. (1982) 'Employment and unemployment over the next decade'. *Administration*, **30**, (1).
OECD (1975) *Education and Working Life*. Paris: Organisation for Economic Co-operation and Development.
Page, G. (1967) *The Industrial Training Act and After*. London: Deutsch.
Parsons, D. (1984) 'Politics without promises, the crisis of overload and ungovernability'. *Parliamentary Affairs*, **Spring**.
Parsons, D. (1986) *Political Economy of British Regional Policy*. London: Croom Helm.
Perry, P. (1976) *The Evolution of British Manpower Policy*. London: British Association for Commercial and Industrial Education.
Pliatsky, L. (1983) *Getting and Spending – Public Expenditure, Employment and Inflation*. Oxford: Blackwell.
Pollard, S. (1983) *The Development of the British Economy 1914–1980*. London: Edward Arnold.
Prior, J. (1986) *A Balance of Power*. London: Hamish Hamilton.
Pym, F. (1984) *The Politics of Consent*. London: Hamish Hamilton.
Quicke, J. (1988) 'The "New Right" and education'. *British Journal of Educational Studies*, **xxvi** (1), February.
Raffe, D. (1986) *The Context of the YTS: An analysis of its strategy and development*. CES Working Paper No. 86/11, University of Edinburgh.
Ransom, S. (1984) 'Towards a tertiary tripartism: new modes of social control and the 17-plus'. In Broadfoot, P. (ed.) *Selection, Certification and Control: Social Issues in Educational Assessment*. Brighton: Falmer.
Redwood, J. (1984) *Going for Broke: Gambling with Taxpayers' Money*. Oxford: Blackwell.
Rees, T. and Atkinson, P. (eds) (1982) *Youth Unemployment and State Intervention*. London: Routledge.
Reich, B. (1983) *The Next American Frontier*. London: Penguin.
Riddell, P. (1986) *The Thatcher Government*. Oxford: Blackwell.
Ridley, P. (1984) 'The Job Creation Programme'. In Lewis, D. and Wallace, H. (eds) *Politics into Practice*. London: Gower.
Robertson, D. and Hunter, L. C. (1970) *Labour Market Issues of the 1970s*. Edinburgh: Oliver and Boyd.
Robinson, D. (1986) *Monetarism and the Labour Market*. Oxford: Oxford University Press.
Robinson, K. (1985) *A Handbook of Training Management*. London: Kogan Page.
Robinson, P. (1989) *Education and Training – Getting the Questions Right*. London: Campaign for Work.
Roderick, G. and Stephens, M. (eds) (1982) *The British Malaise*. Brighton: Falmer.
Rosenbrock, H. (1977) 'The future of control'. *Automatica*, **13**.
St John-Brooks, C. (1985) *Who Controls Training?* Fabian Tract No. 506, London: Fabian Society.

Sako, M. and Dore, R. (1986) 'How the YTS helps employers'. *The Employment Gazette*, **June**.

Sanderson, D. (1985) 'Youth unemployment'. In Johnson, P. and Thomas, B. (eds) *Economic Perspectives on Key Issues*. Oxford: Blackwell.

Sarup, M. (1982) *Education, State and Crisis: A Marxist Perspective*. London: Routledge.

Sheldrake, J. and Vickerstaff, S. (1987) *The History of Industrial Training in Britain*. Godstone, Surrey: Avebury.

Shilling, C. (1989) *Schooling for Work in Capitalist Britain*. Lewes: Falmer Press.

Shonfield, A. (1976) *Modern Capitalism: The Changing Balance of Public and Private Power*. Oxford: Oxford University Press.

Short, C. (1986) 'The MSC and special measures'. In Benn, C. and Fairley, J. (eds) *Challenging the MSC on Jobs, Training and Education*. London: Pluto.

Showler, B. and Sinfield, A. (1981) *The Workless State: Studies in Unemployment*. London: Robertson.

Simon, B. (1988) *Bending the Rules: The Baker 'Reform' of Education*. London: Lawrence and Wishart.

Sinfield, A. (1981) *What Unemployment Means*. London: Robertson.

Smith, K. (1984) *The British Economic Crisis, Its Past and Future*. London: Penguin.

Smith, I. (1986). The British Constitution: unwritten and unravelled'. In Hayward, J. and Norton, P. (eds) *The Political Science of British Politics*. London: Wheatsheaf Books.

Storey, D. and Johnson, S. (1988) *Job Generation and Labour Market Change*. London: Macmillan.

Stringer, B. and Richardson, J. (1982) *Policy Stability and Policy Change: Industrial Training 1964–1982*, Public Administration Bulletin No. 29 (1982).

Swann, B. and Turnbull, M. (1978) *Records of Interest to Social Scientists 1919–39: Employment and Unemployment*. London: HMSO.

Taylor, R. (1982) 'Trade Union influence on industrial performance'. In Roderick, G. and Stephens, N. (eds) *The British Malaise*. Brighton: Falmer.

Thompson, G. (1986) *The Conservatives' Economic Policy*. London: Croom Helm.

Tipton, B. (1983) 'The quality of training and the design of work'. In Gleeson, D. (ed.) *Youth Training and the Search for Work*. London: Routledge.

Tomlinson, J. (1986) *Monetarism: Is There an Alternative?* Oxford: Blackwell.

Training Services Agency (1973) *Five Year Plan*. Sheffield.

Training Services Agency (1974) *Five Year Plan*. Sheffield.

Training Services Agency (1976) *TSA Five Year Plan, Review*. Sheffield.

Training Services Agency (1977) *Young People and Work*. Sheffield.

Trevor-Roper, H. (1973) Address to the Joint Association of Classical Teachers, reprinted in the *Spectator* 14 July 1973.

Walters, A. (1986) *Britain's Economic Renaissance: Margaret Thatcher's Reforms 1979–84*. Oxford: Oxford University Press.

Weiner, M. (1980) *English Culture and the Decline of the Industrial Spirit 1850–1980*. Cambridge: Cambridge University Press.

Weitzman, M. (1984) *The Share Economy*. Cambridge, MA: Harvard University Press.

Wellens, J. (1963) *The Training Revolution: From the Shopfloor to the Boardroom*. London: Evans.

Williams, S. (1985) *A Job to Live*. London: Penguin.

Wolpe, A. and Donald, J. (1983) *Is There Anyone There from Education? Education after Thatcher*. London: Pluto.

Worswick, G. (ed.) (1985) *Education and Economic Performance*. Aldershot: Gower.

Wright, P. (1987) *Spycatcher*. Victoria, Australia: Heinemann.

Youthaid (1984) 'The Youth Training Scheme, Youthaid's evidence to the House of Commons Employment Committee'. London.

Name Index

Subject Index